# THE NEW POLITICS
# OF CLASS

# Theory, Culture & Society

*Theory, Culture & Society* caters for the resurgence of interest in culture within contemporary social science and the humanities. Building on the heritage of classical social theory, the book series examines ways in which this tradition has been reshaped by a new generation of theorists. It will also publish theoretically informed analyses of everyday life, popular culture, and new intellectual movements.

EDITOR: Mike Featherstone, *University of Teesside*

*Also in this series*

**Promotional Culture**
Advertising, Ideology and Symbolic Expression
*Andrew Wernick*

**Cultural Theory and Cultural Change**
*edited by Mike Featherstone*

**Changing Cultures**
Feminism, Youth and Consumerism
*Mica Nava*

**Globalization**
Social Theory and Global Culture
*Roland Robertson*

**Risk Society**
Towards a New Modernity
*Ulrich Beck*

**Max Weber and the Sociology of Culture**
*Ralph Schroeder*

**Postmodernity USA**
The Crisis of Social Modernism in Postwar America
*Anthony Woodiwiss*

# The New Politics of Class

## Social Movements and Cultural Dynamics in Advanced Societies

### KLAUS EDER

SAGE Publications

London • Newbury Park • New Delhi

© Klaus Eder 1993

First published 1993

Published in association with *Theory, Culture & Society*,
School of Health, Social and Policy Studies, University of
Teesside.

 SAGE Publications Ltd
6 Bonhill Street
London EC2A 4PU

SAGE Publications Inc
2455 Teller Road
Newbury Park, California 91320

SAGE Publications India Pvt Ltd
32, M-Block Market
Greater Kailash – I
New Delhi 110 048

**British Library Cataloguing in Publication data**

Eder, Klaus
  New Politics of Class: Social Movements
  and Cultural Dynamics in Advanced
  Societies. – (Theory, Culture & Society
  Series)
  I. Title II. Series
  305.5

  ISBN 0–8039–8687–4
  ISBN 0–8039–8868–0 (pbk)

**Library of Congress catalog card number 93–083773**

Typeset by Photoprint, Torquay, S. Devon.
Printed in Great Britain by The Cromwell Press Ltd,
Broughton Gifford, Melksham, Wiltshire

# CONTENTS

# FOREWORD

In the following chapters I define the 'new politics of class' as the recoupling of class and new forms of collective action which characterize advanced modern societies. This idea presupposes that there has been a decoupling of class and collective action which I call the 'crisis of class politics'. The assumption is *not* that classes no longer exist in modern societies, but that collective action varies 'relatively' independently of the level of class structuring that is represented by the social distribution of resources, such as power, wealth, and cultural capital. In sociology this concern has been the traditional niche for social movement theory, which has developed research agendas for analyzing the internal conditions of collective mobilization, by studying the motives, organizational resources, and media coverage of movements. I claim that such types of research on social movements lack a direct link to social structure in general, and to class in particular. How then can we relate class and collective action in a sociologically meaningful way?

The central theoretical assumption of this work is that culture provides the missing link between class and collective action. I make a culturalist reformulation of both concepts. The 'culturalist' concept of class is made in opposition to the reductionist versions of class that appear in both traditional theories of class stratification and Analytic Marxism. Collective action events are embedded in *culturally defined action spaces*. This implies that the effect of class on collective action is mediated by the *cultural texture* of class. A culturalist version of the link between class and collective action brings the middle classes – by merit of their location and collective mobilization the crux of traditional class analysis – back once more into the framework for class analysis.

My perception of class coalition and conflict makes classes the key for explaining social developments. Classes produce and reproduce the social institutions that maintain social order and control by their interaction. We no longer have to see the social conflicts that actually occur in the world as occurring outside the framework of class. Instead a culturalist refinement of class analysis enables us to see social conflict as the mainfestation of new structural arrangements of classes of people. The new middle class are the decisive actors in this restructuring, and new middle class radicalism is the decisive factor. This innovation retrieves the concept of new social movements from the flawed assumption of the existence of structurally free-floating groups, and places new social movements within the structural configurations of modern society.

Ultimately then, the 'new politics of class' is intimately linked to the discourse of the 'crisis of class politics'. The crisis discourse is a specific part of the discourse on modernity which is a cultural context for society to generate anew these forms of class politics. This means that there is no longer a crisis of class politics, but a discourse on the crisis of class politics; and that this discourse performs the critical function of placing movement politics into social and cultural context and identifying it as the new politics of class.

# ACKNOWLEDGEMENTS

Some of the chapters of this volume are revised versions of previously published articles. I thank the University of California Press, de Gruyter, Suhrkampf, *Telos* and *Social Research*, for permission to publish revised versions in this volume.

I thank Paul Statham for his critical comments and help when writing and preparing this book, and Nancy Altobelli for her constructive editorial skills.

# INTRODUCTION

# CLASS AND SOCIAL MOVEMENTS

---

## 1

## BRINGING CLASSES BACK INTO THE THEORY OF SOCIETY
### Culture as the Missing Link Between Class and Collective Action

### Decoupling class and collective action

We define the 'crisis of class politics' as the increasing decoupling of class and collective action. This decoupling does *not* imply that classes have disappeared in advanced modern societies. On the contrary, it simply implies that – whatever the degree of class structuring in the social distribution of power, wealth and cultural capital – collective action varies 'relatively' independently of these factors.

This hypothesis assumes a variable that has ensured the close connection of class and action, and yet is also the cause of their disconnection. This intervening variable is *culture*.[1] The traditional idea has been that culture is the result of the social interaction of individuals. Thus it could be assumed that the more such interactions take place in a society marked by well-defined class markers, the more action becomes class-specific. My claim is that this assumption does not hold. A series of scholars have deduced from the absence of such an assumed link, that classes no longer exist because no class-specific action can be shown. This argument errs in that it does not consider that it is not class, but the medium connecting class and action which may have changed.[2] Thus we shall look more closely for the intervening variable 'culture', that might prove such a thesis of the end of class to be merely the products of inadequate theoretical models of social

[1] The notion of culture will become analytically more clear in the following discussion. To begin with, culture refers to any kind of symbolic expression that makes sense of the world, of society and of oneself. It contains elements (symbolic means) to express such a sense and structural patterns that organize these patterns into coherent wholes.

[2] This is the famous 'weakest link' in the chain (Lockwood 1981) that has already troubled Marxist theory. So far it remains unsolved in sociological theory as well.

reality. Class then is an inadequate starting point for covering and understanding the rise and fall of collective action in advanced modern societies. It is relevant only 'in context', within a symbolically defined action space to which class refers.

A closer look at culture shows that modern society is characterized by a paradoxical developmental logic. Whereas its class structure develops more and more along complex but clear-cut lines, closing society for its members, culture has developed independently of class toward a system of symbolic orders with another logic.[3] Classes determine the way in which this culture is used in everyday practices, while the usage of culture is dependent upon a social logic, which is less and less a mere transmitter of social differences into conflictual collective action. Culture ceases to directly bridge class and collective action. It becomes an 'intervening' variable in a real sense. What are the reasons for this development?

The answer has to do with the specific logic of *modernity* as a culture. Culture is a means of communication, and the more people communicate, the more they produce social differences in ongoing processes of communication. To the extent that such communications are oriented toward non-class issues, cultural dynamics diverges from class dynamics. The constructivist perspective in cultural theory in the social sciences is a way of grasping the specific dynamics of modern culture. The 'crisis of class politics' therefore is not a crisis in the sense that politics no longer has a class base because class bases have vanished; it is a crisis because collective action can no longer find a legitimate basis in a given class position. The cultural value of class is generated independently of it. Classes have become 'value-free'. Their evaluation follows the laws of the market. Whereas traditional class theory took for granted the moral evaluation of classes, new class theory must treat this moral evaluation as a variable. There is no longer a privilege of the lower classes for high valuation and of upper classes for a low one. Images of class vary with political fashions.

The crisis of class politics, defined as a decoupling of class and collective action, does not, however, necessarily destroy the capacity of classes to act; in fact, it can even increase this capacity. It no longer allows us to reify class as an 'actor'. It is not classes that act but actors, and their action space is only 'structurally' determined by class. This can be taken into account theoretically by defining with more precision what 'structural' means in this context, and how structural determinations can be empirically tested. To make this step, we will move from class to action proceeding through actionalist and culturalist accounts of collective action to the structuralist account. This lays the basis for answering the question of why class matters.

---

[3] This is the topic of the rising tide of literature referring to 'postmodernization' and 'poststructuralism'. See, among many others, Denzin 1991, and the contributions in B.S. Turner 1990 and Featherstone 1992b.

### Collective action and social movements

It is within social movement theory and research that the actionalist account of collective action will be situated. Social movement research[4] has gained in reputation – not because it has become an academically established field of research, but because social movements play an increasingly important role in the modernization of modern society. This has at times led to an overestimation of social movements for the reproduction of society. This overestimation contrasts with the increasing 'normalization' of the existence of social movements in social and political life.[5] They have become one among other collective actors engaged in the reproduction of the institutional frame of modern societies. There is a multiplicity of different collective actors emerging and intervening in the modernization of modern society. This runs against the theoretical model that modernization allows modern societies to become a self-referential system.[6] Collective actors continuously 'disturb' this process. They call for a different relationship with nature, for rights to difference, for participation in bureaucratic decision-making processes, for peace. We cannot understand and explain the reproduction of modern societies without taking into account the role of collective actors.[7]

This is why social movements have gained a prominent place in macro-sociological theory. However, the reintegration of social movement theory and research into sociological theorizing has been less convincing. Over the past few years research on social movements has lost its link to theoretical work in macro-sociology. There are two main reasons. First, it has turned to micro-sociology, overemphasizing the role of activists or supporters, and thus reducing social movements to their manifestations at the level of voting and opinion poll data. In this micro-sociological analysis collective action has been subject to an individualist methodology, which reduces social phenomena to an aggregate manifestation of individual action. This

---

[4] An overview of the 'state of the art' in social movement theory and research is given in Rucht 1991 and in Diani and Eyerman 1992.

[5] This theoretical difference is reflected in two definitions of social movements: defining movements as self-definitions of collective action (Touraine 1981; Melucci 1988) is characteristic for the former approach; defining them as preference structures for change in a society (Zald and McCarthy 1987) represents the latter approach.

[6] Luhmann's systems theory insists on this point. Social movements are considered as a kind of warning system within the system of society. But this warning system varies in different societies. The German case is seen by Luhmann as the most highly developed case (see Luhmann 1989).

[7] This is the reason why Touraine's sociology, even in a time of declining mobilization described as the end of social movements, still offers a challenging and productive perspective (Touraine 1977, 1981). It has only to be integrated into a more systematic institutional analysis that explains the interaction of competing collective actors including movement actors.

research ranges from detailed socio-psychological studies on motivational aspects to studies using rational-choice models.[8] Secondly, social movement analysis has become part of organizational analysis, treating social movements like a business enterprise (Zald 1988). These developments continue, turning attention away from the role of social movements in a given historical socio-cultural context, and towards explaining the emergence of movements and the inner dynamics of the production and reproduction of social movements.

This is part of a general tendency in social theory away from macro-explanations and towards micro- and organizational analysis. This is a costly change when it occurs at the expense of an empirically based understanding and explanation of social movements in a given socio-cultural context. However, the shift away from macro-explanations of social movements is also due to the simple functionalist assumption that guides social movement research. To transform functional analysis into a useful analytical tool for macro-explanations (and we should try to improve this rather than to give it up), we have to replace the micro- and the organizational analysis of social movements into a macro-context. The aim becomes one of reformulating the idea of social movements as a macro-actor in advanced modern societies, by specifically taking into account the socio-cultural context within which social movements produce and reproduce themselves.

I call this macro-context of movement action the *public space*, where social movements represent themselves and are represented by their supporters and opponents. This representation of social movements changes the dominant perspective on social movements, that they are phenomena defined by objective indicators, such as attitudes towards issues, or the organizational resources available to activists. It is replaced by the perspective that movements are *constructed* in the public space, and that their function has to be understood within the process of the public construction of a collective actor. Resources, attitudes, and other indicators, can then be seen as means available to stabilize these social constructions.[9]

There is, however, a systematic limit to such a constructivist approach. It helps to explain the emergence of collective actors; but it does not tell us what happens when these collective actors themselves start to act. Actors are part of a system that defines the social function that they perform. Given a plurality of collective actors, a functional perspective becomes

---

[8] This holds especially true for social-psychological accounts of collective mobilization and forms of analysis that rely on survey data. See, for example, the work of Klandermans (1984), Klandermans and Oegema (1987), Van der Veen and Klandermans (1989), Kriesi (1988, 1992) and McAdam (1988). The recent emphasis on network analysis is a step forward toward a non-individualistic micro-analysis of collective mobilization (Klandermans 1990, 1992; Diani 1992). The rationalistic tradition is best represented by the work of Oliver (1980), Oliver et al. (1985), Oliver and Marwell (1988), and Marwell et al. (1989).

[9] Melucci (1988) made this point very clearly.

even more important. The function fulfilled by social movements (being a special kind of collective actors) is to accelerate the communication of issues in society. Protest actors do not succeed or fail. They are part of a system that defines the contribution of protest – whether failing or not – to the reproduction of society. Social movements have been and are one of the constitutive elements of modern society: they guarantee the communication of issues, a function that persists beyond their concrete existence as forms of mobilization or organization.

This approach to social movements differs from the macro-sociological approaches dominating traditional social movement research. It no longer makes social movements simply additional or new carriers of social, political or cultural change.[10] And it goes beyond the micro-analysis of social movements that restricts the analysis of social movements to the analysis of forms and processes of collective mobilization. The approach I propose is not simply the result of the two dominating traditions. It builds on both traditions, but adds a new element: the interdependence of collective actors in an institutional context. It is an attempt to contextualize micro-approaches to social movements, locating this context within a system of social communication.

The theoretical discussion on social movements thus does *not* lead straightforwardly into the analysis of class. It instead leads us to consider the context which organizes collective action, namely a system of social communication. Social communication is the process by which culture or cultures in a society reproduce themselves.[11] Social movements are more than the aggregates of social actors based on properties in common. Collective action is embedded in a cultural context of meaning and reproduces it by this action. This points to the central role of culture in the analysis and explanation of collective action. But it does not point to the role of class. Why then still bother with classes as an explanatory variable in the analysis of collective mobilization and social movements?

## Why argue about classes?

Given the rise of ethnic and national conflicts, the resurgence of religious cleavages and the increasing importance of race and racism in local, national and global contexts, it seems rather atavistic to propose 'class' as the central category for explaining the constitution and reproduction of

---

[10] This is the classic European type of theorizing on social movements from Touraine to Habermas. It has been taken over by established political science and political sociology. A good example is Kuechler and Dalton 1990; see also the different contributions to this volume. It indicates that social movement research has reached a rather high degree of 'normality' within normal social science research.

[11] Whether culture therefore has anything to do with class and its objective structuring effects would be the next question to ask. But this already presupposes an understanding of the relation of collective action to the culture or cultures that it helps to reproduce.

society.[12] It is obvious that class no longer has the same attraction that it once had as an explanatory category, because it has lost the explanatory power with which it was once attributed. This is the *crisis of class politics*. Before simply dismissing class as an explanatory concept, we must first analyze the reasons for its loss of explanatory power more closely. We will then be in a better position to define with more precision, just what the explanatory power of a concept of class is in modern societies.

Such an endeavour presupposes a theoretical assumption for its legitimacy and usefulness. This assumption is that class has been, and still is, a central structural feature of social reality, and it cannot be too readily dismissed without impoverishing the level of sociological analysis already attained. The problem is in the following: how do we measure its relevance as an organizing principle of social positions and its effects on collective action in terms of the variables that mediate such effects? The example of working class behaviour is revealing. Instead of following its assumed interests, the working class chose to follow political and ideological orientations (such as authoritarianism and nationalism) that were far removed from these assumed interests. There can be no doubt that in the nineteenth century the concept of class grasped an important aspect of social reality. In the above-mentioned example, the effects of class were mediated by 'culture' – i.e. collectively shared patterns of experience and perception that gave a historically specific form to an 'objective' social position, such as a 'class position'.[13] To the extent that the intervening variable 'culture' develops its own dynamics within modern societies decoupling it from social structure, the translation (or 'mediation') of class is becoming more complex, and the link between class and its effects less obvious. This, however, does not exclude the possibility that there is still a link between the two. Assuming that such a link exists, any purely 'culturalist' account of social reality and any 'culturalist' reductionism in social theory, have to be seen as highly questionable.[14]

---

[12] Even this 'object' of social theory already raises controversy. There is no consensus about what society is, whether it has to be understood as a 'social order' (in the Parsonian sense), a 'historical action system' (in the Tourainian sense), a 'social system' (in the Luhmannian sense), or a discursively based 'life-world' (in the Habermasian sense). Nor is there consensus on the method for an analysis of such 'objects'. The chosen formula is still underdefined, except for the claim that – whatever the object is – when analyzing 'society' there are processes of constitution (production) and processes of reproduction at work. Constitution implies that something new is emerging, while reproduction means the opposite. Both cases are ideal types – and this makes them interesting references for theoretical constructions.

[13] This problem has traditionally been analyzed in terms of 'ideology'. This however is an approach that is too cognitivist and too normativist and tends therefore to distort the analysis of cultural belief systems which mediate class positions and their effects.

[14] The theoretical perspective of postmodernism is not free of this implication. The same holds for modern systems theory within which functional differentiation (a catchword by now almost devoid of meaning) is the conceptual element connecting the textual reality of self-observing and other-observing systems to structural features of social reality. See for the second point Luhmann (1984, 1990a, 1990b) and Teubner (1989a, 1989b).

A second series of variables that mediates class positions and their effects concerns the determinants of collective social action. An important point regarding the people's motivation in sticking to collectively shared belief systems and to join collective action has already been made. Research on collective mobilization, public opinion, and social representations has shown that there are interactional, motivational and situational factors which play a role in creating and reproducing collective action. Therefore any simple reduction of this level of analysis to culture would imply gross simplifications. Collective action thus has its own logic which cannot be reduced to 'culture'.

This could also be interpreted as an argument against the explanatory relevance of class. There is a double indeterminacy that has to be taken into account when moving from collective action to class positions. However, the conclusion that class no longer plays a role in the explanation of ideological belief systems and collective mobilization is neither warranted by theoretical nor by empirical reasons. Instead a more complex model emerges. In order to grasp the variables mediating the relationship of class and action a three-layer model is proposed which – seen from top to bottom – consists of a first layer, *class*, which is a structural variable, a second layer, *cultural texture*, which gives meaning to structure, and finally a third layer, *collective action*, which specifies motivations for joining collective action within the context of cultural textures.[15] These three levels are specifications of general analytical concepts in social analysis which are social structure, culture and social action:

| | |
|---|---|
| *class* (probabilistic constructs of aggregates of social positions) | social structure |
| *cultural texture* (values, identities, knowledge) | culture |
| *collective action* (preference structures, normative orientations) | social action |

These levels of analysis show the different ways in which to analyze the constitution and reproduction of society. Action theories take culture and structure as contextual variables, as conditions or constraints of social action. Culturalist theories assume that action is bound to a shared social knowledge that is not only context, but constitutive for social action and the motivations guiding it. Culture is again embedded in structural contexts, i.e. systems of social positions and power that control the production and reproduction of power.

Such a model of levels of analysis forces one to think about relating the

---

[15] An interesting attempt to relate culture, structure and action which is parallel to this conceptualization can be found in Therborn 1991.

different levels. The distinction between the level of collective social action on the one hand and culture and structure on the other has been previously discussed in terms of the problem of the micro–macro link.[16] As the model proposes, the level of culture plays a decisive role in bridging the micro- and macro-levels of analysis. A promising way to conceptualize this intermediate level of 'culture' is in terms of communication and discourse processes.[17] Modern discourse theory and analysis claims that culturally shared knowledge, values and identities relate to context in a double way: as context internalized by actors into their subjective references to culture; and as context objectified in social structures. The former deals with the notion of (collective) action; the latter with the notion of class. This conceptual scheme provides a framework that allows us to understand the possible effects of class through and on cultural texture, and ultimately on action motivations.[18]

In the following sections, the decoupling of class and collective action, which has led to the questioning of the structural effect of class on social action, will be discussed within the proposed framework looking for culture as the missing link and arguing that decoupling is an effect of theoretical assumptions rather than of empirical facts.

### Texture as the missing link

The problem of a cultural context has traditionally plagued the old discussion of class. Class action has always been seen as mediated by *class consciousness*. This consciousness was again seen as determined by class – and thus a circular argumentation emerged. The circularity has been avoided by the two options that were offered within this model: either by the collective consciousness of those acting together; or by the objective togetherness of actors that was given by their class position. This polariz- ation has characterized Marxist discussions on class – without opening up a way out of the theoretical deadlock.

---

[16] A bridge between action and culture is found in interactionist theory. How to go from such micro-theories to macro-theories is the topic of much controversy (Alexander et al. 1987). The most interesting theoretical attempts here can be found in the work of Knorr- Cetina (1981, 1988) and Turner (1988). Whether their conception of the 'macro-level' of social reality is adequate is doubtful. But they offer a perspective that bridges individual and social levels of analysis in an innovative way. A theoretically and empirically promising approach are theories taking 'mediated communication' as their starting point (Anderson and Meyer 1988). I centre my own theory on 'public' communication, which indicates the perspective guiding the present theoretical discussion.

[17] To treat 'culture as communication' is characteristic of recent anthropological and sociological approaches to culture. They combine structuralist and dramaturgical forms of analysis. See, for example, Leach 1976; Wuthnow 1987; Wuthnow and Witten (1988). See also Eder (1992b).

[18] This does not exclude feedback effects of collective action on culture and class, the latter of which will be addressed later.

Recent social movement theory and research, however, has opened up the theoretical space to reveal a way out of the traditional deadlock of discussions on class and collective action. The traditional question was: how are thousands of individual decisions transformed into a collective event that we call social movement?[19] The alternative and new question is: how does collective action constitute and reproduce a symbolically defined action space that is both the condition and outcome of collective action?[20] The central argument is, that collective action events are to be situated in *culturally defined action spaces*. The idea that I propose is, that collective action is embedded in a *cultural texture*, a reality consisting of a specifically organized discourse that is prior to the motivations of actors to act together and even overrides the motivations of actors.[21] It explains what has been called the 'unintended consequences' of social and/or collective action. It is a reality that follows its own specific logic, situated between collective action and class.

Such textures of collective action do not lead us straight into classes, but to cultural forms.[22] Texture refers to cultural life-forms that allow individuals to act collectively. A good example is the application of the 'cultural theory' derived from the work of Mary Douglas (Thompson et al. 1990) to social movement analysis (Johnson 1987). A possible type of texture (among other types) is the cooperation of egoistic individuals. Another type is the subordination of individual actors under symbolically defined orders ('hierarchies').[23] Networks are cases that are neither hierarchical nor systems of strategic cooperation, and that are regulated neither by contingency nor by power; they are systems of interdependencies. According to this cultural theory, these different types constitute

[19] The traditional answers were provided by stage models describing the life history of a collective actor (emergence of collectivities). Recent answers rely on constructivist models that leave open the problem of internal formation and contextual determination.

[20] The analysis of the relationship of culture and social movements belongs to the most expanding areas of actual social movement research. Frame analysis, discourse analysis and communication studies (media coverage of protest events) are examples of this new approach. See Snow et al. (1986); Snow and Benford (1988, 1991); Gamson (1988, 1992); Gamson and Modigliani (1989).

[21] An analogous argument could be made concerning the Chomskyan critique of behaviourism. Behaviourists have never accepted a structuring logic in the learning processes of individuals. Today, Chomsky's argument is generally accepted. Macro-sociology, however, is still behaving on a pre-Chomskyan level as long as it does not take into account the organizing logic of culture (Leach 1976). This also implies that the cultural logic is a determinant independent of the logic of social structure, a claim that has often been countered as metaphysical and anti-scientific.

[22] It should have become clear from this argument that culture is not – as some 'culturalist theorists' want it – an ultimate explanatory variable. Culture is a middle range category which implies an observation perspective that is only partially detached from the observer's position in the world. The class perspective is much more radical: it is – at least ideally – an outside perspective. This makes it epistemologically exciting and difficult to handle.

[23] This distinction has traditionally been discussed under the labels of market, hierarchy and, as a third possibility in recent times, networks (Williamson 1975; Francis et al. 1983).

'life-forms'.[24] Such life-forms are symbolically organized action spaces that coordinate the subjective motivations of people in a non-subjective way, which is governed by a 'cultural logic'. Thus an understanding of the *cultural logic of action spaces* is the key to analyzing cultural texture in research on collective action and collective mobilization. This theoretical element allows us to analyze how and to what extent class determines collective action. The link between social class and movement politics is mediated by a culturally determined action space, which is the basic theoretical proposition of this thesis.

## From texture to structure: a relational concept of class

Cultural texture mediates the effect of class on collective action. It is embodied in *life-forms* which constitute and reproduce an action space.[25] Life-forms are defined as action spaces in which symbols are communicated; they are 'universes of discourse'. Embedding collective action in life-forms excludes a direct determination of class. *Class has effects on collective action through cultural constructions which are generated in historically specific life-forms*.

Going from action to structure through texture is a 'funnel' model of explanation. We start with collective action events, relate them to symbolically defined action spaces (that are produced and reproduced by collective action events) and then ask what is the connection between symbolically defined action spaces and class differences. Thus class comes last: it is the most restrictive variable; it reduces the variability of events that explain what is going on in reality. The explanatory power attributed to class is a claim, namely that class is a determining 'structure' that is 'behind' or 'within' or 'underlying' relationships between groups of individuals.

What does it mean to see classes in terms of *structure*? Structure is generating positions which stand for opportunities (or lack of opportunities) to act. In this sense classes only exist for the outside observer.

---

[24] The concept of a life-form has been advanced by Thompson et al. (1990). It is similar to the concept of a life-world. While the former has to do with a more objectivist idea of a social world outside, open to observation, the latter is linked to a hermeneutic perspective in which the idea of an outside does not make sense except for the reflexive position toward one's social world. The concept of life-forms allows us to replace the traditional idea of class consciousness, both in its objectivist and its hermeneutic versions. It also competes with the weaker idea of a class habitus (Bourdieu 1984) or a class-specific interpretative scheme (Matthiesen 1989).

[25] This systematic argument has been advanced in a narrative form in historical and social-anthropological studies of the 'making of social classes' (Thompson 1968; Calhoun 1981, 1982).

They are 'objective'. This 'objectifying' idea of structure has dominated sociological class analysis from Marx to Weber and beyond. Class analysis and socio-structural analysis have today nearly become synonymous. Structure is defined as the organizing principle of attributes of individuals, and has to do with the distribution of such attributes over a large number of individuals. These individuals are more or less wealthy, more or less educated, more or less young. Structure is then primarily a principle that generates and reproduces different social positions by distributing the attributes of social positions, and secondly, an outcome of the given distribution of attributes of social positions. The attributes of individuals do not have any systematic relationship with the structure they produce. The connection between attributes and structure is reduced to one of probability. It is this objective property of individual properties that allows us to classify people, and separate categories of people into classes. Thus the notion of class is stripped from any concrete references. Class is a probabilistic construct, and therefore a social construction made for identifying the possible effects of objective properties of categories of people. How these categories are separated depends upon the elements that are valued in a society, and this again is a question of culture and social constructions of actors within the limits of their given life-forms.

Such an abstract and 'lifeless' notion of class will certainly provoke negative reactions from those tied to an actionalist oriented class theory. Such actionalist class theory is necessarily caught by the traditional model of a *hierarchy* of classes: it assumes that there are dominating and dominated classes, exploiting and exploited classes, and cultivated and uncultivated classes. The image of top and bottom, the hierarchical model, is still pervasive. But this no longer fits social reality. It is the model inherited from traditional society that is too simple for complex societies. To modernize the notion of class we therefore have to look for an adequate substitute for it. The proposition is to go from a *hierarchical model* to a *network model* of class relationship.[26] A network model of class relationships allows us to make sense of the middle classes as not fitting the image of top and bottom. When we start to think in these hierarchical terms, they belong to both levels simultaneously. It allows us to understand the interdependencies between classes, the dependency of the exploiter on the exploited, the ruler on the ruled, the 'cultured' on the 'uncultured'. These reciprocal relationships are certainly biased – there is inequality built into reciprocity. Inequality, however, does not destroy reciprocity; rather it is a dynamic element in its reproduction.

The transition from the hierarchical to the network model of class relationship has been eased by a critique of the idea of class within the theoretical framework of functional differentiation (Luhmann 1982, 1985). It replaces the idea of top and bottom, the ideal of stratificatory differentiation, by the idea of functional differentiation. When projected

---

[26] A promising way to approach these phenomena can be found in Clegg 1989.

upon the concept of class, functional differentiation appears like a principle that dissolves class relationships. This conclusion implies that classes are necessarily tied to stratificatory differentiation. It should, however, be contested, for functional differentiation is not only a principle applied on the level of social systems, but also a principle underlying the relationships of classes.

Accepting the idea of class relationships at the level of functional differentiation of societies, leads us to the specific organizing principles of class relationships. Within the model of stratificatory differentiation, such organizing principles are based on power and dependency. Within the model of functional differentiation, this type of organizing principle no longer offers an adequate representation. We have to think of interdependencies that go with power. It is not power and dependency, but power and interdependency which are the principles that generate social structures different from those shaping and determining traditional societies.[27]

Our hypothesis thus can be summarized as follows: instead of giving up the notion of class, we only give up the notion of hierarchical relations between classes. The result is a 'modernization' of the class concept. The idea of class has to be stripped from its traditionalist connotations, from its contingent historical forms of manifestation including its connection with the idea of the proletarian and capitalist classes. Class is a structure that translates inequality and power into different life-chances for categories of individuals. It is therefore a structural determination of life-chances, a structure which distributes chances to act, and de-limits action spaces, which are often highly resistant to the attempts of social actors to change them. This structural boundedness of action is what a class theory is supposed to explain. We can then add cultural and socio-psychological variables, which explain the choice of options that is opened up by a structurally determined and culturally textured action space.

This abstract and formal concept of class is not necessarily ahistorical. On the contrary, it allows us to relate class structures to historically specific forms of societies. The probability of life-chances is determined by class structures in a given historical context. Modern society has been traditionally described as a society whose class structure is shaped by its capitalist form of production and reproduction. This form has produced a histori-

---

[27] When applying the idea of functional differentiation between social classes to cultural conflicts in society, we arrive at a model of three interdependent classes: those trying to impose meanings in society, those trying to defend meanings and attack dominant meanings, and those which mediate these meanings. These are three classes in modern communication societies which oppose each other on the level of defining the boundaries between them. To describe these relationships merely in terms of power and dependency is inadequate because it underrates the power of those that have to accept communicated meanings and overrates the power of those that mediate the meanings. The traditional model would run into fruitless discussions on which side (top or bottom of a class hierarchy) to put these mediating agents. And it would not take into account the fact that the more functionally differentiated social relations are coordinated by communication, the more power becomes dependent upon the acceptance of definitions of reality.

cally specific class structure in which the differences in social positions were primarily related to the chances of selling one's labouring. This determinant has been relativized in postindustrial societies which generate new types of disadvantages and dangers by which people are affected. Capitalist exploitation and capitalist work conditions were the conditions within which class structures have developed.

This historically specific context has changed. People's life-chances have more and more to do with conditions of existence that are shaped by collective goods provided for in collective decision-making processes. Instead of the individual labour force, the collective form of life is threatened by social processes. This change has been described as a change toward a 'risk society' (Beck 1992) in which collective goods like a natural environment are no longer guaranteed. 'Risk' is a category used to describe processes of reproduction in which the problem of survival is related to the availability of collective goods. The dependence on such collective goods shapes the new emerging class structures that we call *postindustrial class structures*.[28] Applying the proposed analytical scheme to a 'risk society' enables us to identify three dimensions for analysis:

- an empirical class of people at risk;
- a socio-cultural system allowing for the social representation and communication of the risk a class of people shares;
- a propensity to do something about this risk, above all: to mobilize for or against such risks and thus to reproduce a public image of a class of people at risk.

The postindustrial society can thus be seen as reorganizing its class base and reorientating its forms of mobilization. The relation between class and politics necessarily changes – but class and politics are still the dimensions within which it is possible to understand the dynamics of the emerging society. The crisis of class politics is ultimately the crisis of a vanishing industrial society.

### The making of class in the discourse on modernity

Class and collective action can be analyzed in a *reconstructivist* perspective. Their connection has forced us to introduce a mediating level of analysis, namely culture. The three-layer model has led beyond a mere reconstructivist perspective and forced us to introduce a *constructivist* one. This constructivism analyzes the cultural construction of the norms and preference structures that motivate people to join collective action within the context of given structural determinants. It stops short of considering a

[28] For a discussion of the 'probabilistic' side of postindustrial class structures see Esping-Andersen (1992).

cultural construction of these structural determinants, i.e. a social construction of class [29]

Since the 'activist decades' which began in the late sixties, the constructivist approach has dominated and found its most elaborate expression in the theory of the 'new' social movements. Its constructivism referred to collective action (Melucci 1988); only rarely did the theoretical perspectives go beyond the self-production of collective action.[30] The introduction of a cultural dimension to social movement theory and research, being a recent phenomenon, has opened up the possibility to extend a constructivist perspective regarding the structural context.[31] Thus a constructivist perspective on class consists in extending existing social movement research beyond its self-imposed limits. A constructivist model suggests the following elements of a radicalization of social movement theory:

- Social movements are public constructions of events that emerge in specific aggregates of social actors. The properties of these aggregates can vary – they certainly can no longer be reduced to the criterion of ownership of means of production or of income gained from work.
- Social movements are an aggregation of actors based upon objective properties that make sense in a historically specific discourse in modern societies.

The radicalization consists in analyzing the way in which collective action and class position is thematized in public communications and public discourse, and in the way that this thematization contributes to the construction of collective action and class. This construction is not only the work of collective actors who present an image of themselves to other actors, but also the work of those who react to such presentations of images. The latter can be adversaries of collective actors; they can also be anybody who is observing these actors.

The social sciences play an important role as observers of these actors and necessarily intervene with their analysis in this process of construction.[32] They have effects on the level of the self-organization of collective action – the social sciences are themselves a form of practical action. They affect the socio-cultural level where the social sciences contribute to the ideological reproduction or critique of forms of action and affect the structural level of social reality as well. Classes are – as Bourdieu (1985, 1987) has already pointed out most clearly – constructions of the observer

---

[29] This perspective laid the ground for the idea of a 'making of class' (Thompson 1968). This tradition, however, stops short of its radical implications. Class in this tradition is reduced to collective representations, thereby losing its structural character and becoming a meaningless category.

[30] This is also true for resource mobilization theories as for identity theories. For this distinction see Cohen 1985.

[31] The reference to political or social opportunity structures is no substitute because it considers structure a mere external institutional restraint of action.

[32] This argument is further discussed below in Part II when examining the effect of Bourdieu on present-day class analysis.

(the theorist). Such a constructivist perspective leads us away from discussions of 'postindustrial' class structures (Esping-Andersen 1992) and advances towards a discussion of the 'meaning' of changing social positions, and their mapping onto a scale of unequal social relationships. My thesis is that the discourse on modernity is the field in which social actors define an aggregation of social actors as collective actors, and give them an existence as a social class. Moving from class to movement or from movement to class, is one way of bringing classes back into social theory.

# PART I:
# MODERNIZING THE NOTION OF CLASS

## 2

## CONTRADICTIONS AND SOCIAL EVOLUTION
### A Theory of the Role of Class in the Production of Modernity[1]

### A critique of modernization theory

*The key concepts: differentiation and rationalization*

The classical theory of modernization is based on the general evolutionary assumption that modernization is the result of differentiation (Smelser 1985; Luhmann 1982) and rationalization (Habermas 1984, 1987; Schluchter 1981). However, the extent to which these processes are necessary aspects of modernization is an open question. Discussions of modernization must at least ask about the extent to which dedifferentiation and derationalization are also developmental processes that characterize modern societies (Berman 1984; Moscovici 1976; Tiryakian 1992). If these counterprocesses can be shown to be part of modernization, then differentiation and rationalization are only two among the many possible results of the evolution of modern society. They then lose the explanatory power that is attributed to them in classical modernization theory. The real problem is that differentiation and rationalization are not variables explaining modernization, but processes needing explanation. In other words, I propose that differentiation and rationalization are not causes, but effects of modernization. My strategy is to look for the processes which produce and reproduce these effects. The theoretical starting point then is to look first for the *modus operandi*, a generative structure of modernity,

---

[1] This is a revised version of a paper that was published in *Social Change and Modernity*, edited by H. Haferkamp and N. J. Smelser, pp. 320–49, University of California Press.

and then for the *opus operatum*, that is, differentiation and rationalization
uu possible outcomes.[2]

A starting point would be to restate two classical problems of socio
logical theorizing. The first is the *Durkheimian* problem of relating the
process of social differentiation to the conditions producing it.[3] How does
differentiation come about? What forces underlie the process? Durkheim's
answer is unsatisfactory; it takes demographic growth and increasing social
density as the central causal variables for the progressive dissolution of
collective consciousness (and the individualization resulting from it). Thus
the key to explaining modernization is ultimately demography, something
non-social (but as we know, socially produced!).

The second problem is the *Weberian* attempt of relating the process of
rationalization to the social conditions producing it.[4] How does rationalization come about? Weber gives a historical answer by identifying specific
social groups as the carriers of the process and then relates these groups to
the general social structure – that is, the system of status, class, and power.
Thus modernization is explained through the more or less contingent
historical emergence of specific social groups. For Weber it is history that
ultimately explains modernization.

The alternative theoretical approach to Durkheim and Weber is that of
Marx. Marx's theory states that the evolutionary change of society (a
change that has been conceptualized by later theorists as differentiation
and rationalization) is the product, first, of the contradictions between the
forces of production and the social relations of production and, second, of
the contradictions between social classes. Ultimately, contradictions are
the causes of modernization (Godelier 1973).

Within the Marxian theoretical framework social development is a
process based on two types of contradictions. The first type is a contradiction between social actors – that is, the conflict between social classes.
When contradictions are understood as contradictions between social
groups, the theory explains the development of society through genuinely
social factors. The second type refers to a more abstract concept of
contradiction. In it, social structures rather than social actors are seen to
contradict each other.[5] The configuration of social structure is supposed to

---

[2] Such a macro-sociological focus on the conditions generating society is prominent in
French sociology. For two (very different) versions see Touraine 1977, and Bourdieu 1984. I
take the distinction between *modus operandi* and *opus operatum* from the latter.

[3] Alexander (1992) describes this Durkheimian problem as being one of relating general
models, social processes, and historical analyses of specific strains and tensions. The
argumentation proposed in the following can be read as an attempt to relate these levels.

[4] For a treatment of the Weberian problem see Schluchter 1979, 1981. Going beyond
Weber, Schluchter tries to develop the general model of rationalization, leaving the question
of social processes and historical analyses more or less aside.

[5] This structural notion of contradiction has often been criticized as being 'objectivistic'.
Such a critique can be found in Habermas (1979), who relates this type of contradiction to the
problem of system integration as opposed to social integration. See also Sahlins (1976), who
distinguishes two 'historical materialisms,' one of which is guilty of the objectivistic sin.

set into motion the evolution of society. This abstract use of the notion of contradiction has become important in more recent theoretical thinking: contradictions between systems are seen as leading to self-blockading situations, and contradictions within systems as generating incompatible functions that the systems try to fulfil (Sjoeberg 1960; Offe 1972).

These functionalist reinterpretations run the risk of an analytical nominalism that is empty of any social theory. I consider communication theory to be a more promising theoretical approach to a reinterpretation of the Marxist approach of explaining social change, because it is more adequate to the study of modernization than functionalist and neofunctionalist reinterpretations of Marx (Alexander 1985). In communication theory the analyst can give a systematic place to the concept of contradiction (Elster 1978; Luhmann 1984, pp. 488ff; Miller 1986, pp. 296ff). Reformulated in this way, the concept of contradiction becomes the starting point for a more adequate theory of modernization.

*Evolutionary theory and modernization*

I propose the following preliminary theoretical assumption: contradictions are mechanisms that initiate or continue *communication*. Because societies are the most complex system of communication, contradictions can be treated as the mechanisms for the *evolution* of social systems.[6] This hypothesis entails an evolutionary theory that draws from beyond the old alternatives of an epigenetic mysticism and a Darwinistic functionalism.[7] It takes contradictions as the mechanism producing modernizing processes such as (functional) differentiation and rationalization.

This hypothesis changes in a fundamental way the evolutionary assumptions underlying modernization theory. I shall discuss two modifications noted here. First, modernization theory should not be tied to the idea of a fixed and *unidirectional path* of development to modern society. Differentiation is not an explanatory variable but only a descriptive category that says that there are increasingly more fields of social conflict and struggle. It must therefore be described as the structural by-product of collective practices that produce a modern social order. Second, modernization theory is not to be tied to the idea of a *self-propelling force* (reason or unreason for example) that pushes social development. Rather, rationalization is the cultural by-product of collective practices that construct a cultural order through learning processes and symbolic struggles both of

---

[6] Evolution is not to be conceived as the change of society or of some of its subsystems – to do so would be a case of misplaced concreteness – but as the evolution of structures that regulate the construction of the system (and its subsystems). Such structures are distinguished from other structures by their role in regulating social communication.

[7] The differences between Darwinistic and epigenetic theories can be reduced to differences in the concept of contradiction. Evolution is conceived either as the resolution of contradictions between systems and their environments (the old Darwinistic explanatory strategy), or as the resolution of a general contradiction underlying the history of humankind (an idea that is related to the old progressivist thinking in social theory).

which together establish legitimate authority and generate the symbols society needs to reproduce itself as a legitimate social order.

As a substitute for the two evolutionary assumptions that modernization is self-propelling and unidirectional,[8] I propose the idea that contradictions open diverging and even incompatible paths of development. There is no prescribed way to and through modernity. There are as many ways into modernity as there are historical developments. Therefore, modernization theory cannot be constructed by conceptualizing its outcome but only by conceptualizing the way this modern order is produced.

The problem then is to conceptualize and explain the social production of modern society. The conception I propose is threefold. First, it suggests looking at the learning processes of those social groups that create a new collective consciousness – that is, political and social ideas – to orient individual and collective social action.[9] Because these learning processes are part of a larger historical environment, we must also look further.

Second, we must consider the idea of class conflict. Class conflict should be conceptualized on the level of the system of status and power. To reproduce such a system of status and power, social classes engage wherever possible in struggles to classify and reclassify each other. They struggle to have 'right' on their side. The symbolic universe of right, the idea of morality, sometimes even universal morality, has to be mobilized to secure the reproduction of the class structure.[10]

Third, we have to examine how differentiation and rationalization are related to the evolution of modernity. I explain them as the structural by-products, that is, as the combined effects, of learning processes and class conflict that in turn reproduce these generating conditions. Learning processes and class conflict change the social and cultural dimensions of the structure of society. They lead to what Weber has called the differentiation and rationalization of 'Wertsphären'.[11] This modern differentiation between moral, aesthetic, and theoretical symbols restricts the possible images of a legitimate social order to the moral sphere. In modern times this differentiation of the moral sphere (which is probably the structurally most important one) can no longer be grounded on a holy order – that is, a hierarchy – but only on the abstract and formalistic idea of a social order based on the equal agreement of those belonging to it.

---

[8] For an analysis of the pitfalls of old evolutionary theories see Habermas 1979. For a critique of Habermas's alternative see Schmid 1982. However, the alternative Schmid proposes also remains unsatisfactory.

[9] The following discussion is an attempt to locate the formal structures of learning processes, as described by Miller (1986), within a historical context. For an extensive discussion see Eder 1985.

[10] The role of the symbolic dimension in Marxist thinking has already been elaborated by Godelier. For a short and instructive account see Godelier 1978. An important theoretical reformulation of this problem is given by Bourdieu (1984).

[11] See Habermas (1984, 1987), who uses Weber's distinction of *Wertsphären* for his own attempt to differentiate between different and irreducible claims of validity constituting communicative action.

With this theoretical programme, the reformulation of the notion of contradiction in communication theory should allow for the revision of the theoretical assumptions underlying the conceptualization of differentiation and rationalization as the paths to modernization and offer new grounds for describing the processes of modernization. On a more general level it should allow for the revision of the implicit evolutionary assumptions of modernization theory.

In the following sections I discuss how the concept of the social production of modernity can be made fruitful in a systematic (not historical) reconstruction of developmental processes in modern society. First, I discuss the role of learning processes in the social production of modern society. These processes take place first in 'enlightenment societies' that call themselves 'associations' to differentiate themselves from 'corporations' and from the corporate groups of traditional society such as guilds and estates. These associations contain the elementary structures of specifically modern collective learning processes. Next, I will attempt to locate this evolutionary new type of association within the social structure of early-modern society. Here the specificity of modern social classes and the corresponding class conflict become the analytical focus.

This analysis then allows me to describe the evolution of modern society as one that is generated by learning processes and class conflicts and reproduced by processes of differentiation and rationalization. Differentiation is the key part of the mechanism that reproduces these generating conditions. However, differentiation as such is insufficient; it must also mobilize symbolic resources to continue reproducing differentiation. Rationalization is the process producing the symbolic resources needed for this reproduction. The analysis of the reproduction of modernization by differentiation and rationalization gives some preliminary answers to two central problems in modernization theory: the problem of alternative paths to modernization and the problem of the rationality of these different paths to modernization.

## The social production of modernity

### Association and communication

Since the beginning of modernity certain social groups that are characterized by an evolutionary new form of communication have had a profound effect in triggering modernization processes. Such groups try to organize their mode of association and communication according to the principles of the *equal* and *discursive* handling of disputes.[12] This type of discourse is based ideally on the free and equal exchange of arguments, that is, on

[12] This observation should not be mistaken for the claim that these associations have actually functioned in this manner. I only claim that these principles define the structural model of these associations.

*Aufklärung* (enlightenment). Associations are the social contexts within which this evolutionary new type of discourse can take place.

I would like to distinguish among three historical manifestations of associations in modern society. The first is tied to the rise of groups that since the eighteenth century have identified themselves as the bearers of enlightenment.[13] Within these groups social and political life is discussed in a way that differs fundamentally from the past. This form of collective discussion, which is learned in small political and private associations, forces these associations to describe themselves in a way that is independent of their place in a hierarchy. They begin, instead, to describe themselves as part of a social movement of enlightenment.

A second historical manifestation of the modern type of associations is the one found in the working class movement (Na'aman 1978; Vester 1970; Thompson 1978; Tilly 1978). The culture of discussion found in the working class movement continues the tradition of the Enlightenment. The difference between the associations of the working class movement and the earlier associations of the Enlightenment is in the content of the discussion. The discourse organized in the associations of the working class allows for learning the competence needed for organizing the workers as a collective social force. Thus the specific social experiences of the workers modify the contents, but not the form, of the discourse of the eighteenth-century associations.

A third historical manifestation of the modern type of associations is the one which has emerged since the end of the last century in the petit-bourgeois classes. The social experiences necessary for these 'middle' classes to produce an autonomous discourse arise only in the second half of the twentieth century when the old petite bourgeoisie is complemented and strengthened by a new petite bourgeoisie (Offe 1985c; Bourdieu 1984)[14] that is the result of the increasing professionalization of work. The associations of these new social groups describe themselves today as 'new' social movements. These new associations defend a private 'life-world' that differs from both the just society defended by the working class and the public sphere defended by the bourgeois/citoyen. This new life-world is the private world, the psychic and physical integrity. Thus the specific experiences of these groups modify the content of discourse, but they do not modify its logic.

In these groups a reflexive use of communication is practised. As people learn to communicate about communication, they revolutionize the traditional order. The evolution of modern society becomes dependent on the communication that is the subject of communicative relationships. Reflexivity in communication is the starting point for the social production of modern society. Those who participate in modern associations know that

---

[13] Important descriptions of this phenomenon are Nipperdey 1972 and Koselleck 1973. For a systematic sociological treatment see Eder 1985, pp. 67ff.

[14] See also Part IV in this volume.

they are taking part in a collective learning process. In the enlightenment associations of the eighteenth century (the Jacobin clubs were their radical variants), the associations for the self-education of the workers of the nineteenth century, and the therapy groups of the late twentieth century, the function of learning has become part of the process of communication. The mechanism constituting the modern associations since the eighteenth century can therefore be defined as *discursive communication* (Habermas 1984, 1987).

The form of communication practised by and in these associations throughout modernity changes the form and the content of the learning processes taking place in these associations. Thus the idea of an evolutionary new type of learning is the theoretical key to the cultural consequences of the emergence of associations since the beginning of modern society. Cultural change in modern society is produced by a collective learning process whose logic is defined by the logic of discursive communication. Cultural change, then, is bound to the logic of modern discourse.

*Collective learning processes*

The most important constitutive element of discursive communication is a 'generative', or 'deep', structure. This structure is defined by two principles: *equality* and the *discursive handling of conflicts*. The logic of discursive communication is structured according to the principles that we ascribe as central to modernity.[15] The logic underlying the modern discourse thus allows for learning processes that differ from traditional ones. These modern learning processes are based on the principle of ceaselessly testing the universalizability of the normative order of civil society. Their mechanism is the resolution of contradictions by argumentation or 'critique'. They are modelled according to the logic of a universalization procedure.

A universalization procedure is defined as the impartial consideration by everybody concerned. The basic structure of an impartial judgement is *equality 'more geometrico'*. Equality *more geometrico* means to consider only the behavioural manifestation of an act, not its motivations or circumstances. This basic structure must then be applied to a specific case. First, impartiality can be described as giving everyone an equal chance to act in his or her interest. This condition is the *equality of opportunity*. A second way to construct a situation of impartiality is to distribute chances to act in such a way that all possible positions within the distribution of positions are acceptable to all. This condition is the *equality of differential chances to act*. The logical structure of the operation of the principle of the equal consideration of everybody becomes logically more complex in both

[15] For an interesting theoretical treatment of the model of civil society see Dumont 1967, 1970. For an early treatment of its discursive aspects see Habermas 1989a. For a systematic use of both notions for a reconstruction of modernization processes see Eder 1985, pp. 87ff. An interesting application to recent political developments in Germany can be found in Habermas 1989b.

cases. In the first case it is applied to an abstract other; in the second case the relevant other becomes somebody with needs that clash with yours, a situation that has to be considered within the procedure of universaliz-ation. Going from the first to the second level, the hypothetical operation takes additional empirical parameters into account. The problems inherent in these approaches result in a third way of describing impartiality: the unequal distribution of chances to claim the universality of wants and interests within a process of collective discussion. This condition is the *equality of communicative relationships*.

Thus we can distinguish three steps in the development of collective learning processes since the eighteenth century, interpreting these steps as stages in the unfolding of the logic of universalization.[16] The form of communication invented and practised by the early associations (the societies of enlightenment) has become the foundation for the model of modern society. This model is civil society which sets forth the characteristics of association, the equal rights to free thinking, speech, and association as basic to civil society. The more this complex learning can be organized, the more the idea of a democratic organization of civil society can be radicalized into the postulate of the democratic organization of the well-being of society. This idea culminates in the idea of the democratic realization of the good life by civil society.[17] The theoretical proposition is that these increasingly complex forms of a civil society are incorporations of the logic of the learning processes that have been going on since the eighteenth century. This development, then, can be conceptualized as the manifestation of collective learning processes using the logic of universaliz-ation as its basic mechanism.

## Social class and class conflict

The concept of discursive communication does not adequately explain the production of a social order in modern society because discursive communication cannot control its institutional environment. On the contrary, it sometimes even serves ends contradictory to its intentions. Associations do not exist merely in the thin air of discussion. Being part of a wider social context, they are not independent of the power system inherent in the social order. They are bound to an institutional framework. The symbolic universe produced by discursive communication is used for legitimating purposes within this institutional framework. To grasp this aspect of the

[16] Habermas's theory of communicative action (1984, 1987) can be read as the theoretical programme of the reconstruction of this type of universalization procedure. A theoretical solution to the problem of developmental logic is the idea of a permanent social contract (Eder 1986a). This solution offers an alternative to Kohlberg's (1981) psychological conception of developmental logic. See also Tugendhat 1980.

[17] For a discussion of the development of democratic rights see the classical work of Marshall (1950). However, it should not be forgotten that these ideals are taken from the theoretical work of intellectuals who are tied more or less to the different social and political groups and movements producing modern society.

social reality of modern society, we must look for the social struggles accompanying and controlling the processes of discursive communication.

Associations are part of the class structure of society. This being so, contradiction comes into play as a mechanism of class struggle. Class conflict thus constitutes a social reality beyond the collective learning processes initiated in associations. This social reality has been described since the beginning of the nineteenth century as a reality structured according to class-specific opportunities and rights. Whether such classes correspond to concrete groups has been the object of controversy.[18] In modern societies class has also become a specific way of describing social differences in society. How far the implicit self-description is adequate varies historically.

Since the eighteenth century the classification of the objective positions that separate social classes has followed a different logic from that underlying the previous classification of estates. The transition in early-modern society to a new logic of classification was a result of freeing the social order from traditional bonds and was part of the process of commercializing agriculture and handicrafts. The new social order became sufficiently different from traditional bonds because the unifying hegemony of the church was broken (Thompson 1978, pp. 133ff). The neutralization of the church gave rise to a society without religious bonds. To substitute for hierarchical classification, a new classification system had to be built into the social structure.

During the transformation of traditional society into early-modern society, social relations remained organized around the bonds of patron–client relationships. Class relations were established, as Thompson (1974, pp. 382ff) puts it, between the patrician culture and the plebeian. The patrician culture was organized around the idea of autonomy and self-determination in private life. The plebeian culture, however, was organized as a 'moral economy'. The moral economy was opposed to the market economy; it defended 'just' prices against market prices and the principle of concrete reciprocity against the principle of subjective rights. Taking the example of eighteenth-century England, the structure of these class relations can be described as gentry–crowd reciprocity.[19] The gentry, which is defined as a polite culture dissociating itself from the plebeian culture of the crowd, employed the classical means of control: the majesty

---

[18] For a new sociological look at the concept of class see Luhmann (1985). Luhmann treats classes as emerging from processes that make interactive relations increasingly secondary for social structure. But his discussion suffers because he confuses class structure and differentiation as stratification.

[19] For this 'cultural' definition of class relations see Thompson (1974, pp. 397–8). This definition is formulated in opposition to those definitions of class societies that are too narrow and too economic in nature. The same may be said of Calhoun (1982). It is important to see not only 'class' but also 'class relations'. This point has been emphasized by Kumar (1983), who points out that class action cannot be explained when classes are seen as isolated entities with no relationship to other classes.

and terror of law and the symbolism of their cultural hegemony. Both contributed to the theatrical representation of patrician culture. The plebs, however, had at their disposal the elements of a traditional culture: the moral economy. The struggles between social classes were still struggles for the reconstruction of the traditional good society and were struggles between traditional status groups. Thus the conflict between these class cultures functioned like a bridge between the old and the new.

When class conflict is identified as concerned with the social organization of industrial work the classification underlying class conflict becomes more clearly defined. Social classification starts to be thought of as the result of individual effort. However, the classification of social reality can still be reduced to a dichotomy: to the contradiction between capital and labour. Classes are constructed around the contradiction between those who sell wage labour and those who buy it.[20] Contrary to the preindustrial phase of modern society, both factors, capital and labour, are defined in ways that are independent of cultural or political traits. Culture and politics become the superstructure, something secondary in describing the class structure of industrial society. The further development of modern society, however, has called this dichotomy into question.

Later, with the withering away of the industrial model of development and the coming of 'postindustrial' society, a new contradiction appears between social groups defending technocratic progressivism and those defending a communicative life-world. Today class conflict is being transformed into a fluid antagonism that reaches into every aspect of social life. Class conflict has expanded in time as well; it has become permanent class conflict. The social reality created by this permanency is a system of classification that radicalizes the individualist premises of the modern system of classification. This system of classification that compares individuals and that counts the (economic and cultural) capital they own results in the highly individualized class structure of modern society.[21]

These ways of classifying people create a power discrepancy between social groups that has to be shown to be normal; the discrepancy must be seen as legitimate.[22] Class conflict is necessarily accompanied by practices that generate the legitimating symbolic order. The purpose of legitimating

[20] This interpretation of classes differs from the conceptions that see classes as concrete social groups. Rather than try to identify the groups that constitute a class, my theoretical approach constructs classes theoretically and tries to find out whether historically these classes actually emerged. I expect that any identity between theoretical constructs and historical classes will be an exceptional case.

[21] This development can only be grasped by a theoretical approach that constructs classes as clusters of indicators that are shared by individuals. When such indicators become diversified, empirical classes are increasingly less like a single or several concrete social groups. Today classes can be described as highly 'individualized'. For this point see Beck 1983, 1992.

[22] Bourdieu (1980, 1984) has developed at length the idea of collective illusions as systematically distorted visions of the world. Theoretically, this notion is, so far, the most interesting sociological reformulation of the old concept of ideology.

practices is therefore to make the existing relations between individuals appear to be normal relations. Resolved in this way, legitimating these practices allows for the symbolic reproduction of the class structure of a society. The symbols favoured by those who are on top are symbols claiming universal validity because such symbols produce the most perfect image of legitimacy for the class structure of modern society. Thus on the level of class conflict, another logic of cultural change intervenes. Cultural change is not only the result of learning processes but also the result of class-specific symbolic practices.

### Legitimating practices

The production and reproduction of class structure is dependent on the symbolic practices by which classes try to maintain their differences. For this purpose symbolic resources are used to legitimate the class structure.[23] Class conflict produces not only a social relation but also a symbolic one. This symbolic relation serves as a specific mechanism for organizing and reorganizing the symbolic universe that legitimates modern society.

A look at modern history might clarify this point. In the sixteenth and seventeenth centuries princes and the newly established parliaments tried to break the sovereignty of religious authority by postulating a new basis for legitimizing political domination: the welfare of the people.[24] This secular ground for domination legitimated either the absolute sovereignty of the king or the representative sovereignty of the estates. The plebs still lived in the old world of the moral economy, which was culturally opposed to both the world of the absolute prince and the world of the new estates. The ensuing struggles on the symbolic level were struggles between the modern and the traditional world. Thus the symbolic practice of the absolutist state (constructed as the practice of the rule of law) was opposed to the symbolic order of traditional life (defined as the practice of customary law) that was defended by the lower classes.

At the beginning of the industrial revolution a new field of symbolic struggle was added. The dominance of the old class cultures was broken by the rising bourgeoisie, which transcended these cultural worlds with its idea of an individualistic and competitive society, a society based on 'industria'. It was legitimated by a radically individualistic ethic, the

---

[23] For a systematic treatment of processes of classification in modern societies see Bourdieu 1984. This implies a critique of Touraine's central assumption that the concept of society is no longer adequate as a description of modern social life. Touraine's idea of centring social theory on a modified version of class conflict is insufficient to tackle the developmental processes going on in the cultural representations of society. For this perspective see Touraine (1981).

[24] The collected papers of Hintze (1970) are still the best systematic analysis of this period. For a more recent treatment see Mousnier 1974, 1980.

Protestant work ethic, and its *telos* of never-ending maximization and perfection. This class made the individualistic society of a market economy the symbolic world shared by both the upper and the lower classes. The legitimating practices based on this symbolic world led to the model of class relations that was created in nineteenth-century Europe between the labour movement, on the one hand, and the organizations of the industrial elites on the other. This model conceived of this relationship as a game between pressure groups bent on maximizing power and interests.[25] It conceived of the capital–labour relationship as a bargaining one. This symbolic world created the illusion that was necessary for the reproduction of this individualistic and competitive society. It was precisely this illusion that helped to reproduce, at least for a time, the class structure of modern society in its industrial phase of development.

The developmental dynamic of advanced industrial societies again changes its field of symbolic struggle. The world of the unlimited development of the industrial forces of production is replaced by a new legitimating practice: the programming of the economic, cultural, and social reproduction of society. The cultural world opposing such an encompassing programme developed in both the working class and the bourgeois classes. This development took the form of a romantic culture emphasizing naturalistic sentiments that are opposed to the 'coldness' of modern economic and political life. In late-modern society a new 'green' philosophy, trying to develop another moral image of the good world, carries on this tradition of a culture that is opposed to a world controlled by the bureaucratic welfare state. The 'new' social movements are explicitly opposed to the welfare state; they speak instead of health, green nature, aesthetics, they generalize the idea of the 'good life into all fields'.[26] The ensuing symbolic struggles between different 'modernities', that is, between modernity and romanticism, legitimate a society with a highly individualized class structure.

The winners in these symbolic struggles try to produce the image of defending claims that are universally valid. The claim of universalism is, at least in modern societies, the most promising strategy to reproduce a given class structure of society. If symbolic struggles arrive at defining the symbolic world of the upper classes as the legitimate one, the lower classes have to see their existence as an illegitimate one. The degree of legitimacy becomes the reference point for distinguishing social groups. The history of

[25] A general history of the labour movement seen from a trade-unionist perspective is contained in Kendall 1975. A theoretical version of this perspective can be found in 'analytical Marxism' (Elster 1985a, 1985b). A critical discussion can be found in Offe 1985a.

[26] The bureaucratic welfare state manifests a conflict about the type of professional knowledge that should be used for the reproduction of society. For the green movement see Galtung 1986. Theories of postindustrial societies – with the exception of Touraine (1981) – generally miss this point.

legitimating practices[27] is therefore the key to an understanding of the processes that constitute the symbolic universe of modern class society.

The symbolic universe of law offers the exemplary case of the processes of legitimating the class structure of modern society. On the one hand, legal norms fix the objective classification of legal rights. On the other hand, law has symbolic power because it claims to have morality on its side.[28] Law is a mechanism that is used in different contexts for the symbolic reproduction of an institutional order. To analyze this function of the symbolic universe of the law, I use examples from the history of legal and political thought.[29]

At the beginning of the sixteenth century both traditions adopted the new premises that there no longer existed a metaphysical order on which political and social life could be built and that the anthropological nature of man is the basic fact. These new premises emerged from the reflexive structure of modern social thinking: social thought had become dependent on the thinker (and his nature) as such. Hobbes's *Leviathan* and the radical Puritan theories of the covenant are examples of this radically new social thinking; they mark the beginning of the evolution of modern representations of society. The symbolic authority of the modern legal order is based on these new normative grounds. There are three key ideas: that order has to be maintained by the rule of law; that the state's function is to maximize the welfare of its constituents; and that a good way of life must be defended against the consequences of uncontrolled progressivism. Order, welfare, and a good life are the normative grounds for the symbolic authority of modern law.

The images of a legal order constructed on such principles are the most effective mechanisms in producing the illusion that is necessary for the reproduction of society. The more complex the social structure of modern society, the more complex these images become. The first idea, that of a formal legal order founded on the universalistic principle of the reason of state, structures and legitimates the absolutist state that ended the religious wars by guaranteeing indifference to religious and social differences, thus creating order through law. The second idea of a legal order takes into account that the modern state has taken on the regulation of the economic sphere, which up to that time had been integrated into traditional forms of living. The *telos* of a legal order is maximizing the welfare of a society through law. The third idea emerges from the dysfunctional consequences of maximizing social welfare. Because perfect order is no longer produced

---

[27] For a sociological approach to the history of social movements and cultural struggles in modern society see Eder 1986b. See also Eisenstadt (1981, 1992), who focuses on the complementary aspect of the elites.

[28] The old and polemicized problem of the relationship between the moral and the legal is restated here in a new way. For the classical sociological treatment see Durkheim 1969.

[29] For a history of political thought that takes this perspective see Skinner 1978. For legal history see the abundant nineteenth-century German literature. For the sociological use of this literature see Eder 1985, pp. 329ff, 396ff.

by regulative law, 'progress' has to be corrected or, better, planned 'by the people'. The law then distributes the chances to participate in the planning of society. Law, conceived primarily as procedural law, becomes the incorporation of the democratic creed.[30]

Against the majesty of law the lower groups either mobilize a cultural world beyond the law or they subject themselves to the law, accepting its authority and thereby contributing to it. In both cases, law serves for legitimating class structure. Legal practices are the most important among the symbolic practices reproducing the power structure of society.

## The evolution of modernity

### The social reproduction of modernity

In the preceding section I laid the foundations for a theory of the social production of modernity. I identified the mechanism that launches processes of social and cultural change, but I have not yet described the specific nature of these processes. The processes that are seen as crucial by traditional modernization theory are (functional) differentiation and (formal) rationalization. Whether they are the master trends of change in the course of modernization is a question that must be answered now. My answer covers two aspects. First, differentiation and rationalization can take different courses than those ascribed to them in classical modernization theory. Second, there are differences in the 'functionality' and 'rationality' of these processes that have to be explicated.

The first of these processes, differentiation, is a structural arrangement to meet the functional consequences of two types of modernizing forces: modern associations and modern class structure. This structural arrangement has to reproduce these generating forces. Otherwise, modernization cannot go on. Thus, differentiation can be defined within my theoretical framework as the mechanism for the *social* reproduction of these modernizing forces. A theory of differentiation describes how the *opus operatum* reproduces the *modus operandi*.

Classical modernization theory states that in modern societies differentiation takes on the course that is functional differentiation, a course different from the traditional course of stratificatory differentiation. The decisive innovation is the functional autonomy by which structural arrangements are *equally* and without external constraints able to accommodate[31] the functional consequences of the modernizing mechanisms. By separating and multiplying the fields in which the construction of modern society

[30] A short description of the stages of legalization can be found in Habermas 1987, chapter VIII.

[31] The concept of 'accommodation' has been proposed by Smelser (1985, p. 124). This concept allows for the development of a more adequate idea of the functionality, or 'success', of differentiation.

can take place, functional differentiation makes this accommodation possible.

Thus differentiation allows modern societies to accommodate learning processes and class struggles by structurally separating the specific spheres of action that are the objects of these collective actions. For example, the economic system and the religious system are based on functionally specific ways of accommodating the consequences of modernizing activities. Economic class struggle is no longer logically adapted to enactment in the religious sphere of action (as in traditional society). However, there are still social struggles within the religious sphere: for example, in conflicts between religious professionals and the lay public. Specific class conflict occurs in the economic sphere and is manifest in the distance between capital and labour. Analogous struggles take place in the political and the cultural spheres. The most conclusive example is the effect of differentiating the educational system from other systems. The modern educational system reproduces the class structure of modern society much more efficiently than before, while guaranteeing the cognitive skills a complex, modern society needs for its reproduction.[32] Functional differentiation is the mechanism by which the dominant elites reproduce their positions in an increasingly complex modern society.

Such differentiation is not a master trend; it is the trend of the masters. This observation implies that there is more than one path of differentiation in modern society. Functional differentiation, I propose, reproduces class structure by producing a distinctive structure for the formation of autonomous elites and for the deformation of the people as the clients of these elites. Whether dedifferentiation takes place depends on whether social forces are strong enough to get rid of their confinements to the specific social spaces that, from the perspective of the elites, are rational and to redefine the social space in which they act. Such dedifferentiation mobilizes class conflicts that generate collective action beyond the established networks of communication to involve those who do not yet communicate with each other.[33]

Thus those who argue that the formation of elites is the most important function of structural arrangements have to plead for functional differentiation. Those who argue that the organization of the collective interests of the lesser classes is the most important function must plead against

[32] The functional differentiation of class conflict is normally thought of as the end of class conflict. This notion, however, presupposes a realistic definition of class – that is, it implies that we already know what a class consists of. I argue that differentiation allows for the reproduction of class structure. The best example of this phenomenon is the role of the educational system. For the reproductive role of the differentiated educational system see Bourdieu 1984.

[33] An interesting concept trying to mediate between differentiation and dedifferentiation is the concept of 'uneven' differentiation (Colomy 1985). But, ultimately, Colomy remains tied to the elitist perspective complemented by the idea that there must be structures providing a refuge or haven for critical (i.e. powerless) elites.

functional differentiation. Ultimately, functional differentiation is an option, not a fate. It is a possible but not a necessary trend of modernization. Using it as a master trend implies a value judgement. To give theoretical distinctiveness to it contributes to its image of being 'rational'.

## The cultural reproduction of modernity

The ability of functional differentiation to dominate the process of modernization depends on its ability to reproduce the image of an egalitarian social order. Thus a second form of the reproduction of modern society has to be considered: rationalization allows for the *cultural* reproduction of modernity.

As I have already indicated, in modern society rationalization is the result of a double production of culture: learning processes and practices that legitimate class differences. Collective learning processes constitute the discourse within which modernity is made possible. Symbolic practices try to mobilize the universe of discourse produced in these learning processes in order to legitimate existing distributions of power and positions in modern society. The mechanism generating rationalization is, first, the discourse in associational life and, second, the interest of social classes in legitimating their position and illegitimating the positions of others.

Rationalization is the result of two types of generating conditions and can assume different forms. What holds for differentiation is also true for rationalization: there is more than one path of rationalization in modern society. Rationalization is part of both the disenchantment and the reenchantment of the world.[34] The difference between the two processes can be traced back to the differential rationalization of high and low culture in modern society. They can be seen as constituting two ideal types of rationalization: disenchantment, which is related to the dominant groups in society and has become the 'official' image of rationality, and reenchantment, which is related to the dominated groups and has become the 'unofficial' image of rationality. The Weberian perspective of a historical vacillation between rationality and irrationality is thus translated into the image of a rivalry between an official and an unofficial type of rationalization. This rivalry has become central in deciding the course of modernization.

Among the best examples of the 'official' version of rationality is legal rationality. There are, however, other symbolic universes based on this type of rationality. For example, the symbolic universe of political discourse and that of scientific discourse contribute in their specific manners to the official rationality of modern society. Rationalization

---

[34] The discussion about disenchantment and reenchantment refers above all to the religious aspects of rationalization (Tiryakian 1992). Lechner (1985) also takes reenchantment into account but reduces reenchantment to a form of social discontent: that is, to a negative orientation toward social action. Thus the elitist theoretical stand can be kept.

triggered by these forms of rationality ends, as Weber has argued, in disenchantment.[35]

Rationalization takes a different course when strong cultural movements contest a society's accepted practices and ways of thinking: that is, its hegemonical symbolic order.[36] Such movements can be brought about by psychic or ecological crises that cannot be resolved by purely political or economic means. Rationalization that takes a direction other than the official one ends in reenchantment. Whether rationalization really takes this direction depends on the developmental paths set by such cultural movements. Reenchantment does not necessarily mean 'irrationalization'. Reenchantment can be based on the old symbolic resources of religious orientations.[37] For example, we know the extent to which Catholic and Protestant ideas still influence individual and group choices in the continuing path to modernization. We know the effect of non-Western religious traditions on the process of the social production of the modern social order. Weber has proposed the difference between this-worldly and other-worldly orientations to distinguish between different symbolic logics.

Another form of reenchantment is the attitude toward nature. This form of reenchantment challenges the productivist image of modernity, which is defined by its instrumental relation to nature, with a romantic image of another modernity that is defined by the integration of society into nature. This reenchantment leads to a rationalization of a more moral kind. Weber called this moralization 'material' rationalization.[38] It questions the dominance of formal rationality and serves as the vehicle, as Weber saw it, of an irrational rationalization.

This interpretation is misleading. Both processes are contradictory forms of rationalizing the modern world. In traditional societies cultural differences centre on the poles of orthodoxy and heterodoxy. In modern societies they centre on the poles of formal and material rationality. How do we decide their respective degrees of rationality?

*Falling short of modernization*

The question of rationality comes up not only on the level of rationalization, but also on the level of differentiation. When functional differentiation is substituted by segmentary forms of differentiation, a social structure emerges that is unable to reproduce the class structure of modern society. Moreover, when rationalization is replaced by a new magical

---

[35] These examples of rationalization are ones identified by Weber. For a systematic discussion of the different aspects of rationalization see Habermas 1984, Chapter I.3.

[36] Cultural movements and countercultures are a difficult subject for theoretical treatment. For one attempt see Yinger 1982.

[37] Reenchantment, conceived as the development of posttraditional religion, is then a counterprocess to the process of secularization. For such a restatement of the notion of secularization see Werblowsky 1976.

[38] The concept of material rationalization was originally developed by Weber using the example of the legal postulates for justice.

image of the world, a cultural system emerges that is unable to reproduce the collective practices underlying the production of modernity. In this case a manifest regression occurs. Can we describe such a development as 'irrational'? In addition, on the levels of differentiation and rationalization, we are also confronted with antagonistic paths to modernization. Whether one of these paths is more rational than the other becomes a problem for a theory of modernization. The key to these problems is not the theory of differentiation, but the theory of rationalization because this theory contains the double problem: to look at the way the social order is rationalized and to identify the criteria for distinguishing what is to be considered as rational. Thus the theory of rationalization cannot escape the process of rationalization of which it is part.[39]

There are only two ways out of this problem: either to postulate a substantive normative criterion of rationality or to identify the social conditions that are necessary for rationalization to occur. The first solution is tautological because such a postulate becomes part of the symbolic struggles pushing rationalization in whatever direction. The second solution is to see the social conditions of rationalization as the 'procedural' norms[40] that are necessary for rationalization and to examine whether they are in evidence and if so, to what extent they are given or not.

Reduced to its procedural form, the ultimate ground of the rationality of modernity is that we can choose our symbolic orders, that we are not stuck with any one type of rationality, and that we can at any time abandon what we have ceased to accept rationally. Whether or not such a rational outcome is to be expected has to be treated as an open question. Classical modernization theory seems to have already decided this question by describing modernization as rationalization. In the following section, however, I show that this modernization is not necessarily a rational one. Therefore modernization theory has to incorporate a more explicit notion of rationality into its conceptual framework. I suggest that we look for procedural rationality on the level of the conditions generating what has been called rationalization.

As I have shown, rationalizing the modern social order is dependent on two mechanisms. First, rationalization is the net result of social struggles between social classes. Second, these social struggles are dependent on collective learning processes to reproduce the cultural conditions of their existence. Thus two mechanisms are necessary to arrive at a modern social order. Although difficult to achieve, such a social order is even more difficult to reproduce. It must be assured that learning processes and class conflict can continue. When reproduction fails, then social development regresses or is rigidified. The historical process becomes 'pathological'.

---

[39] The reflexivity built into the idea of rationalization has been treated by Habermas (1984, chapter I.2). It has been radicalized by Giddens (1990) and Beck (1992).

[40] The concept of procedural norms has close links with communication theory. This point is examined later in this chapter.

The result of blocked class conflicts and blocked learning processes is the pathogenesis of modernity.[41]

Historically, pathological processes seem to predominate. Collective learning processes are more often blocked than released. Associations more often turn into forms of interaction producing enemies rather than forms favouring learning processes. The history of modern associations is closer to history of private feuds than a history of learning. The same applies to class conflict. Often class conflict is neutralized by populist appeals or reduced to an elitist struggle.[42]

Either way, the result is cultural conflicts which try to mobilize either the moral majority or the moral minority. Fascism radicalizes the moral majority: it offers integrative formulas with racist, nationalist, or imperialist orientations. Terrorism is the radicalization of a moral minority and is exemplified by the Jacobin terror after the French Revolution, the terror of Stalin, and that of the Khmer Rouge. Whether class conflict ends as fascism or moral terror depends on the cultural logic of a modern society.

This conceptualization allows us to tackle the problem of pathological developments in a more promising way. Although associations 'learn' and social classes 'struggle' with each other, modernization nevertheless fails. Nationalism mobilizes expressive resources that are not rationalized by the former factors. Fascism mobilizes sentiments that cannot be controlled by the modern political and social movements. The following questions arise as a result: Why do such pathological developments occur? Why are learning processes blocked? Why is class conflict negated? What are the cultural foundations that make possible such outcomes?

A provisional answer to these questions can be given here. Ultimately, it is the symbolic universe in which a society lives that determines whether modernization, once triggered and set into motion, will succeed or not. Variations in the degree of associational life and class conflicts in modern societies raise questions such as: Why is there no socialism in the United States? Why is there such a strong tradition of class conflict in England? Such factors determine the tempo of modernization and the injustice tied to it, but they do not block modernization.

The crucial question, then, is why does modernization as such fail in some societies – at least for some time? It does so because there are cultural traditions that become dominant in specific phases of modernization. An example is the German modernization experience in the second half of the nineteenth and the first half of the twentieth centuries.[43]

---

[41] The pathogenesis of modernity has been the topic of the classical discussion concerning the 'German road to modernity'. The central problem of this discussion has been whether there is such a thing as a 'normal' road to modernity that can be attributed to a particular country.

[42] This critique of an elitist or populist transformation of class conflict is found, for example, in Touraine 1981.

[43] For a discussion of the concept of social pathology see Eder 1985; for the idea of blocked learning processes as indicators of social pathology see Miller 1986.

Although starting modernization like the other European nations, collective learning processes and social struggles over the cultural orientation of modernization were blocked in favour of a civil society that was controlled by the state. The state took a tight control over associations, thereby controlling the collective learning processes. The state also neutralized class conflict, thereby imposing a symbolic order on modern society. The modern culture was created in an authoritarian manner. As long as this type of creation remains dominant, the possibility of pathological cultural evolution exists.

Therefore, the key to explaining the path of development leading into modernity lies in the learning processes and the symbolic practices in the sphere of culture. These processes and practices determine not only the type of rationalization (disenchantment or reenchantment) that will take place, thereby restricting the possibilities of structural differentiation, but they also determine the degree of rationality. Thus we will be able to regard the counterprocesses to functional differentiation and formal rationalization not as simple aberrations[44] from the path of modernization but as possible outcomes of modernization. The normality of differentiation and rationalization is precisely not the point. Rather the question of normality and pathology is one of the social conditions generating differentiation and rationalization. Only by considering the conditions that block collective learning processes and symbolic struggles will we be able to explain pathogenetic forms of differentiation or dedifferentiation, of disenchantment or reenchantment. The description of modernizing processes as pathogenetic developments is a communication about the conditions which trigger collective learning processes and change the universe of discourse used in class conflict for legitimating practices. Such communication about the pathogenesis of modernity cannot exclude, but can minimize, the possibility for the pathogenesis of modernity.

## Contradictions and evolution

### A theoretical treatment of contradictions

The analysis of the social production of modernity can be done on three levels: collective learning processes, class conflict, and reproductive structures. This analytical distinction of levels allows for localizing both the structure and the functioning of contradiction as the mechanism for originating and reproducing communication. This implicit notion of contradiction must be clarified in the following sections.

Contradiction can be defined as a social event where someone opposes what someone else says or does. This definition leads to a *first thesis*: the

---

[44] Although it has often been mentioned that different paths to modernization cannot be reduced to aberrations from a master trend leading to modernity, seldom have the necessary theoretical consequences of this observation been considered.

notion of contradiction presupposes the notion of communication. Without communication, contradiction is a meaningless category. Only within a communicative relationship can contradiction occur at all.[45] This thesis leads to the following *corollary*: contradictions work on different levels of social reality.

On the level of associations, contradiction is the mechanism by which participants in a collective discourse can construct a shared world of meanings. Such a shared world relies on concrete interaction, which forces those engaged in it into a logic that transcends their personal involvement and egoistic interests. A communication on the level of concrete interaction that uses the mechanism of contradiction is bound to the logic of argumentation. Argumentation is in turn a mechanism that binds all engaged in it to a collective reality, one defined by the learning process triggered by communication. Thus contradictions are fundamental for a first type of social reality: the reality of social *groups*. On this level we have to deal with concrete actors trying to communicate with each other.

Contradiction can be pushed to the point where argumentation is itself put into question: one side can argue against further argumentation and start to resort to power. The reproduction of communication in the group is interrupted. A substitute for the social basis of communication must therefore be found. The new basis is constituted not by social relations between persons but between classes of people. On this level communication is a mechanism for locating and relocating classes in relation to each other. The mechanisms that force social classes to communicate (through struggles) with each other are those of the marketplace because those who do not participate are necessarily the 'losers of the game'. At the same time this situation forces institutional agreements to reproduce the marketplace. Generating distinctions, that is, a world of social classification, is the result of communication on this level. Thus contradictions are fundamental for a second type of social reality: that of social *classes*.[46] On this level we have to deal with social classes communicating by struggling with each other.

However, there is still another type of contradiction that escapes the description of contradictions given so far. These are the contradictions built into the structural effects of group and class action, into differentiation and rationalization. This type of contradiction is different from the one between society and its environment because society cannot contradict its own environment. Luhmann (1984, pp. 191ff, 498ff) has defined the environment of society by the property that it does not communicate. The contradiction I refer to is still within society. Thus we arrive at the broadest and most fundamental level of social contradictions: the level of structural contradictions that constitute the social reality of *society*. Structural

---

[45] For the centrality of the concept of communication for a sociological theory see – each following different intentions – Habermas 1984, 1987, and Luhmann 1984. For the cultural anthropological point of view see Leach 1976. In the following I draw heavily on Miller 1986.

[46] To insist on the difference between group and class implies the critique of classical conflict theory as developed by, for example, Dahrendorf (1959).

contradictions do not constitute communication, but they allow for the reproduction of communication, both on the level of group and on the level of class.

The levels of the communicative constitution of social reality can be summarized as follows:

- The first level concerns contradictions between actors communicating with each other. This level constitutes the social reality of the *group* and the learning processes triggered by communication between actors.
- The second level concerns contradictions between groups engaged in classifying and reclassifying each other. This level constitutes the social reality of *class* and the social struggles going on between classes.
- The third level concerns contradictions built into the developmental processes that are the structural effects of learning and class conflict. This level constitutes the social reality of *society*.

Contradictions on all three levels work together to produce social evolution. The implications of this conceptualization for the theory of social evolution can now be clarified.

*Contradictions and social change*

This discussion of the communicative function of contradictions on different levels of social reality shows that contradictions are the medium and the *telos* of communication. The *telos* of communication is not the resolution of the contradiction – for that would imply the end of communication. Rather, it must assure an ongoing and continuous stream of communication which demonstrates that social reality is something always in flux.

This relationship between contradiction and communication discussed here opens up a new theoretical perspective on social change. The *second thesis* concerning a theory of social change follows: contradictions generate social change and these changes are the mechanisms of evolution.[47] This proposition differs from usual conceptions of social change in one fundamental respect: it tries to explain change not by changes in factors outside the system but by internal generating mechanisms. Social change is itself a social product. A *corollary* of this general assumption is the following: contradictions are constitutive of social change; they produce social change in constituting social reality.[48]

[47] The difference between my approach and the Marxist strategy consists in differentiating between the changes produced and the evolutionary process that handles these changes. My approach avoids the problem of 'misplaced concreteness', which is tied to theories that try to deduce social developments from observed actions.

[48] Here, some possible misunderstandings should be mentioned. The centrality of contradiction does not imply that contradiction is the guarantor of rationality; those who contradict do not necessarily understand those whom they contradict. This also applies to contradictions in class conflict; the result of class conflict is not rational *per se*. The same applies also for the

Social change is constituted on the level of association by the very fact of 'contradicting' (in the literal sense). Communication exerts a specific constraint: it forces those participating in communication to learn or not to learn. Contradictions can be used to reinterpret the world; if this reinterpretation is blocked, those engaged in the communication must explicitly negate the possibility of learning that is offered to them. In either case social reality changes. In this problem, the theory of practical discourse has its generic field of application: it is an ideal model of the constitution of social reality. It leaves the other levels of social reality to other theories, such as systems theory.[49] Contradictions on this first level produce social change by triggering *collective learning processes* (Miller 1986; Eder 1985).

However, these learning processes are not sufficient in explaining social change because not every learning process survives on the level of the institutional order. Social change can therefore be perceived on the level of the institutional order as the result of struggles between groups interested in classifying or reclassifying others or themselves. Contradictions on this second level produce social change by forcing social classes into *class conflicts*.[50]

These conflicts, whether they are described as class struggles or as forms of status politics, have structural effects beyond their intended effects. The structure of communication producing these effects causes a type of contradiction beyond the actors and classes of actors. Contradictions on the level of the reproduction of the conditions generating society produce social and cultural change by mobilizing antagonistic models of reproduction (i.e. differentiation and rationalization) that take their theme from the structural basis of communication.[51] Thus Marx's idea of the contradiction between the social relations of production and the forces of production

idea of rationalization; the empirically given process of rationalization (what is real) is not necessarily rational. None of these empiricist presuppositions has to be made. The only thing that counts is the fact of contradiction. Reality is nothing but the environment, which is a continual resource for changing the conceptions of reality.

[49] This is the theoretical strategy of Habermas (1984, 1987), who has combined communicative action theory with systems theory thus producing a kind of division of labour among social theorists. However, these theories have different normative implications which do not necessarily amount to a fair division of labour.

[50] The theoretical treatment of classification leaves open the question of the mode of differentiation used in classification. Whether there is functional, segmentary, or other differentiation remains to be seen. For an interesting treatment of this problem see Schwartz 1981.

[51] This observation points to the central place that a theory of reproduction has for sociological theorizing. A sociology of culture is a necessary and important part of such a theory of reproduction, but it has to be complemented by a sociology of social structure. A new approach to such a sociology can be found in Bourdieu (1980), who works with the concept of a social topology. He speaks, in a manner similar to the language of differentiation theory, about the logic of different fields of action, the homologies concerning the social positions in these fields, and the homologies of these fields within the general society that both reproduce society as a classified reality.

is abstracted to become a contradiction between the antagonistic forms of differentiation and rationalization that are to be specified on each level of social evolution.

### Evolutionary mechanisms

This discussion still leaves open the problem of how contradictions on the different levels of reality are related to one another. How are contradictions that generate learning processes related to contradictions on the level of class conflict? How are the contradictions on this level related to contradictions on the level of the reproduction of society? This problem leads to a *third thesis*: the social changes on these different levels are the mechanisms of social evolution.[52] Evolutionary changes are the result of the combined effects of contradictions producing changes on different levels of social reality. This thesis implies that it is neither collective learning processes nor class conflict nor structural strains alone that explain the evolution of society, but it is their evolutionary interaction. Collective learning processes function like the mechanism of mutation, offering varying patterns of social reality produced in various social groups. Class conflict functions like the mechanism of selection, favouring the patterns of social distinctions that will be integrated into the institutional system of society. Differentiation and rationalization function as a mechanism of reproductive isolation, stabilizing the system of society.

However, there is a problem in grafting such an evolutionary-style theory, well designed though it may be for biological evolution, onto the process of social change. The processes described are not tied to a specific evolutionary mechanism. The evolutionary mechanisms these processes serve are interchangeable. This implies that learning processes, class conflicts, and structural antagonisms can all be selection environments. Mutations can result from any of the social processes mentioned. The same reasoning is valid for the mechanism of reproductive isolation (stabilization). The possible recombinations of mechanisms and processes thus strongly suggest a theory of evolution with a highly complex structure. An important *corollary* goes with this theory of evolution: given these mechanisms, a strict Darwinian theory, which may be defined as a theory that assumes no relation between mutation conditions and selection conditions (Harré 1980, pp. 293ff), is not feasible. A Lamarckian theory would work better. This approach, which assumes a strong relation between mutation conditions and selection conditions, is better suited for explaining the interchangeability of mechanisms and processes in the theory of social evolution. It would allow us to anticipate that the mechanism of stabilization could be transformed into the mechanism of mutation when structural antagonisms became the topic of communication in groups. It would also allow us to anticipate that the mechanism of

---

[52] For these discussions on the relevance of the biological model see Plotkin 1982; for a sociological application see Eder 1987a.

stabilization could be transformed into the mechanism of selection when the description of structural antagonisms became a weapon in the hands of one class against another class of actors.

The analysis of modernization, then, demands a much more sophisticated theory of evolution. Evolutionary theory, itself a product of modernization, is a way of describing modern society. As such, it must take into account the force of collective action as well as the dimension of social and cultural conflict. And it must be able to account for the success or failure of historical developments. It seems that only an evolutionary theory that leaves open the question of what a modern order is about and that concentrates on the question of the social production of modernity will be able to grasp the changes occurring in society. These are changes that, after all, often contradict the theory of modernization that sociologists have formulated concerning this type of society. Perhaps this contradiction is still another mechanism of change in modern society.

# 3

# BEYOND CLASS AS A HISTORICAL SUBJECT
## Towards a Theoretical Construction of Collective Actors[1]

### From metaphysics to sociological analysis

The idea of a historical actor being discovered and brought to light by social analysis has always been a tempting question in the field of social thought. Such questions range from secularized messianic hopes via Marx up to Touraine.[2] Social theory has developed in permanent contrast to and a distancing from such theorizing. This has been its function in theoretical discourse in sociology. It provoked structuralist theory, explaining social change by structural configurations of variables, thereby correcting for the overestimation of actors; as well, it provoked methodological counteractions, with positivism being the most radical one.

Both in times of crisis as well as in times of collective rage the idea of a historical collective actor has gained ground. He was the one to guide society out of its troubles. The historical subject replaced the king as the person embodying the society subject to him,[3] and also became the secularized version of the holy body of the king. It is therefore an invention of modernity, having become one of its constitutive elements. Marx has given the idea of a historical subject its foremost theoretical expression.[4]

---

[1] A first version of this article appeared under the title 'Au-delà du sujet historique: vers une construction théorique des acteurs collectifs' in *L'homme et la société*, 25, pp. 121–40, 1991.

[2] This genealogy of messianic thinking in social theory still has to be reconstructed. This would not simply be an exercise in scientific critique but an exercise in a sociology of scientific development, and as such it should be interpreted as being an aspect of disenchantment to which all the assumption guiding such a reconstruction will have to yield too.

[3] The king as a symbolic representation of the whole society has been treated in different ways: either as representing all its evils or all its goodness. This again can be approached as an empirical variable. It depends upon society's organization which one of the two possibilities it will choose.

[4] Its most interesting and revealing development can be found in Lukács's work (Lukács 1971). It ultimately prescribed history's course and thus exposed itself to historical refutation. We have to find means for refuting theories that do not need such a long time period for proving or disproving theories. Social science is only an attempt to make a more economic use of time in processes of evolutionary learning, i.e. to shorten the amount of time necessary to unlearn.

There were lesser thinkers to rely upon it, and they can be found in all political camps, from the right to the left. Whether it is race, class, gender, or age, we find any category being used as describing the historical actor of modern society.

This already gives us a key to its use: social categories were used to define a historical actor; they were metaphors in the social construction of a historical subject. Understanding this social construction shows us that the attribution of it to a social category is itself a social production. Some claim this attribute for classes, others for races, and still others for the subject as such. These are everyday theories that do not meet hard scientific standards because they do not examine the degree to which such claims are based on reality. However, they are good theories because they indicate the way in which individual actors try to develop a collective identity with the capacity of 'agency'. They are thus social facts that play a crucial role in the process of transforming individual action into collective action.[5]

I intend to deal with the problem of how collective actors emerge in social reality and how they are related to social reality. I will begin with the assumption that historical actors are a real phenomenon that emerges in certain times at certain places. It has its specific conditions of existence and its specific conditions of reproduction that vary over time and space. Therefore, I will collect the variables used in the analysis of collective action and develop some hypotheses on how these variables are related to each other on different levels of social reality. This will allow me to describe the historical subject as the result of a specific type of collective action capable of constituting itself on the level of society. Collective action on the level of society is then seen as the condition for the emergence of a collective actor that can be called social movements. The historical subject is 'disenchanted'; the more we find social movements, the less their description as a historical subject makes sense. Social movements are as normal a phenomenon as any other collective phenomenon in modern society. There is nothing special in and around them. However, we can draw another conclusion: the more we have collective actors on the level of society, i.e. social movements, the more the idea of 'agency' becomes important. The more we give up the idea of a historical subject the more we are capable of thinking of society and social change as the outcome of collective action shaping the course of history. This action perspective does not necessarily lead to an 'agency' perspective that identifies collective actors struggling intentionally to shape the course of history and producing society. Actors rarely make history, and it is up to sociologists to identify the processes that make it a rare phenomenon. The problem therefore

---

[5] This problem has normally been dealt with as the problem of aggregation. But aggregation is not enough: it is necessary to understand the mechanisms that coordinate actions before people start to coordinate their action by intentionally relating to each other.

is not to bring collective actors back into sociological theory, but it is *how* to bring collective actors back into social theory.[6]

### Theoretical approaches to collective action

#### The end of class as a collective actor

This question implies that collective actors have been excluded from social theory, where they had once been a central element. Looking back into the history of social theory, the idea of a collective actor arises with the emergence of modern social theory: the Enlightenment was thought to be the emancipation of *civil society* from traditional bonds. Civil society was thought of as a collective actor, as the association of equal human beings, or in one word: mankind. It was a collective actor based on sharing human rights – a powerful social construction in modern history. The rational belief in this collective actor emerged only 200 years ago – the bicentennial anniversary of the French Revolution reminds us of this fact. This belief could not uphold the social reality. The labour movement indicated a further step in the development of modern society and replaced this collective actor by another one: the *working class*. This produced a puzzle: a part was thought to represent the whole; a class was thought to be a historical collective actor. A condition had to be fulfilled, namely the need for class to possess class consciousness, a rational consciousness about its class existence. This Marxist idea has found an elaborate formulation in Lukács's idea of the proletariat as a historical subject (Lukács 1971). Today even the assumption that a class constitutes a collective actor has to be abandoned.[7] We are faced with the existence of collective actors (in the plural!) that have neither to do directly with civil society nor with class. They seem (!) to exist independently from such structural and cultural conditions, and have to react to this theory. Simple social structural determinism forbids itself – and the problem is to find out how structures play a role in the rise and fall of social movements and other collective actors in modern societies.

However, social theory is badly equipped to react to the rise of new collective actors in developed and developing countries and to the effects of these collective actors upon the modernization of modern societies. The reasons for this are to be found in the distinction between agency and

[6] The allusion to a famous ASA presidential address is intended. However, we aim to bring collective actors back into theory, rectifying structural-functional objectivism in sociological theory.

[7] This assumption has presumably always been utopian, but it influenced a lot of sociological work done in the area of collective consciousness. I will argue later on for a reversal of the perspective upon the relation of class and its existence as a collective actor: I will argue for a primacy of collective actors over classes in the description of social phenomena. Classes are a hidden mechanism that allows for an (at least partial) explanation of the existence of collective actors.

structure that dominates both action theories and system theories. Present-day social theory looks at collective actors either from the perspective of individual actors or from the perspective of social systems without arriving at the phenomenon to be explained: forms of collective action that manifest themselves as countercultures, corporate actors or social movements.

System-theoretical approaches do not explain the rise of collective action nor do they explain the role of collective action in the production and reproduction of social systems. Collective action is treated rather as noise-making. Thus their explanatory power is reduced to identifying barriers to collective action, the most important one being the functional differentiation of modern society. The central problem of action-oriented approaches is the concentration on individual action and constructing collective action from the individual point of view. However, the individual is a highly particular social construction – its existence is still debated (Pizzorno 1986); the individualization of society is still something to come (Beck 1992). Thus the emergent properties in the constitution of collective action tend to be reduced 'ultimately' to properties of individual action. This, by the way, explains why system theories have had no problem showing that structures are stronger than actions. It explains why the 'objectivity' of structure has so easily been played off against the 'subjectivity' of action.[8]

The concentration on the dichotomy of structure and action has disabled action theories and system theories to grasp the phenomenon of collective action. When we start from individual action, collective actions are nothing but aggregated individual actions. A necessary reductionism is built into theory construction. Starting from systemic properties of social structures, collective action appears as a mere medium of the reproduction of systemic forces. However, there are collective actors emerging from diverse forms of collective action. The idea of explaining the emergence of collective action out of individual action and systemic constraints therefore is only the first step toward a theory of collective action. This is not yet a sociological theory. A sociology of collective action begins when we want to find out how collective action is constituted through interaction in micro-social situations and how through collective action social structures and processes are reproduced. Instead of arguing for the conceptual difference between agency and structure, the difference of micro-social processes and macro-social processes is made and their genuinely social character is emphasized (Knorr-Cetina 1988). Thus what I am aiming for is a *sociology of collective action* beyond agency and system.

[8] The problem of individual actors again complicates the discussion. Those looking at actor-oriented approaches reinforce the hiatus between structure and action. Here, the only way out is to radicalize the voluntaristic theory of action into a theory of the creativity of social actors or an 'agency' theory (Joas 1989). Then, however, we have to give up most of our sociological knowledge. A pertinent critique of agency theories is found in Collins 1992.

*The theoretical construction of collective action*

We therefore have to explore the possibilities of a level of theoretical analysis where action and structure are related in a way different from traditional theories of action. This level of analysis is realized – as I see it – in the problem of the *coordination* of individual action (Becker 1986; Miller 1986). There has been much theoretical work done on individual actors and interaction between individual actors and on how they construct a collectively shared world by mutual (mis)understanding. From symbolic interactionism up to the theory of communicative action the idea of a collective construction of reality has become an important strand of sociological theorizing apart from system-theoretical approaches. This can be considered a starting point. The next step consists in giving up the perspective of the individual actor.[9] Thus the starting point can only refer to actions that produce a double social reality: the reality of systemic structures and the reality of actors.

In the following, the emphasis will be on the social construction of social actors. The empirical reference will be – due to their central importance in social life – the social construction of collective actors within processes of collective action. To start with such a sociology of collective action it is necessary to conceptualize collective actors without falling into the traps of 'collectivism'. This is an important question because the history of social theory has given us a series of negative examples of this way of thinking.

The traditional *mass-psychological approach* sees collective action as driven by irrational motives – LeBon (1963) represents the classic mass-psychological approach. The idea of the irrational crowd needing guidance by rational leaders is highly suggestive. A specific version of it is the Marxist idea of class as a collective *historical subject* with its potential of a class consciousness that will realize the potential suppressed by and in bourgeois society; this collective actor is at first not very much different from the mass as LeBon conceptualized it. Embedding this irrational crowd in a theory of collective consciousness raising the irrational crowd is transformed – the divergence from the mass-psychological approach begins here – into a rational actor. However, the idea of a collective actor situated between collective crowd psychology and philosophy of history has not gained reputation – on the contrary. The way out of this conceptualization is certainly not the return to either mass psychology or philosophy of history.

How to avoid such implications? We must abandon the idea that there is something 'basically' irrational in collective action. This is the basic assumption underlying an approach to social movements that deals with socio-psychological explanations for joining collective actions and social

---

[9] We have to see the individual actor as a social construction that is used in the reproduction of interacting collective actions.

movements.[10] This approach looks for the motivations using (and some-times going beyond simplifying) assumptions about rational behaviour. Rational motivations can also be moral motivations; some preliminary research has been done on the relation of stages of moral consciousness and participation in social movements.[11] Theoretically, this 'particularist approach' (as it has been called by Eyerman) is based on a rationalist reinterpretation of the mass-psychological paradigm. This 'particularist school' of analysis investigates social movements as vehicles for political socialization – it is explicitly centred on the 'concrete' individual and its experiences and perceptions as well as learning capacities.

Following such premises we will not grasp the phenomenon of a collective actor emerging from collective action. We will only find a class of individual actors motivated in a parallel manner. Sharing similar motivations is taken as the foundation of 'acting together'. Instead of leaving this question aside or to objective forces in history we will provide a genuinely sociological approach to account for such sharing as emergent properties in collective action. We will look for the processes that generate shared collective feelings and orientations of action. The collective actor as the emergent social reality is not to be sought outside the process of collective action, neither in the psychology of individual actors nor in the teleology of history. He is to be located *within* the process of collective action.

Such a theoretical approach will give us the tools for an empirical analysis of collective actors. It will allow us to treat collective actors beyond the metaphysical constructions of historical subjects that have up to now dominated its theoretical discourse. We will begin not with the theoretical construction of collective *actors* as the carriers of collective *action*, but vice-versa, with the theoretical construction of collective *action* within which emerges a collective *actor*. This theoretical perspective is due either to the failure to identify in collective actors a historical subject or to the failure to understand the rational element in collective mobilization excluded in the notion of collective actors as irrational masses.

Leaving the problem of the individual actor to psychology and the problem of the historical actor to philosophy, sociology might be able to treat the problem of a collective actor emerging from collective action more adequately. With the following analysis I will show that there are interesting developments in the research on collective action that can be

[10] Socio-psychological literature has gained a prominent place in social movement research in recent years. Important is the work of the social psychologist Klandermans (1984, 1988, 1992). Another approach which is related to the rational choice tradition is represented in the work on the 'critical mass' in movement mobilization (Oliver et al. 1985; Oliver and Marwell 1988; Marwell et al. 1989). See also Opp 1989 for a radical example of applying rationalist assumptions to movement mobilization.

[11] This strand of research has been overpowered by the rise of rationalistic approaches in action theories. Nevertheless, this area still represents a potential that has not yet been fully exploited.

taken up by theory. It is the *theory of social movements* that has become the key to the theoretical problem outlined above. Social movements are collective actors as well as collective actions. Both perspectives converge in the phenomenon of social movements. Therefore, we should not be surprised to find the theoretical alternatives in the midst of social movement theory and research.

### The European/American divide in the study of social movements

The research on collective action, pushed in recent years by the rise of social movements in Third World countries as well as in Western and socialist countries, is characterized by the so-called 'great European and American divide' (Eyerman and Jamison 1991). There is – as usual – a gulf between American and European sociologists in the understanding of present-day social movements. In Europe it has become common to analyze movements as carriers of political projects, as (more or less) 'new' historical actors or 'new' social movements (Touraine 1977, 1981, 1985, 1992; Habermas 1987). Collective action is situated in a historical environment. Theoretically, the European school is close to the philosophy of history paradigm; variations within this school can be reduced to its positive or negative interpretation. The American approach has been dominated by what has been called the resource mobilization approach (Zald and McCarthy 1979, 1987). The central idea here is that movements exist through movement organizations that recruit members and money, or human and material resources. Thus the development of movement organizations and of a movement industry has been the centre of analysis. The ambiguous figure of 'historical action' is replaced by the conception of 'organized action'. The American school, contrary to the European one, begins with a more rationalistic theory of action environments to account for the emergence and persistence of collective action.[12]

Varying solutions combining the American and the European approaches have been examined. Cohen (1985) proposed to combine both by specifying the complementarity of perspectives: the complementarity of resource mobilization and resource generation. The idea of resource generation takes up the idea that collective actors can also become producers of new collectively shared cultural orientations.[13] Another solution is to generalize the concept of 'resources'. Why not mobilize moral resources or even generate them? A recent proposition (Klandermans et al. 1988) suggests centring the analysis on the problem of *consensus mobilization* where

---

[12] A good overview discussion of the difference between the European and the American approaches with further references is found in Klandermans 1991. An excellent overview of the 'state of the art' can be found in Neidhardt and Rucht 1991.

[13] This is the point made by Touraine and his collaborators against resource mobilization theory (Lapeyronnie 1988). See also the similar critique of Kitschelt (1991) and the interesting response by Zald (1991).

consensus is the result of a screening process (100 feel motivated to act, 5 will do it). However, such propositions ultimately do not solve the problem inherent in both approaches, namely to explain the social processes underlying the definition, generation and mobilization of resources. They reduce the problem of explaining collective action to the problem of explaining the emergence of a group of consenting people. Thus we arrive at a theory of movement or protest elites who share some ideological and strategic visions of the world and monopolize the world of protest communication.

I would like to propose another solution to the problem of explaining the making of a collective actor. A theory of consensus mobilization has to consider its social (not psychological!) conditions on the micro-level and its embeddedness in a socio-historical context as well as the interrelationship between both levels. This theory will be based on two related arguments.

The first argument is that we have to distinguish three phases in the production and reproduction of collective actors. The first phase can be described as the process of the *constitution* of a collective actor by acting together. The action oriented toward producing this good is a collective action. The second phase comprises the process of identifying a collective actor by defining the *boundaries* of collective action. Collective action is no longer restricted to its internal making but marks boundaries between itself and its social environment. It thus becomes identifiable as a social entity, i.e. as a collective actor. The third phase is characterized by processes that allow for the reproduction of this identity. These processes can be called *cognitive practices* (Eyerman and Jamison 1991). Cognitive practices stabilize the identity of a collective actor by his capacity to describe himself and his relationship to a social environment. A collective actor reproduces himself through cognitive practices of self-representation, thereby adding reflection as a mechanism of reproduction of collective action. This opens up the possibility for collective actors to learn and to transform themselves without having to return to the first phase of the constitution of a collective actor through collective action. This is my first theoretical argument to bring collective actors back into social theory.

The second argument is that we have to distinguish between three levels of analyzing the production and reproduction of collective actors. The idea of consensus mobilization as a *micro-level* analysis of collective action provides a powerful, but very limited methodology in social research on collective action. My claim is that the analysis of social movements can be improved by developing the micro-foundations of the analysis of collective actors more systematically. By relating the economic approach to theories of moral learning processes in the micro-analysis of collective actors, we could gain a more thorough understanding of the processes of the formation of collective actors on the micro-level. This will transform the economic (or market) model into a more dynamic one while sensitizing to the processes of communication while acting together. The next level of analysis forces us to go beyond the interactionist model and to contextualize the micro-level analysis. Consensus mobilization needs more than mobilized motivations; it needs power and resources. The American school analyzes collective action at this *meso-level*. On the meso-level, collective action manifests itself in organized pressure groups that relate to an institutional system, to a 'political opportunity structure'. The research on collective action shows that European studies traditionally have concentrated research on the *macro-level*. On the macro-level, collective action manifests itself as social movements transcending the limits of an institutional system and relating to historical alternatives of societal development. Viewed from this perspective, Americans stop at the meso-level (which is, as the work of Tilly has shown, extremely helpful for historical–empirical research). Europeans are more caught by their revolutionary past and see collective actors primarily as potential social movements, thus locating themselves on the macro-level (which has produced the privileged stand of European social theory in critical diagnoses).

References to the micro-level relate mainly to political socialization or moral learning processes, to the degree of moral consciousness and their reproduction in collectively shared worldviews, and to the development of linguistic capacity and their class-bound realization. The American type meso-level analysis of pressure groups contains references to economic theories of collective action as well as to cultural factors. Resource mobilization through social movements organizations is seen as a mechanism used to surmount the difficulties of generating collective action. On such grounds the theory of resource mobilization and the macro-theory of social movements can be reformulated within a theory of consensus mobilization. This is the second theoretical argument to bring collective actors back into social theory.

In the following section, a sketchy outline of the stages in the formation of a collective actor going from the micro-level up to the macro-level will be given. On each level the problem of the emergence of a collective actor from processes of collective action will be discussed. Based on such a theoretical construction of collective actors, we will avoid reifications of collective actors as historical subjects. Moving beyond the classic paradigms will allow us to conduct research on collective actors avoiding the historical irrelevance of micro-analysis and the empirical irrelevance of macro-analysis. The discussion will be restricted to the analysis of a specific collective actor, namely protest actors.[14] This does not exclude the applicability of this theory to other types of collective action and other

[14] The phenomena I have in mind when discussing this theoretical scheme are the diverse elements of the ecological movement: namely its 'grass roots', its effective and professionalized social movement organizations and its anchorage in specific social groups and classes as the carriers of cultural change in the process of modernizing modern society. But it should also be applicable to other collective actors, to counterculture groups, to symbolic crusades (anti-alcoholic or anti-smoking movements, for example), to countermovements (such as pro-life movements as countermovements to pro-choice movements) or to regionalist and nationalist movements.

types of collective actors such as business lobbies and governmental actors. On the contrary, it allows for describing social reality beyond the individualistic paradigm without giving up the idea of an actor constructing his social environment. It will, however, provide some argument against a theory of agency as natural outcomes of rationally motivated collective action.

## The micro-level analysis of collective actors

### Collective action at the micro-level

The introduction of a micro-level analysis of collective action implies a sharp break with what I have called the particularist school. Motives are not given but are themselves produced within the process of collective action. People do not decide to join collective action but their motives to do so are generated and produced in acting together. Thus the problem of the coordination of actions replaces the problem of psychological motivation.

The transformation of theories of action into theories capable of explaining the coordination of social action, has – and this is not surprising – refreshed the old European and American divide in social theory. We can choose between two competing theoretical strategies of explaining the coordination of action. The attempt to systematically grasp the interaction effects of individual actions has led to the development of two promising developments in social theory: *rational choice* and *argumentation theory*.[15] Both theories are only a beginning still tied to the old theoretical battles. They open a new ground, and they do this in two respects:

- First, in relating rational and symbolic actions with each other specific interactive effects are produced; the key situation underlying the rational-choice approach is the *prisoner's dilemma*, a situation where interacting rational actors try to maximize their profit in a situation of insecurity where they do not know how the significant others will act. The key situation underlying the communicative action approach is the *discursive situation*, where actors are forced to base their actions upon collectively agreed arguments in processes of argumentation.

---

[15] It may come as a surprise to treat rational choice theories as non-psychological theories. There is, however, a decisive difference between behavioural psychology and rational-choice theory although rational choice theory once emerged from behaviouralist assumptions. Rational-choice theory has developed in such a way that it has been freed of such assumptions. It provides models for the coordination of action that can be initiated by any kind of motivation (as built into the preference structure of individuals). This has softened rational-choice theory, a process that is to be seen very clearly in the recent work of Elster (1989) where he emphasizes the role of norms in shaping social relations. Social norms, for example, shape wage negotiations as well as self-interest, namely norms of equality, equity and fair division. This shift could even become a possible bridge to argumentation theory.

- Second, both approaches can be described as ideal models of coordination. In the first case an attempt is made to find out the best strategies for all engaged in a competitive situation. In the second case an attempt is made to discover a collectively shared interpretation of the situation (a temporary consensus). The coordinating mechanisms turn out to be two polar models of cooperation: *market* and *discourse*.[16]

Both models explain the coordination of social action by crediting it – to use some classical sociological categories – either to material or ideal interests. The material interest is to get, in the long run, the best out of a situation. This is the message of Axelrod's theory of the evolution of cooperation (Axelrod 1984). The ideal interest is to uphold a moral level of human existence. This is the message of Kohlberg's and Habermas's theory of the development of moral consciousness (Kohlberg 1981; Habermas 1983). Both interests are – as Weber has taught us – equally present in historical life, but have been the locus of fierce ideological battles. Elster has applied rational-choice theory to Marxian theory. My own argument can be read as a communicative reconstruction of rational-choice theory. The old ideological battles are over. We must lay the ground for new ones.

A first objective to be met is the clarification of the empirical status of these idealizing models. The problem is not only that people are less rational and less communicative than the theory predicts, nor that people deviate from these models in a systematic way; this is normal. The problem is that there are socially structured patterns of being rational and communicative. This is the central empirical problem that both a micro-theory of collective action and a micro-level analysis of the formation of collective actors have to deal with.

Empirical propositions to deal with this question have come mainly from rational-choice theories of collective action. They point out that group heterogeneity (not homogeneity!) will serve the constitution of collective action, that group size plays an important role, that a critical mass of activists is necessary to generate collective action and to mobilize a following. Communicative-action theory has also made some propositions, a first one being that the structural features of communicatively organized groups will be a decisive variable in the constitution of collective action (Eder 1985). A second one is that the communicative basis of these groups will make them the privileged collective actors in the defence of the life-world against the domination of system imperatives (Habermas 1987).

These general empirical propositions run into complementary problems. Rational-choice propositions neglect the communicative nature of collective action, while communicative-action theories neglect the strategic side of collective action. Therefore, a thorough examination of the simultaneous incorporation of these propositions into a wider theory is to be

---

[16] Contrasting market and discourse implies a common ground for comparison which is its mode of social coordination of action. Elaborate models of markets are found, beyond the pioneering work of Williamson (1975), in Reddy 1985, Zelizer 1988 and Lane 1991.

looked for.[17] Based on such a micro-theory of collective action the emergence of a collective actor from collective action can be described and analyzed.

### The formation of a group and the reproduction of a group identity

On the micro-level, the collective actor emerging from collective action is the 'group',[18] exerting pressure upon its members and integrating individual actors into the ongoing process of collective action. The reality of coordinated individual motivations produces the reality of group pressure. The existence of a group is not only the effect of individual decisions, be they motivated by egotistic or altruistic sentiments, rational or moral decisions. The group is also a social fact that precedes such sentiments and exerts social control over such decisions and sentiments. To account for such group processes we have to understand the nature of social relations emerging from interactions of rationally or morally motivated actors. The emerging collective reality of a 'group' is a social construction produced by actors drawing boundaries between the collective action they contribute to and its environment.

By defining the boundaries of collective action an identity emerges that transforms collective action into a collective actor. A micro-level analysis of group identity is the key to a more refined theory of the formation of a collective actor. This refined theory extends the theory of group identity to a theory of the self-production and self-reproduction of groups through *cognitive practices*, in the ideal case through *collective learning processes*.[19] Cognitive practices and collective learning processes are processes in which people interpret the modes and ways of their collective action. The problem of collective action cannot be separated from the problem of interpretation. The problem of interpretation gives a dynamic dimension to the model of the market because interpretation presupposes communication and communication over the validity of interpretations is bound to the logic of argumentation. Thus we have to look at the processes of communication through which a group identity is reproduced.

An interesting proposition of how to analyze such cognitive practices and processes has been made by Snow et al. (1986), who try to identify different forms of 'frame alignment' among social movement participants

---

[17] This has affected research in an characteristic way: the rationalist theorists have used data from police records to find out about the character of collective actions. The communicative theorists have rather used self-descriptions as a source of data on collective action. The first are more inclined toward quantitative, the latter more toward qualitative analysis of empirical data.

[18] Theoretical formulations of the concept of groups are rare. See an interesting attempt in Moscovici 1979. A historical application is found in Eder 1985. See also the foregoing chapter and its further references.

[19] The idea of collective learning processes in social movements has been treated in Miller 1986. A good discussion, relating this idea systematically to Habermas's theory of communicative action (of which it is an offspring) is found in Strydom 1987.

(i.e. protest groups). They distinguish between 'frame bridging' (simply mobilizing people with similar outlooks, for example by direct mailing), 'frame amplification' (the clarification and reinvigoration of an interpretive frame), 'frame extension' (frame generalization that makes frames attractive to a greater part of the population), and 'frame transformation' (i.e. producing new frames of interpreting specific or general aspects of the world). Their research points to dispositional factors, be they formal (such as stages of moral consciousness) or substantive (some ideological creeds), as secondary factors to the recruitment process and the frame alignments going on within them.

Engaging in collective action is therefore not only an effect of having rational reasons for participating nor an effect of group pressure and group power. It also triggers reflective cognitive processes. As collective action produces the reasons for joining a collective action, it becomes itself a mechanism of collective learning. Thus market models and discourse models are related to each other in the way that mechanism and logic are related to each other. This therefore does not imply rejecting rational-choice models. On the contrary, these models show some structural conditions necessary for reflective processes to take place. Such variables are group heterogeneity, group size, and the relative number of activists. Considering the communicative nature of reflective processes in groups these variables can be reformulated in a discourse theoretical way: group heterogeneity provides for argumentative conflicts, thus feeding the dynamics of communication. Group size is the classic variable accounting for the possibility of discourses (an old argument of democratic theory!). Activists are those who dare to talk in public and consequently fuel communicative struggles. Thus we arrive at an impressive list of variables on the micro-level that can be related with each other to explain the emergence of a collective actor from collective action. Cognitive practices create a group identity, allow members to identify with the group beyond the grip of group power.

These reflective processes can finally lead to collective learning processes. Two types of collective learning can be distinguished: *moral learning processes* that thematize and change the normative context of strategic cooperation, and *strategic learning processes* that use and instrumentalize moral arguments in a rational-choice situation, in a cooperative game. We can derive from these two types of learning processes two forms of 'distorted learning processes': and in moral learning processes, for example, processes of ideological and terrorist transformation (the French Revolution!), in strategic learning processes, for example, the self-destructive exploitation of others.[20] The type of learning processes that will

---

[20] A systematic description of distorted learning processes is found in Miller 1986. See also Eder 1985. Such a theory presupposes a clear theory of 'normal' learning processes the foundations of which are sought in the theory of communicative action and discourse as developed by Habermas (1984, 1987).

dominate depends on social conditions beyond the reach of the processes constituting a group. To clarify these social conditions I will turn to the meso-level of analysis of collective action.

## The meso-level analysis of collective actors

### Collective action on the meso-level

The reasons for which some collective actors stay in contention longer than others, and why some do have greater and more enduring success, are changes in opportunities and the expansion and appropriation of material and symbolic resources through *organizing* collective action. We have introduced the meso-level earlier by referring to the theory of resource mobilization central to the American tradition of social movement research. The problem of how to mobilize people for collective action and collective goods is solved – as the theory of resource mobilization holds – by organizational resources.

The organization of social protest has been regarded in traditional social movement research as the end of the life history of a social movement. This is not true as far as the bourgeois and workers' movements are concerned. With regard to the new social movements, this law does not hold either. Organization is not the end, but the normalization and stabilization of collective action. Social movement organizations have been the mechanism devised to overcome the improbability of individual actors joining collective action. This hypothesis can be elaborated more clearly when contrasted with traditional forms of mobilization, which are based upon preexisting social networks (Oberschall 1973). Without the possibility of creating ties beyond traditional network structures, movements in premodern societies never succeeded in surpassing short life cycles. Social movement organizations ('SMOs') are the characteristic invention of modern social movements to stretch their life cycle.

Such 'SMOs' are oriented toward the patronage of constituencies who do not act on their own (such as the blacks in the United States in the sixties). They are supported by communication professionals and thus allow for the representation of interests not capable of doing so on their own. Outside leadership, full-time paid staff, small or non-existent membership, speaking for others rather than for an aggrieved group – these variables characterize a type of organization of collective action emerging in modern society (McCarthy and Zald 1973).

This intermediate level is decisive for understanding the role of collective action within the institutional system of a society. When the problem of mobilizing people into collective action has been solved by SMOs, three further problems arise. The first is the emergence of a new type of institutional structure. Each SMO will act by looking at other SMOs, thus producing a social movement industry (SMI) of interconnected and interrelated SMOs. Greenpeace, Friends of the Earth and WWF are good examples of a professional division of labour between protest actors that constitute an SMI in the ecological field. The second problem refers to the relation of SMOs with the historically established collective actor we call the 'state'.[21] Today we tend to speak of the political opportunity structure as defining the space for movement organizations and thus allowing collective action to play a role in the field of bargaining on the institutional (meso-)level. The third problem relates to the question of different logics of collective action implying unequal capacities in mobilizing resources (Offe and Wiesenthal 1980).

On the meso-level, collective action is constituted through social relations that no longer depend exclusively on interactional ties. It is coordinated through organizational ties that differentiate between activists and supporters (the 'constituencies') and thus make organized collective action relatively independent from the everyday motivations of the actors. The differentiation of a meso-level from the micro-level is a process that started with the rise of modern forms of protest. It has been put into question by movement activists and ideologically criticized as a separation of activists from the people. Thus the structural phenomenon of organized collective action is reflected as a problem in the subjective experience of mobilization. Considering this specific structural property of collective action the emergence of a specifically modern type of collective actor can be analyzed.

### The formation and reproduction of corporate actors

These forms and mechanisms of generating and stabilizing collective action through formal organization and resource mobilization contribute to the formation of an *organized collective actor*. Collective mobilization generates a 'corporate actor'. This collective actor is normally called a 'pressure group'. Pressure groups can be distinguished based on their concerns: these concerns can be moral (the classic example being the pro-life/pro-choice groups concerning the abortion issue)[22] or material (the classic example being syndicalism). The context of organized collective action is in the rules of the institutional game and the public resonance to collective action. This gives public communication and the media a preponderant

---

[21] The role of the state has so far been analyzed mainly in terms of a repressive organization. This has to do with the close connection made between social movements and violence or terrorism. The analysis of cooperative relationships between movement organizations and the state is a more recent phenomenon. A historical account can be found in Birnbaum (1988), who has lucidly analyzed the interaction of the state and protest actors in modern European history. Gale (1986) has given a systematic framework for analyzing the relation of social movements with the state using the example of the relation between the environmental movement and government agencies. Approaches to this question from very different theoretical starting points are found in Hirsch 1988, McCarthy and Wolfson 1990 and Zald and Useem 1987.

[22] A good example is the discussion in McCarthy 1987. Organized collective actors concerned with moral (or moralized) issues have gained in recent years the attention of social movement researchers. See, among others, the work by Gusfield (1981a).

role in explaining the context of organized collective action. The central problem is how to conceptualize theoretically the dynamics of such concerns in the formation and reproduction of organized collective actors.

On the meso-level, we can observe the transformation of organized collective action into organizations as acting entities. The examples of Greenpeace, the WWF and other movement organizations show that organizations act and are perceived as acting entities. This capacity of organized collective action has to do with the capacity of these organizations to develop an identity. This process has been recognized in organizational analysis which has contributed to a growing literature on organizational culture and organizational symbolism.[23] To understand the emergence of organized collective actors, a 'corporate protest actor', out of organized collective action the analysis of the symbolic representation of collective action is essential. The development of social movement organizations towards symbolic forms of organized action is the necessary condition for representing an organization as a social actor because it is through such action that movement organizations produce a coherent symbolic identity.

This emerging type of organized collective actors is dependent upon its recognition as a collective actor by others, above all by other cooperative or antagonistic collective actors. Bound to a system of competing collective actors, the capacity to adapt the organization to the demands of its environment is a question of survival in the market of organizational identities.[24] This leads us to the question of collective learning processes of organized collective actors.[25] The problem of collective learning processes arises here when the rules of the game are changed by the interaction of organized collective actors. I think of new legal forms of controlling and regulating the interactions between different collective actors and the related discourse on the democratic meaning of these changes. The

---

[23] There is widespread discussion on organizational culture and organizational symbolism that is pertinent to this discussion. Important has been Meyer and Rowan 1977, which treats the formal structure of organizations as myth and ceremony. See also Meyer and Scott 1983 on the connection of ritual and rationality in organizational environments. This discussion has been expanded by Mangham and Overington (1987). An overview of the current debate is given by Alvesson and Berg (1990). An application to types of organizations (non-profit organizations) that also emerge within the movement sector is found in DiMaggio and Anheier 1990.

[24] This argument can rely upon recent developments in organizational and institutional analysis and attempts to grasp the new institutional order resulting from the 'new' collective actors in the institutional game. For the point on the programmatic statement of an institutional analysis of politics see March and Olsen 1989. For an interesting assessment on the latter point see Streeck and Schmitter (1985), who emphasize associations as an institutional and organizational element beyond the market and the state.

[25] A review of the literature on organizational learning is found in Levitt and March 1988. This literature relies – due to the symbolic nature of organized collective action – on theatrical metaphors and on a theory of dramatic appearances and dramaturgical action. See on this point also the collected papers of Kenneth Burke (1990), including the introduction by Gusfield.

significance of informal modes of conflict resolution (especially in environmental issues) is controversial; they are, for example, interpreted in
political discourse as well as in theory as either contributing to democratic
institutions or as blocking the democratization of institutional frameworks
of modern societies.

The institutional context is again embedded in the wider context we call
society. Therefore, the analysis of collective actors needs to be pushed
beyond the meso-level. The formation of political actors (or pressure
groups as they have been traditionally termed) is an intermediate, not yet
final stage in the formation of collective actors. Collective actors do not
only intervene as organizations into the process of social production and
reproduction. In the following we have to look at a third level of collective
action: the macro-level of collective action and the emergence of social
movements as collective actors.

## The macro-level analysis of collective actors

### Collective action at the macro-level

The traditional macro-level answer to the question 'How is collective
action possible?' has been that there are class-specific ways of experiencing
and perceiving the social world that generate collective action. *Class* thus
defines a specific capacity of collective action. The description of collective
action by reference to class-specific schemata of practices and action has
been debated because the traditional classes no longer define the speci-
ficities of collective action on the macro-level. Regionalist and nationalist
mobilizations, gender-specific forms of mobilization and environmental
protest do not fit the model of economic classes we have inherited from the
last century. People are mobilized across traditional class lines.

Whether social class is a collective actor has become a still more debated
question. This question is complicated because we do not know anything
about the processes that generate class-specific collective actors. Action
theories are – as Lockwood (1981) has pointed out – 'the weakest link in
the chain' from class position to class action. The relation of class location
and collective action has lost (if it had ever existed) its close relationship.
This critical argument can be turned into a constructive one by distinguishing analytically the level of class as a context for collective action and the
level of class as a collective actor emerging from class-specific collective
action. Describing collective action on the level of class is distinguished
from the level of organized collective action by the criterion of a similar
form of being involved in social problems in issues. This is what is meant by
the term of being 'socially determined'. There is a commonality of
experience given by a specific location of 'classes' of people in a society.[26]

[26] This abstract notion of class has been introduced and defended in the foregoing chapters.
It allows us to decouple the concept of class from its economic interpretation, inherited from
the nineteenth century.

On the macro-level, the way in which collective action is socially constituted not only runs into problems of forms, but also into problems of substance. We have to consider that collective action of social classes is realized in a more complex manner than traditional analysis had claimed. There are different types of collective action, each with its own specific logic. The classic two-class model of modern society has led to the idea of two logics of collective action (Offe and Wiesenthal 1980), one constitutive for the working class, the other for the class of employers. Bourdieu (1984) has generalized this idea, deriving the logic of collective action of social groups from a class-specific 'habitus', a class-specific form of experiencing and perceiving the world. People diverge from this logic only within the confines of statistical variance. In this way, a social structure (which is a macro-level phenomenon) as the context of collective action can be identified. Class structures are the environment within which collective action produces and reproduces itself on the level of society. However, classes define only the macro social space within which collective actors emerge; but they do not determine it.

### The formation and reproduction of social movements

The collective actor emerging from such structurally embedded collective action has been called a 'social movement' since the rise of modern society, but without giving this term a precise meaning. The working class had its movement in the same way as the political class of citizens and the petit-bourgeois class had their own movements. The reason why social movements so easily become an ideological subject of analysis is the imprecise nature of social movements (which has often been compensated for by deterministic theories of class).

This ideological analysis has prevailed in the theory of social movements. We have to break with this tradition. Social movements are not the most conscious part of a social class, be it the bourgeois or the working class. The historical development of modern society has produced a multiplicity of social movements and because of this created additional problems for this tradition. We have to reformulate the way in which different class actors relate to each other. Today's social movements are therefore still less the outcome of the will of a class than the traditional social movements were. They have to be related to social class – and this opens the possibility of theoretical and empirical research on the relation of social class and social movements.

This level of analysis has been explicitly avoided by Tilly (1978) and others, who point to the difficulties of adequately putting into operation such a level of analysis.[27] This fluidity of the concept might explain why the research on new social movements on the macro-level has been theoreti-

---

[27] The fluidity of rendering this phenomenon operational can be illustrated by a definition given by Zald and McCarthy (1987): social movements – contrary to social movement organizations – are defined as preference structures for social change in a population.

cally weak. Most of the research is either merely descriptive (NB: research institutions still do nothing more than produce chronologies of protest for future generations of researchers with a convincing idea of how to treat such data!) or it is action research, engaged research. Literature abounds with forms of description. If there is analysis, it is socio-historical, a form of 'contemporary history' using social science terminology. These ways of looking at collective actors lack something constitutive for science: the capability of producing a counterintuitive perspective, of objectifying the intuitive perception and experience of reality, or, to use Bourdieu's words, to objectify the illusions constitutive of the historical meaning of the new collective actors.

How do we deal with this phenomenon without reifying social movements? On the meso-level, the solution has been to look at the organized collective actors that mobilize 'preference structures for change' (Zald and McCarthy 1987) in a population. On the macro-level we have to relate such movement organizations to a wider context. This context will be defined as the context of public communication. Macro-level analysis of collective action refers to identifying the context of public communication within which collective action reproduces its conditions of existence. This implies leaving the context of organization behind and locating social movements in the public sphere. The public sphere is the macro-condition *par excellence* of the constitution of collective action. The collective action ascribed to social movements exists only because their existence is constructed in public communication.

Touraine (1981) claims to have grasped theoretically the cultural dimension of collective action to which sociological theories of action are not well suited. Rational-choice theories take a highly specific culture for granted.[28] Theories of communicative action tell us that emancipation will come out of a discursive way of acting together, but they do not tell us how such outcomes come about. The theoretical task that we have ahead of us is to develop these theories in a direction that allows them to grasp the process of generating collectively shared meaning systems. Theories of social movements as collective learning processes assume that the self description of a collective actor as a social movement places him beyond the institutional framework. Whether this claim is warranted or not, collective actors become, by this self description, part of the historical action system.

The context within which such theoretical developments have originated are societies shaped by the dynamics of present-day social movements. These developments have challenged the established idealized models of social order and stimulated a more dynamic approach to the theory of reproduction of social systems. They have also pushed towards a shift in action theory from individual to collective action. It is this development, the rise of new collective actors and the related theoretical challenge, that

---

[28] This is an old argument, but it is still valid. The best formulation is found in Sahlins 1976.

offers some exciting new perspectives on the way class and politics are related. Classes are no longer historical actors; but they function like a *social opportunity structure* for collective action that underlies movement politics. Class no longer is a determinant; it is a restriction and a chance. But this is more than enough to keep the notion of class while decoupling it from the idea of a historical actor.

## Conclusion

The historical subject is dead. However, a multitude of collective actors is still alive. This forces us to reconsider our theoretical tools for understanding and explaining collective action. We made four basic propositions:

1. Bringing collective actors back into social theory leads us beyond Marx and Marxism. The question of historical actors has become an empirical one. There is no social location that is a privileged locus of generating social movements. Collective mobilization depends on the cultural orientations contained in collective actions.

2. Bringing collective actors back into social theory forces us to change the individualistic bias of post-Marxist social theory. The theory of communicative action is only a first step away from Marx, for it remains within the individualistic paradigm of social theory that has led to the theoretical split of structure and action. The empirical analysis of present-day collective actors and movements might help us to overcome these restrictions and push theoretical development into a more promising direction. The alternative approach is a collectivistic reconstruction of the theory of communicative and rational action that at the same time brings modern (Luhmannian) systems theory down to earth. This would enable us to grasp more adequately the phenomenon of collective action upon which a theory of the formation of collective actors has to be built.

3. Instead of relying upon sweeping theoretical generalizations and functional explanations, social theory should give a more sophisticated account of social action that produces and reproduces social reality. This applies above all to macro-theoretical accounts of the role and function of social classes as collective historical actors. To avoid functionalist or philosophy of history type of explanations, a genuinely sociological analysis has been proposed to look at social classes as collective actors and to use elements of social movements theory as it has evolved since the late seventies.

4. To explain the effect of social classes or groups on social reality (which is the project of a theory of praxis) we have to analyze the formation of collective action and the emergence of collective actors from collective action on different levels of social reality, going from the micro- to the macro-level. Using insights from theories of rational action as well as from theories of communicative action, the idea that collective action

has to do with rational behaviour as well as with the problem of communicating such rational behaviour by ascribing good reasons to it has been developed. This could explain how social movements emerging from rational behaviour are transformed into collective practices, or more generally, how individual rationality is transformed into collective rationality without basing the latter on sweeping functionalist or historicist accounts of collective practices.

# PART II
# RECONNECTING CULTURE AND CLASS

## 4

## CULTURE AND CLASS
### Bourdieu's Culturalist Refraction of the Traditional Theory of Class[1]

### The three-way refraction of class theory

Among the attempts to revive a class analysis of advanced modern societies the contribution of Bourdieu has a central place.[2] His work is best understood as the attempt to push class analysis beyond Marx and Weber rather than beyond status and class. Bourdieu does not simply combine Marxist and Weberian elements of class theory – looking at how the self-understanding and interpretations of theory correspond. Moreover he gives the concept of class – this being the fundamental starting point – a genuine *culturalist twist*. This culturalist twist cannot be dismissed as a mere 'extension' or as another 'rescue-act' for class theory. Indeed, its significance escapes the critics who question the concept of class and class analysis.

This new approach to empirical class analysis[3] implies a *three-way refraction* of traditional class theory. First, it breaks with the separation of base and superstructure in class analysis; secondly, it integrates the analysis of class action into a theory of class-specific cultural practices; and thirdly it analyzes the theoretical description of class structure as itself an instance of that class structure. In the following this three-way refraction is discussed to determine exactly what this 'new' approach implies.

---

[1] This is the English translation and a revised version of the article 'Klassentheorie als Gesellschaftstheorie. Bourdieus dreifache kulturtheoretische Brechung der Klassentheorie', published in *Klassenlage, Lebensstil and kollektive Praxis*, edited by Klaus Eder (pp. 15–43), Suhrkamp Verlag, Frankfurt. It has been translated by Paul Statham.

[2] Notwithstanding the fact that Bourdieu has turned away from class analysis toward cultural analysis in his more recent work.

[3] Bourdieu's contributions to class analysis and class theory are outlined explicitly in Bourdieu 1966, 1974, 1984, 1987. See also 'A reply to some objections' in Bourdieu 1990. For a detailed discussion of the cultural sociological aspects of Bourdieu's class theory, see Joppke 1986.

The *first* culturalist refraction of traditional class theory is linked to the attempt to make the occupational basis of class positions the key to the class structure of modern societies. The empirical assumption that facilitates this break is as follows: having an occupation is increasingly determined by cultural resources. The vesting of the labour force with 'cultural capital' is partly a result of the wide-reaching changes in the structural characteristics of objective class positions.[4] Culture is a capital that determines the human labour force. One consequence of this is that objective class positions are increasingly determined by institutions other than the legally defined labour contract. The cultural restructuring of the occupational organization of the workforce denotes what specifically is 'new' in the modern class structure. It is tied to a primary fundamental revision of the Marxist concept of class.

The *second* culturalist refraction of traditional class analysis concerns the problem of how the objective class positions that are increasingly being constructed on the basis of cultural capital are reproduced. Traditional class analysis determines the problem of reproduction as a problem of the constitution of class consciousness. Bourdieu goes beyond this determination, when – abstracting from categories of consciousness – he speaks of the schemata of collective experience and perception as the medium for reproducing objective class positions. Bourdieu thereby eliminates the search for a 'class consciousness'. He replaces this concept with the concept of 'class habitus'.[5] Having opinions on what is good, beautiful, and just, counts as an indicator for class habitus. These opinions are not the result of individual choice from the range of possible viewpoints, but the selective outcome of a class-specific habitus at any given moment in time. The decisive break with the classical idea of a class-specific collective consciousness lies in the fact that identifying the social presence of classes is no longer dependent on class consciousness. It is dependent only on the cultural coding of a class action, and this primarily occurs unconsciously. To this extent class habitus can be understood more as an expression of collective class unconsciousness than as an expression for collective class consciousness.

The *third* culturalist refraction is a methodological one. It consists of interpreting the discourse on social classes as a part of class reality. This reflexivity of class analysis based on the sociology of knowledge makes it possible to avoid both the class-theoretical objectivity of Marxist class analysis and the class-theoretical subjectivity of voluntaristic class theory.[6] Thus Bourdieu advances a debate that is employed by Marx and has proceeded little beyond Lukács's *History and Class Consciousness*. He

[4] On the concept of cultural capital and its significance for class analysis the works dealing with the sociology of education and the theory of capital are the most important. For these concepts see Bourdieu 1970, 1984, 1986).

[5] The concept of class habitus is covered mainly in Bourdieu's writings on the theory of praxis. See Bourdieu 1980, 1984.

[6] On the self-reflexivity of sociology and the problems related to this, see Bourdieu 1987, 1990.

stands the debate – to follow Marx's dictum – from its head onto its feet by putting sociological demystification in the place of philosophical grounding, showing that philosophical grounding does not prevent ideological functions from fulfilling the reproduction of a class structure, and by indicating that even the philosophical dissociation from class society has itself a social function for the reproduction of that class society.

These three culturalist refractions of traditional class theory supersede the *materialist* conception of social class, which forms the basis of traditional class theories. Indeed, the specific achievement of this approach does not lie in signalling the end of class analysis, but, on the contrary, in making a theoretical abstraction that facilitates a more precise empirical perspective on the class structure of advanced industrial societies.[7] The cultural theoretical refractions of the class concept allow Bourdieu to replace the traditional 'materialist' concept of class with a 'constructivist' concept of class, and hence make the class structure of societies visible (and not just that of contemporary French society!). In the rest of this chapter I show how this is done in relation to each of the cultural theoretical refractions of the class concept.

## Culture as a characteristic of objective class position

### Occupation as a primary indicator of class position

To determine the extent of class structuring in modern societies requires more than merely referring to income differentials. Income differentials historically signify class differences only under very specific societal conditions. The conceptualization of objective class positions is more complex for advanced industrial societies.

The attempt has been made to comprehend objective positions in complex societies within the framework of research on stratification by combining objective characteristics of individuals. These characteristics were in particular income, level of education, and occupation (whereby occupation was also supposed to gauge the power, or lack of power, that an individual possesses in relation to others, as well as the prestige one possesses in a particular occupation). Making social aggregates of these characteristics, and hence strata, necessitates the use of a parameter of hierarchy. The simplest method is arithmetic: separating the income scale

[7] This sets Bourdieu apart from other critics of class theory, who are content to throw the concept of class onto the scrapheap of intellectual history. An outstanding example for this is Luhmann (1985). Another example who opposes this is Elster (1985b), who attempts to reformulate the concept of class with theories of rational choice. The alternative strategy involves generalizing the concept of class and making it a universal characteristic of socialization (*Vergesellschaftung*). In this case it is no longer the difference between class society and non-class society that counts, but the relatively fine distinctions between class societies at different levels of societal complexity. This is the strategy I propose. On this see my previous contributions in Eder 1987b.

into quintiles and correlating this income scale with other variables. The incremental units of characteristics that result from this are then colloqui-ally reinterpreted and described as upper class, middle class, and lower class. What this technique actually measures is the level of crystallization of status in predetermined groups of individuals. Whatever does not comply with these statistically constructed classes of individuals is described as 'status inconsistent'. In particular, the change of educational status from the growth of widespread education generated this phenomenon of status inconsistency. Thus the increasing lack of relevance of differences between the strata was proven, and was used even further to demonstrate the absence of social classes.

Yet there is nothing more unsociological than linking social classes (or strata – at this analytic level they are exchangeable concepts) to criteria of *individual* status consistency. Such a claim completely fails to comprehend that even those individuals who are status-inconsistent are classified objectively, and that they are able to constitute a social class or a social class fraction. Micro-sociological perspectives of research on stratification tend to derive objective class positions from individual characteristics, instead of proceeding the other way around and showing that the aggregation of individual characteristics of status is an outcome of social processes of distributing status characteristics of this kind, and that what matters is determining the structure of this process of distinction.

The intersection at which social processes are translated into individual characteristics, the intersection between society and individual, is increas-ingly signified by the *occupational role* in advanced industrial societies. The role of occupation determines attributes of status such as income, prestige, privilege and power, for the societal standing of an individual is usually deduced from the role of occupation. Occupational role has therefore a societal history. In this role the inequalities that are produced by social background and social career (a history of education, training, and profession) constitute a unit. Someone who has an occupational role, has thereby already dealt with social inequalities.

Inequality that is mediated by these processes is constituted by having an unequal amount of capital at one's disposal that counts on the economic market. Objective class position is defined by possession of this 'capital'. In Marx's time this basically meant control over the means of production, and hence economic capital. In any case, one would get no further using these criteria for analysis even today. Indicators for economic capital are self-explanatory: house ownership, possessing a top range car, having a yacht, spending holidays in a three-star hotel, are all indicators of a type of economic capital that cannot simply be reduced to ownership of the means of production. Social background and social career also place a type of 'capital' at one's disposal that is of a non-economic nature: i.e. the social and cultural qualifications with which one acquires and/or can stabilize status. With the spread of education the factor of 'cultural capital' in the form of educational and training certificates and titles is becoming increasingly important.[8] The significance of economic capital is diminishing relative to cultural capital (traditional electoral research also reflects this when it maintains that political electoral behaviour can increasingly be explained by education rather than income).[9] The relationship between background and education, however, is more complicated, since the information on education is variable once more in its dependence on social background. This means: that the higher the social background, the more meaningful the level of education becomes.

Thus the question arises of how these displaced characteristics are to be fitted together into new class characteristics and new objective class positions. This problem already implies a fundamental distance from all materialist conceptions of social class. Social classes are theoretical constructs – consequently Bourdieu describes his methodology as that of a structuralist constructivist (Bourdieu 1990, p. 123). The analytic status of the concept of class is far removed from the idea that a social class has to coincide with a social group. The analytic status of this concept lies in its being a 'model' of social reality. Social class is hence nothing other than social class 'on paper'.

## The cultural constitution of occupation

To grasp the multi-dimensionality of objective class positions in theoretical terms, Bourdieu proposes constructing social class positions with a three-dimensional model: the volume of capital (i.e. the sum of economic and cultural capital); the structural location of the two types of capital (i.e. the relation between economic and cultural capital); and a time dimension, that sees the combination of the two locations of capital as being dependent on life courses that are generation-specific. This last dimension enables class analysis to be connected with the developmental trends in a society (even with demographic trends that are significant for the changes in the quantitative position of the various social classes).[10] From these three criteria the groups of occupations can be placed together and distinguished from one another as objective class positions.

'Cultural capital' plays the key role in this reformulation of class analysis. Objectively defined positions are differentiated from one another

---

[8] There is a growing literature on this point. See for the German case Weymann 1987. See as the most recent comparative analysis Blossfeld and Shavit 1992.

[9] However, there seems to take place a general upgrading of educational title that compensates for levelling effects of more people acquiring higher educational positions. See on this point Blossfeld 1990, Blossfeld and Huinink 1991 and Blossfeld and Shavit 1992.

[10] There is a growing body of specialized literature on this aspect of reproducing class relations. See as an overview Mayer and Blossfeld 1990. The methodology that is capable of taking the time dimension into account is event history analysis (Blossfeld et al. 1989).

by cultural characteristics. These characteristics function as 'objective' factors in the production and reproduction of class structures. This theory of class does not acknowledge only a cognitive-instrumental form of expressing class structure: the occupation that determines rights and material advantages in society. It also recognizes a cultural form of expression: the knowledge and education that are acquired in having an occupation.

This conceptualization goes beyond the attempt of traditional stratification theory to determine the cultural side of class positions, and in particular beyond the traditional surveys on occupational prestige. Occupational prestige has been used as an indicator for objective class. It was even called a 'cultural' variable. However, it was not used in the sense of a cultural logic but only as an indicator for something else, i.e. strata or class positions. This reductionist work on the classification of occupations by prestige not only underestimates the function of classification as a mechanism for the reproduction of objective class positions, but also the objective function of prestige as a medium for societal distinctions to delimit the exclusive parameters of an occupation (Wegener 1985). The result of class struggles on the social worth of occupational positions and hence social power is embodied in occupational prestige.

A 'cultural capital' is adopted in occupations that extends beyond the classical requirements of a class position ('economic capital'), which itself can no longer simply be related to the concept of 'possession of crude labour', if labour is increasingly determined by cultural definitions. Primarily, the training acquired in learning processes at school and work as well as elements of social capital (as social relations and contacts or the mastery of modes of behaviour) are the key to a statistical construction of class structure from occupational statistics. It is unnecessary to add that we are dealing with sociological constructs, which – and this is the claim – depict the world more accurately than traditional constructs have been able to do.

I thus claim that a more adequate answer can be given to the problem of class structuring in complex societies with these concepts and theoretical constructs than that given by the classical pieces of research on inequality. An empirical analysis based on these same structural and constructivist theories and methodologies can start from the premise that having an occupational status and having a culture are both a prerequisite and effect of social class positions. We are dealing with a circular determining relationship that has its decisive instance in the *reproduction* of a structure. There are no independent variables: every independent variable is itself already the effect of this structure.

This 'structural class analysis' is only a preliminary (however a theoretically rich one) step beyond the class analysis of Marx and Weber. The second step would consist in naming the empirical mechanisms of reproduction from the classes that are constructed 'on paper'. Sociological analysis only succeeds in moving closer to reality to the extent that these 'objective class positions' are adapted into the process of reproducing these class positions – a particularly constitutive problem for sociology (Matthes 1985). Thus to speak of social classes one must indicate how their 'objective class characteristics' are reproduced by social actors (whether in a direct, or in a systematically distorted way, or indeed not at all).

Finally we have to examine to what extent the constructivism of the theoretically informed observer corresponds to the constructivism underlying the practical logic of social actors. Finding out how a theoretically constructed class structure is reproduced thus requires taking a step beyond mere social structural analysis. It involves clarifying how the various characteristics of objective class positions 'really', i.e. in social praxis, relate to one another. It involves explaining whether behaviour, attitudes, opinions and actions can be assigned to theoretically constructed classes, whose practical logic can be understood from the theoretically constructed context of a class position. With this debate the traditional requirement that a theoretically constructed class ought to correspond to a real group is pushed of the agenda once and for all – and hence the theoretical aim of the second culturalist refraction of traditional class analysis is implied.

## The reproduction of class positions

### Opinion as a secondary indicator of class positions

The second cultural theoretical refraction of the classic materialist concept of class relates to what are called the 'subjective factors' in traditional class analysis. The Weberian criterion for evaluating class positions maintains that a society is structured into classes, when the 'inner destiny' – i.e. subjective attitudes, opinions and cultural practices – can be identified as an expression of such differences. This is where the concept of 'subjective consciousness' is joined onto the concept of 'objective class position'. This criterion offers a 'softer' concept of the theory of subjective class position than the Marxist criterion for collective class consciousness. This Weberian proposition has dominated analysis of a 'subjective factor' in class analysis up to the present day.

Here Bourdieu also goes beyond Marx and Weber. The conceptual key to the revision of the traditional idea of a subjective factor in class analysis is the concept of 'class habitus'. The concept of habitus is not orientated towards individual ideas, personality traits, or attitudes, but towards the collective schemata of experience and perception that delimit the available 'subjective' ideas, personality traits, and instances of consciousness. The concept of 'habitus' describes a structure beyond the actors, that is acquired by the actors in specific social processes and is selectively stabilized by specificity of occupational career and adapted in relation to the economic and political conditions.[11] We can speak of 'real' social classes to the extent that such forms of 'habitus' reproduce objective class positions.

This sort of 'reproduction perspective' makes traditional class analysis (and research on stratification) involving the search for 'analogies' to objective factors at the subjective level obsolete. These types of class analysis only enabled one to speak of social classes when objective and subjective characteristics concurred. Complying with this demand necessitated a series of 'homogeneity tests'. I shall refer only to a few. One means involved using scales of occupational prestige from which subjective classifications could then be ascertained. Another classic method involved the use of subjective self-evaluations of status. One could speak of social class, when the occupational prestige, subjective self-evaluation, and the objective class position are in correspondence. If the subjective representations of class position are found, one can then examine whether political or religious differences concur with these differences in class.

The general outcome of these sort of homogeneity tests is predictable: it is discovered that there is no class-specific orientation of values and modes of action in common, ergo, there are no longer any social classes. This conclusion infers the absence of classes from the absence of a correlation. If culture has become a non-class-specific concern, then – and this is the good news for modern societies! – we are also approaching the end of class society.

How are homogeneity tests of this sort lacking? They predetermine a social classification in 'subjective' variables. An example might be the relation between social strata and rice-eating: the lower stratum may eat more potatoes, and the middle and upper strata more rice. What does this explain? Nothing, because it is unable to determine what eating rice signifies for different strata. Refined rice may appear on the plebeian dining-table and curry rice may be a typical dish of the new middle class, whereas unrefined rice may hardly refer to any specific group in the life-world. The rice one eats may thus define a social difference. The stance of the two variables is not as explanatory variables; on the contrary, they depend on something quite different: rice eating facilitates a structural ordering in society. The difference in meaning splits between classes of social actors; we need therefore to clarify to what extent these *real* differences can be associated convincingly to the *theoretical* construction of a society divided into social classes.

[11] A 'structuralist' invention of this kind can be related to a tradition of empirical social research that due to the dominance of quantitative methods was only able to survive in cultural anthropology and social anthropology and likewise in the Weberian sociology of religion. The analysis of the protestant ethos and its role in the ascending bourgeoisie as the driving force behind capitalist productivity, hence the analysis of its class-specific meaning, is one of the key pieces of sociological research, which generations of field researchers could still live off today and continue to do so in the future. An actual example of this kind of 'structuralist' research strategy is provided in the research by Matthes on religion, where oral life histories form the text from which the researcher aims to become familiar with the specific structure of rules, that form the basis for the manifest religions, political and social behaviour, and opinions of social actors (Matthes 1984, 1985).

One may choose a less 'materialist' example and consider the question of religion (i.e. the spiritual pole of cultural practices) and ascertain that class position (defined as belonging to a stratum) correlates with religion (operationalized as religious activity in Church or religious consciousness). Then what do we learn from this? Nothing, because the decisive question is not addressed: what meaning does religion (either going to Church or consciousness) have for the different social classes? This hermeneutic step is missing in traditional social research – yet it is able to indicate in what way religion incorporates the social division of society into classes. The *relation* to religion – how we already knew before – is status-specific. The old dichotomy between popular religion and intellectual or theologian religion (or, as social anthropologists say, between 'practical' and 'theoretical' religion) is further strengthened in modernity by increasing social differentiation.

The statistical correlation game is pursued to absurd lengths by several new comparatively orientated and operationally expensive research projects on socio-cultural value distributions. For example, Kaase and Klingemann (1979) relate the variable 'Church connection' along with social stratum, age, and education, as independent variables that are supposed to explain value distributions such as religiousness. Church connection is related to the frequency of Church attendance, which leads to the supposition that the frequency of Church attendance 'explains' religiousness (since religiousness diminishes with a decrease in Church attendance). It is difficult to see what this is supposed to prove, Church attendance being an independent variable and religiousness being a dependent variable as opposed to turning the frequency of Church attendance into a dependent variable; one would have to impute a connection between thought (religious thought) and action (religious action). One might expect religiousness and the frequency of Church attendance to have a different meaning for the working stratum than the old middle class, and the rural population to have a different one than the new middle class. To answer this question, however, one only has to know the self-evaluations 'very religious', 'fairly religious', and 'not religious'.

The absence of a correlation between stratum and religiousness would be more likely to imply political preferences rather than type of stratum or religion. The amazement over the correlation between type of religion and political preference indeed turns to out be based on a failure to comprehend that political socialization and religious socialization are two sides of the same coin, i.e. a specific subcultural socialization into the social system of values (the high level of correlation is then hardly surprising). Specifically, this perspective misses the point that in both the cases of politics and religion the dependency of a stratum is neither maintained in its orientation to the left or right nor in its orientation to being religious or secular, but on the contrary in the distinct subcultural relation that one can have towards politics and religion.[12] This type of homogeneity test that has employed generations of survey researchers is based on an unsociological illusion, which is that men are equal and they all perceive religion and politics in a similar way. Analyzing social inequality this way requires overlooking the point that this egalitarian misrepresentation necessarily hinders the empirical perspective. It does not just concern what specific opinion one may have, but whether one has an opinion at all. This is what sets men apart from everything else.

At the level of empirical perspective a subsequent sociologization is already possible. Opinions and their contents are uninteresting in themselves, but the structure and the process of selection from the possible range of opinions that one may hold are not. This structural perspective involves identifying the schemata for collective experience and perception that regulate the social reproduction of opinion. Bourdieu calls these collective schemata *habitus*. One can talk of *class habitus* to the extent that these schemata are structurally distinct from one another and allow for a class-specific reproduction of culture.

### Habitus as a collective class 'unconsciousness'

The decisive step in Bourdieu's analysis of class habitus is in the distance it keeps from all types of 'consciousness analyses'.[13] Class-in-itself is a theoretically constructed class. Class-for-itself includes the instance of class praxis. That does not, however, have to be related to class consciousness. It occurs unconsciously too – and yet is more than class-in-itself. It is the rehearsed self-descriptions and practised modes of perception and experience, and not the reflexive consciousness of class presence, that determine the cultural reproduction of social classes.

In attempting to identify structural differences beyond differences that

[12] This theoretical postulate can, however, only be empirically realized with difficulty. It has been pointed out for instance that the regulations for child education are universally distributed these days, and that the mass media are involved in implementing that sort of general ethos for education into society. This argument overlooks the point that such regulations for educating children are regulations that claim cultural legitimacy in our society. If you do not abide by them, you drop out. Who wants to be considered old-fashioned? Recognizing the modern or new regulations of child education no longer means that such regulations are considered relevant. The relation that one takes with respect to the regulations of child education is what is decisive. This relation to the regulations of educating children may vary in different subcultural 'milieus': a liberal style of education implies something different in the old middle class than the new middle class, never mind the lower strata. And regarding the mass media it concerns what the advertising psychologists have long since recognized: that media consumers select the perceptions for each day that confirm their own class ethos.

[13] Here I am concerned with the idea that class-specific worldviews contain something similar to a collective repression; there are many methodological difficulties tied to this conceptualization. These are – and here I oppose a strong positivist position – unavoidable when one makes collectively distributed worldviews the subject for empirical analysis. One cannot simply dismiss as non-empirical the historically preexisting normative standards that are deposited in the collective consciousness of society. They belong to the cultural 'background' that facilitates the production of the unity of variations behind all the differences that are specific to class.

relate to having individual opinions, Bourdieu tries to move away from the trend that is built into opinion research towards 'de-structuring' social reality. Indeed he attempts to oppose the effect of this research that emphasizes an image of progressive social 'individualization'. The survey researchers who are orientated towards stratification have seldom even managed to contradict that old sociological attempt claiming that modern societies are on the path towards a mass culture, where traditional cultural differences tend to disappear and social differences become more contingent (especially as individual differences!), that can once more only be seen as further proof of the obsolescence of class theory (Beck 1983, 1992).

Other than these individualizing ways of looking at social milieu or the life-world, there is another tradition of research which has expounded a view on the systematic differences in cultural orientations: namely research on value change.[14] The paradox of research on value change is that it does not describe change, but on the contrary it identifies fundamental differences in the differentiation of a before and an after in society (Eder 1988b). It gives pointers to the new cleavages in society in mass-cultural consciousness, which advocated a thesis of 'mass culture' prior to the thesis of a 'cultural balkanization' in modern societies. One can read the research on value change as a contribution to the reformulation of class-theoretical explanations of high modern societies.

In research on value change the quantifying empirical social research has shifted from the futile search for statistical correlations of objective and subjective characteristics and has analyzed the world of subjective characteristics as a social reality *sui generis*. This survey research on the distribution of value orientations has unearthed an increase of postmaterialist orientations opposing the materialist orientations in society. Increasingly, values of self-fulfilment became favoured in opposition to the classical values of achievement and duty. A grand theory of the decline of asceticism and the protestant work ethic is deduced from this and a fundamental cultural change in society is claimed. It almost seems as if society is tending to split into two great cultural classes, the Postmaterialists and the Materialists. Instead one could – taking on Bourdieu at this point – pursue the thesis that this phenomenon is related to changes in class structure, i.e. to internal differentiations in the petite bourgeoisie, and therefore to social structural changes in the middle classes.[15]

[14] This research tradition has been established by Inglehart (1977, 1990a). For critical comments on this research tradition see – among many others – the contributions to Luthe and Meulemann 1988.

[15] Bourdieu's structural analysis of this phenomenon shows that we are dealing with nothing but a new variant of the old petit-bourgeois asceticism and thus with merely a change of some contents of the same ethos of duty: the duty towards work becomes – as Bourdieu formulates it – a duty to pleasure. The protestant ethic of this new middle stratum becomes compelled by relations that no longer offer work – transposed to the field of self-discovery, and looking after oneself. This implies that a quantitative aggregating analysis cannot on its own even recognize the questions that are really interesting let alone examine them. See also below Part IV, Chapter 9.

Klages (1984) has relativized this empirical field and indicated that the majority of the population have a mixture of both value orientations; they therefore witness a simultaneous co-existence of materialist und postmaterialist orientations. Most people in our society – according to Klages – maintain both types of value orientations and so are particularly capable of reacting according to requirement: they can be postmaterialistic if it is necessary (that happens in particular when one is without work or in a job one considers inadequate), and they can be materialist if it is necessary (that may be the case for all those who are well integrated into their working lives). Klages' idea amounts in the final analysis to the subjective grounding of value opportunism.

We get an analogous result in a piece of research from the fifties, in Lipset's thesis of 'working class authoritarianism' (Lipset 1959) which is cited by Bourdieu (Bourdieu 1982, pp. 677ff). Workers are illiberal in political matters (political rights of freedom and egalitarian expression in the family count little for them); they have a manichaean idea of politics. In contrast, bourgeois strata hold a non-repressive idea of politics and even emphasize political freedoms in particular. This division of authoritarian and liberal vanishes into its own one-sidedness, if one considers that the liberal bourgeois strata become less liberal and more conservative in political deeds when social changes disturb the basis of their privileges. And, similarly, lower classes often hold a non-conservative position in political deeds, particularly when concerning issues of distribution and changes in social relations.

If we perceive value orientations as the outcome of class-specific practices, then the earlier research on value change – contrary to its intention – can be read as a contribution to a theory of class-specific forms of habitus. This implies only that the concept of habitus could be substantially clarified with the help of such traditions of research without extending the analytic explication of the concept (Miller 1989; Matthiesen 1989). A more precise class-specific analysis of forms of habitus (even the split between materialist and postmaterialist values in the middle classes) on the one hand would do away with the traditional fixation of class theory on research into class consciousness (or research on workers' conscious-ness) and yet at the same time not neglect to take into account the objective structuration (or even 'structuredness') of subjective factors. Sociology can only look for the social force of class-specific schemata of experience beyond the price that is paid for the blindness of the empirical perspective.

To this extent the analysis of 'class habitus' is not only the central problem for class analysis but also for society in general (and diagnoses of society must also justify themselves in these terms!). Class habitus is a concept which on one side structures the form of perception and experi-ence of the world and on the other is necessarily drawn to its own position in 'social space'. This characteristic allows us to understand the way a habitus works and functions within its objective context.

Even if all cultural expressions (such as political, religious, and aesthetic beliefs and opinion) are elements in the reproductive relationship of a class structure, one can still consider 'opinion' or 'meanings' on social inequality to be a privileged field for the construction of a class habitus – yet opinion and meanings relate thematically to explicit effects of a class structure. A differentiation of the world of symbolic forms can be shown from a perspective of the constitution of class habitus and 'objectified' at three levels:

- at the level of the *perception* of social inequality as a disequilibrium in potential to perceive;
- at the level of the *experience* of social inequality as a disequilibrium in potential to grasp the conditions of social inequality;
- at the level of *consistency* in knowing about social inequality as a disequilibrium of potential for producing a publicly effective explication of a consciousness of injustice.

This kind of analysis allows a distinction between type of class habitus in relation to one's potential for acting in the social world. A 'volume of competence' is added to 'volume of capital' as the starting point for constructing class positions, and this can also become the starting point for constructing the forms of a class habitus. Class analysis then culminates in proving the correspondence between a structural division in the volumes of capital and the structural division in the volumes of competence.[16]

A new problem arises from radicalizing class analysis in this way: how is it possible to avoid seeing class analysis as simply an expression of 'intellectual' class habitus? This question leads straight into Bourdieu's third culturalist refraction, where he provides a new and useful answer to the old problem concerning the role of a theorist in society.

[16] Hence class analysis is a reconstruction of 'having' the capital and competence that facilitates distinction from others. In this process of distinction the lowest go to the dogs: he who has neither capital nor competence is excluded. It begins with the primary characteristics of having a job. Those who just work but have no profession hold a precarious position in modern work society. The lower the position, the less the profession of work is credited. The case of the unemployed is an excellent example of this. An unemployed person is someone who requires re-qualification (which is a euphemistic way for describing the status of being excluded). The 'unemployed' who is defined as insufficiently qualified is excluded from the world of work and yet at the same time is one of its constitutive elements, for he is the point of reference from which a new logic of vertical classification functions. The unemployed are needed to distinguish who has work. This is the starting point of far-reaching distinctions in which it is important to have income, qualifications, taste, and morals. The underlying logic for classification signifies the 'culture of possession' that is the outcome of new types of class displacement which the discourse on equality has introduced. This culture of possession is the key to the class structure of modern society. It is the culture of a new rising social class: the new middle class. On this see Eder 1989.

**The cultural thematization of class structure**

*The social scientific discourse on inequality*

The third culturalist refraction of traditional class analysis concerns the reflexivity of the idea of class structure, which has an increasing significance in the cultural reproduction of class structure on account of the 'socio-scientification' of society. This aspect directly concerns the development of the social sciences. The changes that can be observed in intellectual culture in the earliest period, in both positive and negative directions, are frequently related to the social sciences. It would be an exaggeration of the effects of socio-scientific knowledge to claim that the social sciences are 'responsible' for these changes. It is obvious, however, that they have something to do with them. The social sciences are themselves part of the discourse of intellectual culture. They relate to one another reflexively in this culture. They attempt to produce knowledge on the role of this discourse in society. Hence a double role is attributed *a priori* to sociological knowledge. Not only does it analyze objects in society, but – constituting the societal object that it is – it is also analyzing itself (Bonß and Hartmann 1985, pp. 1–46).[17]

This double function of socio-scientific knowledge is becoming virulent in the very type of socio-scientific research that has already been constitutive for the emergence of sociology as a discipline, i.e. in the sociological analysis of inequality. The division of bourgeois society from traditional society and the regulatory idea of equality that is related to bourgeois society is the starting point for modern social research, such as the studies on pauperism and social statistics of the nineteenth century (Jantke and Hilger 1965). This social research has not only produced knowledge on existing society, it has also to a certain extent changed the consciousness of modern society by carrying out research on inequality as a means of 'class analysis'. It has made the 'social question', which became the empirical point of reference for the self-descriptions of modern society in the nineteenth century, into an ideologically effective theory on this society. Undertaking research on equality as a form of class analysis has not up to the present day lost this function – despite society becoming more egalitarian. One example is the public and everyday discourse on inequality in education.

The relation between socio-scientific knowledge and socio-scientific theory on one side and societal change on the other has become even more complicated with the differentiation of the socio-scientific knowledge from

---

[17] For a discussion on the self-demystification of social science see the contributions in Bonß and Hartmann 1985. 'Useful research' is nothing other than empirical social research that is sympathetic to this kind of 'reflexive sociology'. For a theoretical discussion see Giddens (1990, 1991), Lash (1990) and Beck (1992), who have developed a coherent theoretical framework of a reflexive sociology.

other types of knowledge that works on these changes. One of the complications is that the social sciences have unintended consequences even when they are attempting to reduce social inequality. An example would be the problems that arise from increasing egalitarianism in the field of education. This experience of unintended consequences has given rise to changes in the self-description of modern societies: whether it concerns reactionary correcting mechanisms, where the unavoidability of inequality becomes a regulating insight into the structure of modern society; or alternatively, whether it concerns the self-correcting mechanisms of liberal and radical thought that try to bridge the gap between intention and effect. The sociology of sociology that thematizes the problem of unintended collective effects is moreover – and that implies a further reflexive spiral in the reproduction of socio-scientific knowledge – part of this self-correcting process for the forms of consciousness in the structuring of classes in modern societies.

However, sociological analysis of the theoretical dispersal of research on inequality – as far as it goes – is largely descriptive. The societal conditions that are examined do not go into a sociological analysis of the theoretical use of the research itself. Hence these analyses remain largely pre-sociological. Above all in the case of research on inequality that treats knowledge as the central problem of modern societal reproduction, a concrete analysis of the actors who appropriate this research is particularly necessary. This problem does not merely concern the use of the knowledge, the 'use of research' in the classic sense. It concerns the social groups who take up research on inequality – and that includes the social scientists themselves when they begin to undertake such research as an analysis that is led by theory. It concerns the socio-scientific 'self-use' of produced knowledge. That implies placing class analysis as a form of appropriation of research on inequality in the context of theoretical praxis. If one adds to that the fact that research on inequality is a form of socio-scientific research that is specifically normatively equipped, then it becomes clearer why indeed class analyses and the theoretical debate over their sense and purpose are placed so highly – both emotionally and ideologically.

In this respect the most interesting idea and hypothesis that Bourdieu has produced – despite the idiosyncratic mode of its presentation from time to time – is the assumption that socio-scientific knowledge has itself become a mechanism of the reproduction of class structure in modern societies. The sociological debate concerning the inegalitarian consequences of the expansion of the education system is the field on which this reflexive discussion is now concentrating. In this field Bourdieu formulated his thesis of the 'cheated generation' (Bourdieu 1982, pp. 241ff). We also find the most interesting and intensive debates on the 'theory–praxis relation' in the German 'debate on use' in this field (Weymann 1987; Beck and Bonß 1989).

The methodological consequence of this involves understanding socio-scientific reflection on the implications of its own usage not just as a repetition of the objectifying idea to its object, but as an opening of communicative processes that are based on their own implications of usage. This implies a reconstruction of the appropriation of empirical research by socio-scientific experts in the form of theories and other cognitive forms of appropriation (even in the form of an 'evaluation' of socio-scientific research results) as a social process that exists within a class structure of society and not as an independent social field. Even with the best of critical intentions, intellectual discourse cannot avoid the problem of social inequality and itself being a part of the relations of reproduction that operate in a class structure. This makes the analysis of social inequality the privileged object for a self-reflexive sociology.[18]

If sociological discourse has its origins and function in society, which at the same time it is examining, then the question arises of how this discourse is ever able to escape such a determining relationship. Bourdieu's radical proposition is that sociology does not describe reality as an objective description but on the contrary as the discovery of illusions about social reality. 'Sociological de-illusionment' consists in attributing the thematization of social injustice to actors (including theorists) as a mechanism of the cultural reproduction of basic class structure. 'Sociological de-illusionment' involves recognizing that the discourse on inequality itself contributes to the reproduction of the basic class structure. The good will that this discourse carries has social effects, that the discourse itself is only too ready to overlook. Shattering this illusion constitutes part of the third culturalist refraction of class theory: every theory of class has always to reflect upon the relation of its own usage, if it aims to be more than a misinterpreted element in this process of reproduction.

### Sociological de-illusionment: a learning process?

The rehabilitation of a class-theoretical perspective by Bourdieu is necessarily at the expense of another perspective, i.e. the perspective on *learning processes* in a society which change or dissolve this structure of classes. This question relates to the mobilization of classes or the consciousness of classes of themselves and the effects this can have on the class structure of a society. The reverse of this perspective – which corresponds to the optimistic belief that modern societies can steer themselves – refers to the

[18] A possible topic for research that arises from these considerations would be the example of consciousness of injustice among social groups, examining the significance of social scientific knowledge for the reproduction of a class structure. Two aspects of the problem are thereby addressed. The first concerns the interaction of the 'theoretical discourse' of (social) science with the 'practical discourse' of social actors already standing in a class-specific relation to one another. Thus one could deduce which organizational and rhetorical forms seek to distinguish themselves from 'everyday discourse' with the help of 'refined discourse'. The second aspect concerns the role that the 'refined discourse' of science plays in the stabilization of a class-specific consciousness of injustice and hence for the reproduction of class positions. The solution to this involvement in the class structure lies in the demystification of the illusion of not being an element of this class structure.

problem in terms of looking for possibilities and links for learning processes in the process that reproduces class structure.

In any case the Bourdieuian analysis offers little on this point. To recognize the possible amount of consciousness, i.e. of learning processes that force reflection on their own class position, would require a practical form of research that examined the effects arising from the piece of research itself.[19] However this requires different methods than those facilitating the reconstruction of a structure that as a social process has already 'run its course'. Methods of this kind would be:

- first, making an analysis of the effects of interaction into the interview situation with the help of proceedings from group discussion analysis, that in the meantime has become a societally normalized 'natural situation';
- second, making an analysis of the effects in the public discourse using content analytic and discourse analytic methods.

These sorts of methodological proceedings in any case go beyond those which Bourdieu requires to sharpen the 'class-analytic perspective'. Such methods aim once more to grasp the sociological, i.e. that which arises from undertaking sociological de-illusionment. For even the strategy of sociological de-illusionment does not escape the society that it de-illusions.

These critical conclusions are not just to be read as a *critique* of Bourdieu's class analysis. They can also be as an *advance* from Bourdieu's class analysis, for the analysis and reconstruction of learning processes presupposes a recognition and clarity of structure that learning processes block or distort. The objective possibilities for learning processes are given only in the case of the non-identical, that is brought to light by an analysis of class structure that attempts to de-illusion. To this extent the strategy of a 'cultural' class analysis for sociological discourse aims to be 'positive', or, in less banal terms, aims for the conditions that facilitate change.

Empirical social research that does nothing differently than what we already know, is bad sociology, and it confirms something as 'empirical' thus covering rather than uncovering the aspects that have already been hidden by consciousness in society. If there is to be a justification for the existence of sociology as a science, then it must de-illusion that which it explains and reject the self-evident truths through which everyone sees his

---

[19] This aim relates to a new development in sociology that was sociologically radicalized by Touraine, namely the idea that producing sociological theory (and data) is part of a system of historical actions, at least in societies of our type (Touraine 1981). This occurs independently of whether the relation of this is an emergent phenomenon or not; it is the theoretical consequence that is decisive. The social significance of socio-scientific knowledge arises from the relation of this knowledge to other forms of knowledge. Hence there is no knowledge that exists beyond society. The concept of society as a 'material' thing is relinquished for a proposition that favours a system of relations between distinct discourses and perceptions of the world.

own little world and that of others. Empirical social research under-estimates its own social function, when it just runs after society like a book-keeper saying that 'there are 2% more postmaterialists and 5% fewer industrial workers' and uses this among other things to speculate on trends. Empirical social research is supposed to make visible in society that which consciousness would like to keep invisible. Once and for all, it should have as part of its aims: the advance of knowledge on the societal relativity of consciousness that each of us in society possesses; the rejection of ethnocentricity within one's own society; and thus the development of a reciprocity of perspectives that is the prerequisite for a culture in society that does not simply reproduce the culture of a minority. For if it is only made relevant to a few of us, how can the project of modernity help the majority through discursive communication? Empirical social research cannot avoid this normative question, unless it devalues its own social function.

# 5

# THE COGNITIVE REPRESENTATIONS OF SOCIAL INEQUALITY
## A Sociological Account of the Cultural Basis of Modern Class Society[1]

### The discourse on social inequality

*Inequality: social fact or interpretative scheme?*

Social inequality is one of those issues that simultaneously mobilizes moral outrage, political engagement and social analysis. The discourse on social inequality understandably functions as a container for all expressions of disadvantage, repression, desire and hope in our society. Sociological theorizing on social inequality is nothing but a special contribution to this discourse, adding empirical data that give scientific backing to one or another opinion. Yet even scientific discourse on social inequality does not escape the social function of this discourse: to produce a cognitive representation of social inequality. A sociological analysis considering this implication thus treats social inequality not only as a *social fact*, but also as an *interpretative scheme* of social reality and asks for the function of this scheme in social reality.

The sociological 'objectification' of the concept of social inequality presupposes a theoretical perspective that locates the discourse on social inequality within the social reality that produces it. My thesis is that the modern discourse on social inequality is shaped by the collective experiences and perceptions of the social world that emerged with the bourgeois classes in the eighteenth century and that today are culturally dominated by the middle classes. The actual research and theorizing about social inequality[2] thus can be explained – to use a provocative formulation – as an

---

[1] This is a slightly revised version of a contribution to H. Haferkamp (ed.), *Culture and Social Structure* (pp. 83–100), de Gruyter, Berlin.

[2] As overviews of the recent theoretical discussion on social inequality see Kreckel 1983 and Mayer and Blossfeld 1990. Completely separated from this discussion is the normative discussion on justice that has developed in reaction to Rawls's *A Theory of Justice* (Rawls 1971); as an example see Lukes 1991. Thus the liberal strand of thought on questions of injustice and the socialist/welfarist strand are opposed as normative versus empirical approaches, which has hindered any fruitful cooperation.

outcome of the dominance of the middle classes in modern sociological thinking.[3]

## The universality of vertical classification

The sociological 'objectification' of the concept of social inequality will be described in two steps. First, the existence of social classes in society will be identified as the objective base underlying the discourse on social inequality. Second, the subjective conditions of reproducing social classes will be examined. We will show that with the emergence of the bourgeois discourse on equality, the discourse on social inequality starts to assume a central role in the reproduction of the class structure.

Social inequality is – as many theorists propose – a universal social phenomenon (Tumin 1967), equally present in simple, traditional and modern societies. This claim, however, provokes that question of what is the reality represented by the concept of 'social inequality'? What is the 'signifié' that belongs to this 'signifiant'? The facts that underlie the discourse on social inequality are the social differences between social actors, differences in hair colour, income, aggressiveness, attractiveness, and taste. What we must first explain is why some of these differences are used by people or those doing research about them (or both) for separating social classes of people. This is the classical question concerning the origins of class society. Then we must explain why class differences are perceived by these people as inequality.[4]

Thus to speak of social inequality involves making use of two types of cognitive operation. The first is to classify differences vertically. The second is to describe the classified social world as a deviation from an ideal of equality. Vertical classification is universal (Schwartz 1981).[5] All societies separate people vertically. In simple societies the classification is based on sex, age and lineage. Traditional societies add estates and castes as criteria. Modern societies substitute individual achievement. What

---

[3] Nothing is more opposed to sociological thinking than attempting to explain the origin of social inequality through human nature. Yet this approach is still implicit in modern economic explanations (Elster 1986). These are logically unsatisfactory because changes toward social equality would have to entail changes in the nature of man. We, however, assume that human nature does not change. Thus the social and cultural context of human nature becomes the central explanatory variable. A sociological reformulation of the problem to be explained is: What are the mechanisms contributing to the definitions and redefinitions of the 'context'? The sociological answer is: Permanent classificatory activity is the mechanism of defining the context that is described as social inequality.

[4] Social inequality can refer to a wide spectrum of conditions. So many different things are called 'unequal' that we can with reason begin to doubt the thesis that it is universal. Moreover, its wide distribution forces us to specify the cultural dimension of this term. Social inequality is not only a social fact, but also a cultural representation of social facts (Giesen 1987; Berger 1988).

[5] The simultaneity of universality and specificity of social inequality that is implicit in the discourse on social inequality makes distinguishing between them difficult. Schwartz's approach, taken from the sociology of knowledge, avoids the difficulty by restricting the discussion to vertical classification as a cognitive operation.

really distinguishes modern societies in this scheme, however, is that they are the first ones to call themselves class societies. They interpret themselves as unequal societies. This shows that the concept of social inequality is an evolutionary-specific interpretative scheme (Giesen 1987) bound to the emergence of the discourse on equality that is characteristic for modern culture.

In simple societies the socially significant differences are between age, gender and lineage groups. The principles underlying this type of class formation are based upon ascriptive criteria. An extreme example would be the Australian tribe where older men can marry as many women as they can handle. The younger men have to wait until the old men die before gaining the advantageous positions within this wife-distribution system. In practice, this means waiting until they are forty years old. 'Membership' in an age class therefore is the specific basis of social class in this society.[6] As outsiders we might feel that such practices would have to produce the idea of social 'inequality' between the old and young men (apart from that produced between men and women). Tribe members, however, experience and interpret this social inequality as part of the order of nature. The conclusion drawn by diverse theorists of simple societies – that because there is no conception of social inequality there is no social inequality – is wrong. Although social differences are perceived as representing an order inherent in nature, there is real social inequality.

In traditional societies differences that can be made the basis of vertical classification increase. Class formation is no longer strictly dependent upon 'natural' indicators (age and sex), but upon indicators that are the result of an increasing division of labour. Additional differences, such as those between peasant and craftsman and between craftsman and lord, emerge. In such societies social inequality is perceived as part of the divine order. The principles of vertical classification are represented in a specific theory of social inequality: in the theory of a 'hierarchy' of estates or castes. An extreme example is the Indian caste system (Dumont 1967). The literature about its modernization shows to what extent the notion of hierarchy contributed to preventing the caste system from being seen as an expression of an unjust social inequality (Béteille 1965; Meillassoux 1973).

Modern societies enlarge even more upon the differences between social actors (as any opinion poll or the official classifications of occupations show). To the extent that these societies foster the 'individualization' of life-chances, social actors become still more different and still more unequal (Beck 1983; Berger 1986, 1987, 1990; Berger and Hradil 1990). Life-chances are increasingly determined by manifold and crosscutting classificatory strategies (Bourdieu 1984). Statistical analyses, however,

---

[6] This difference has even been named by some authors as the fundamental determinant of class in simple societies (Meillassoux 1976). Other authors, using other examples from socio-anthropological research, perceive the division of labour between women (collectors) and men (hunters) as the primary mechanism (Moscovici 1972).

show that these individualizing traits 'cluster'; they show that there is a hidden class structure behind the image of an individualizing society. This image rather helps to represent class differences not within the model of hierarchy – as traditional societies have done – but within the model of equality. At times the modern bourgeois classes engaged in the discourse on equality have difficulties harmonizing the reality of class structure in modern society to this discourse. Such difficulties lead to descriptions of those forms of social inequality that proceed from modern class structure as legitimate forms of social inequality and to the theories of social inequality. Then, as these theories take hold, they gain a paradoxical function: they have to legitimate social inequality and also uphold the idea of equality. This paradox has been resolved by individualizing social inequality; inequality is represented as the outcome of individual achievement and competence. Thus theories of social inequality in modern society serve the function of representing the class structure of this society. Once done, the only problem left is whether we should undertake some affirmative action for those who lose in the struggle for the better social positions or not. This allows for reducing social inequality to a political issue.

The more modern society advances, the more the forms of representing the class structure within theories of legitimate social inequality gain importance while the idea of equality remains a latent source of critique of these theories. The discourse on social inequality therefore becomes a very dynamic force in modern society. The critique can manifest itself in questions as to the justice of existing social inequality and pleas for redistribution bringing about a closer approximation to the ideal of equality. This approach treats social inequality as a temporary phenomenon. Another manifestation of the critique accepts the functional importance of social inequality but pleads for the equality of chances within it. A third manifestation of the critique acknowledges social inequality with regret that the world is not such as it should be and explains social inequality as the outcome of human nature. The sociological theories of social inequality express these variants according to their epistemological bias. These cultural representations serve as a mechanism of the cultural reproduction of class positions in modern societies similar to the way in which their cultural representation as estates or castes did it in traditional societies. Just which theories are used by what social groups or classes is an empirical question to be treated later.

To summarize my hypothesis developed so far: Social inequality is an interpretative scheme produced for a specific cognitive representation of modern society and then projected upon other societies.[7] The discourse on

---

[7] That class divisions are not described as social inequality sometimes leads to the conclusion that there is no inequality in simple societies; more precisely, that there are no classes in simple societies. This is obviously erroneous. In this sense social inequality is also a socio-centric category.

inequality is a specifically modern form of the cultural representation of class divisions in modern society. The discourse on social inequality is nothing but the legitimation for continuing strategies of classifying and reclassifying existing differences in society. It is rhetoric, apology and also rationalization. A sociological theory that simply continues this discourse of representation takes part in the legitimating discourse in society instead of analyzing its origins and functions.

## Class position and social inequality

### *Four forms of classificatory struggles*

To analyze the cognitive representations of social differences as 'social classes' it is necessary to examine the specific classificatory practices characteristic of modern society. Any critical understanding of the theories of social inequality must be preceded by an analysis of the real social differences these theories refer to. Thus we do not dismiss the concept of class as suggested by diverse theoreticians (Luhmann 1985), but feel it needs to be theoretically constructed in a more adequate manner.

With the evolution of advanced modern societies, a shift in emphasis of the dominant dimensions of classification can be shown. The theoretical problem resulting from this shift away from income as the standard of class can be formulated as follows: What are the effects of new classificatory practices on class structure? The key to explaining class positions is – and Bourdieu (1984, 1987) especially has stressed this point – understanding the strategies of reproducing existing classifications, viz. mutating strategies of classification and declassification, the struggle of the classifiers to classify the social reality to their advantage. The starting point for an empirical treatment of social class in advanced modern societies is to generate a typology of classificatory struggles that define the relevant dimensions of social inequality.

The struggle for income belongs to the type of conflict bound to the institutionalization of the antagonism between capital and labour. To some extent this struggle has smoothed out differences in income, but it has not equalized them (Bellmann et al. 1984). More important is that some groups, especially those involved in practising alternatives to conventional work and business (Benseler et al. 1982), have withdrawn from this struggle and now wage their classificatory struggles in non-economic fields. That their alternative economic practices have been described (and thus classified!) as self-exploitation already points to changes in what counts in classificatory struggles.

Today, the classical struggle for income is complemented by new types of classificatory struggles. The following three can be distinguished: the struggle for formal qualification, the struggle for taste, and the struggle for moral excellence change the class structure of modern society. They are at the core of what has been called the 'new social inequalities'.[8] The struggle for formal qualification has dramatically altered the differences, both qualitative and quantitative, between the middle and the lower classes. The key figure in this new struggle for status is the skilled worker who, having acquired new formal qualifications, has distanced himself from the normal unskilled worker and joined the ranks of the old lower middle classes. His struggle, made possible by the expansion of the educational system, has become a central type of struggle in advanced modern societies (Blossfeld 1985). The working class is going to be separated into the core workers and marginal workers. Upward qualification and downward qualification are the result of new ways of constructing occupational roles in the labour system (Kern and Schumann 1984).

The struggle for taste, the central topic of Bourdieu's analysis of social distinctions (Bourdieu 1984), is tied rather closely to the struggle for formal qualification. The positions gained in this struggle often are explained as the result of the struggle for informal qualification. In this struggle symbolic capital (like the intuitive knowledge about the correct behaviour in a given situation) is used to stabilize or improve an actor's position in the class structure of society (Wippler 1985, 1990). Informal qualifications crosscut income differences in the same way as formal qualifications do.

The struggle for moral excellence is an attempt to mobilize the moral weight of a group against that of other groups. The petite bourgeoisie, both old and new, is the group that has most promoted this type of struggle (Gusfield 1966, 1981b; Part IV of this volume), thereby attracting much public attention and succeeding in organizing its moral claims in 'new' social movements. The struggle for moral excellence is – beyond its mobilization into a social movement – part of a larger system of moral classification and declassification. It denotes a specific class-bound moral lifestyle. Against the morality of the petit –bourgeois lifestyle other types of moral lifestyles are directed: those pleading for a utilitarian morality (the neoliberal lifestyle), for obedience, duty and order (the traditional lifestyle), and for a morality based on universal principles (the intellectual liberal lifestyle). Because they tend to be the best explanatory variables for forecasting voting behaviour, such classifications of moral lifestyles have become a favourite topic in sociology.

From these different types of struggles result vertical classifications that redefine the class structure of modern society, dividing it into social classes according to the quantity of material and symbolic resources they dispose

[8] The issue of 'new social inequalities' has been a fashionable topic over the last few years. It has been treated theoretically in very divergent forms. The range of interpretation goes from 'continuity of capitalist class structure' through 'new middle class society' to 'individualized society'. See among many others Beck 1983; P.A. Berger 1986; Bischoff et al. 1982; Hradil 1987.

of. The dominant classes can be distinguished from the middles classes and the dependent classes by differences that refer to claims of a 'higher' moral consciousness, to a 'higher' judgement of taste and to a 'higher' formal qualification.[9] The interdependence of income and qualification on the one hand and of moral and aesthetic competence on the other allows us to identify the social distribution of quantities of competence making up the class structure as it developed in advanced industrial societies.

This theoretical reconstruction of the modern class structure takes into account the changes resulting from the increasing relevance of formal qualification for the distribution of work among the workforce. This distributive process produces 'losers' and 'winners' (i.e. those who lose or win social status, when rationalization changes the social and technical organization of work). The measure 'control of the forces of production' has lost its classical relevance. The power accumulated in occupational positions via strategies of social and cultural closure has rather become the basic mechanism in the formation of social classes and class relations in advanced modern societies. This also draws a sharp line between those having an occupation (i.e. those who are not unemployed) from those who don't have an occupation. These phenomena show that the social construction of an occupation has become the most basic mechanism of changes in the modern class structure and they show that occupation (and no longer the position in the social relations of production) has become the most important measure of the modern class structure.

An actor's occupation, however, is not yet sufficient as a class marker. He also needs culture. The indicators of culture, however, defined as secondary characteristics of social classes complementing the primary characteristic denoted by the occupation, have also changed. Nowadays, to have culture means to have opinions. Opinions related to politics and morals or to art and technology now tend to be the marker replacing the classical indicator of distance from the sophisticated high culture. For an actor to have opinions allows for his vertical classification according to the criterion of cultural competence.[10] It allows us to distinguish between those with opinions, to approve of those who know what opinions to have (which only a few people can know) and to pity those who do not. Ultimately we defer to those who create opinions and define what the right ones are from those who can't.

[9] This distinction corresponds to the one Bourdieu makes between cultural and social capital. See Bourdieu 1986.

[10] The success of market-dominated relations, even in those subsystems or fields to which a specific internal logic (art, religion, science or political culture) has traditionally been attributed, transforms culture into something that can be measured and therefore classified. It is moreover not the market that dominates but the model of communication that it makes possible. This model establishes a standard that allows for aggregation but the place of money is increasingly taken over by competence which thus becomes the new medium of communication. For this reason culture becomes 'countable' as if it were economic goods. This underlies the sociological meaning of statistical analysis: to correspond to the reality that it tries to measure and to represent.

## The theoretical construction of the concept of class

There are two categories highly suited for the statistical construction of social classes in advanced modern societies: occupation and opinion.[11] Both are achievements of modernity where one's occupation and one's opinions characterize one's social existence on a basic level. The proposition to see occupations and opinions as the central indicators of class positions claims not to be a universally valid description but a historically specific theoretical construction of social classes. The concept of social class that we can construct starts with characteristics that are themselves the results of the modern discourse on equality. The prominence of formal qualification in determining professional or occupational status can be explained as the result of an educational system under democratic pressures. The differentiation of society along the lines of differences of opinion can be explained as the result of a democratic political culture. The effects of an egalitarian culture, occupations and opinions, are equally the constitutive elements of the class structure of these societies. Occupations and opinions have become the privileged object of vertical classification.

The class structure of modern society becomes more abstract the more social classes are defined by individual differences. Clearly visible differences, based for example on gross differences in income and consumption patterns, tend to dwindle in importance. Eventually, the class structure can be made visible only by measurement procedures, and statistical analysis, the description of classes as statistical clusters of individual characteristics, becomes the privileged instrument. Classes tend to have a mere statistical 'existence' (Bourdieu 1987). Thus we are forced to conceptualize the notion of class beyond its existence as a concrete entity into a logical category.

What then constitutes the standard that allows us to assign status to occupations and opinions? Who defines what is high and what is low? There is no standard that is not the result of a class-specific perspective. Outside the class structure there is no criterion of inequality. There is no standard of inequality that escapes the context within which and for which it is formulated. Even the most complex indicators offered by the techniques of empirical social research cannot neutralize the sticky fact that even researchers have to commit themselves to normative criteria that define some difference as inequality.

---

[11] Research on occupations and professions and opinion research belong not coincidentally to the best developed strands of social science research. They measure the two central types of competence that generate and reproduce social inequality in advanced modern societies. These competences can be substituted for each other. Someone who has no occupation or a bad one might emphasize his culture, and vice versa: someone who lacks culture seeks a better classified occupation. It is possible to compensate. Combining occupation and culture thus seems to be an adequate measure for identifying the class structure of advanced modern societies. Such a theoretical construction of classes contains at first glance very different groups, such as social workers and programmers. What makes them part of one class is the net amount of competence they have.

How then, do we identify the criteria that underlie the vertical classification by occupation and opinions? What is the specific logic of this process? The traditional theory of class does have a criterion that works when the primary struggle is for income: the criterion of the degree of exploitation. This criterion is also expected to explain the logic of vertical classification in modern capitalist societies, but this alone is no longer sufficient. We propose what will function as a workable standard for vertical classification derives from the logic inherent in the idea of competence. Competence is a criterion that allows for the transformation of quality (i.e. cognitive, aesthetic or moral quality) into quantity (i.e. cumulation of first-level competence against second-level competence and so on according to the number of levels of competence that are distinguished).

Thus vertical classification in advanced modern societies tends to become dependent upon the logic of 'having culture'. The measure of this vertical classification is the quantity of competence. To have an occupation presupposes a cognitive-instrumental competence (Beck and Brater 1978; DiMaggio and Mohr 1985; Bourdieu 1984). To have an opinion presupposes a moral-aesthetic competence (Bourdieu et al. 1981; Wippler 1985, 1990). Evaluating the immanent logic of these competences allows us to explain the class structure made visible by statistical analysis. What distinguishes among people is a differential amount of competence. Defining these differences solely in terms of 'capital', of 'market value', a solution proposed by Bourdieu (1986), is insufficient. It is rather the 'use-value' attributed to cultural qualities that counts. To conceptualize the dimensions that determine life-chances in an adequate manner we need a notion of culture that neither reduces culture to what people want to buy and have nor reduces culture to what philosophers think about the world.

The distinguishing characteristic that such attributions of quantities of competence have is an implicit criterion of value. To have greater or lesser competence can then be said to render a person or a group of persons better or worse. To the extent that 'stages' of the development of competence (in the sense of Piaget and others) are theoretically distinguished, classes of people can be distinguished in a legitimate way. The more society distinguishes people according to their amount of competence, the more this standard of competence (itself legitimized by scientific theories of stages of competence!) becomes the principle underlying a theoretical construction of social classes. This point will be elaborated later.

To summarize, we would like to distinguish two dimensions of competence that can combine and be transformed into each other and that together determine the quantity of competence, this specifically modern parameter of vertical classification. The relevance of the cognitive-instrumental competence is self-evident. The idea of a meritocratic social order as a realization of the modern principle of equality separates social classes according to quantities of cognitive-instrumental competence. The second dimension of competence, the moral-aesthetic one, has to do with orientations that have characterized modern society since its beginnings and that have gained new meaning within the moral and aesthetic protests of the rising new middle classes and the social movements these new middle classes have formed.

A system of vertical classification can be constructed using these two indicators. The quantity of competence is the result of a specific combination of these two dimensions of competence. Such a model of vertical classification representing the class structure of advanced modern societies is a modified version of the model developed by Bourdieu (1984). Whether this class structure develops into the direction of a preponderance of the cultural element in constituting and reproducing the class structure of advanced modern societies, has to be treated as an empirical question. The decisive point is that to explain this class structure, the recourse to material production and the material economy has become insufficient. We have to consider more and more the phenomenon of cultural production as the mechanism of vertical classification. Only such a theoretical perspective gives us some theoretical tools that hinder our seeing in advanced modern societies nothing more than individualization everywhere. There is no 'beyond status and class' (Beck 1983) in modern society.

Vertical classification according to quantified, value-designated competence thus characterizes a new evolutionary level in the realization of a class society. This means analyzing the mechanisms that attribute positive or negative competence; this means generating a typology of classificatory struggles of 'recognizing' and 'decognizing' competence and defending the proposition that in advanced modern society a class structure based on the quantity of competence emerges. However, when dealing, in sociological analysis, with theoretically constructed and statistically identified classes (*Klassen an sich*) the question remains open whether these classes can become 'real' classes (*Klassen für sich*). This question leads to the old problem of 'subjective' conditions of the existence of social classes, a problem that will be taken up in the following considering the objective changes in class structure described above.

**Beyond class-specific subcultures**

*A critique of the discourse on class*

The first example of an influential theory of class trying to identify a 'real' class is the Marxian one. It is, however, tied to social conditions that no longer exist and perhaps never did. The Marxian concept of a 'real' class (*Klasse für sich*) starts with two assumptions that have been seen as constitutive for modern society: first, the separation of labour from its traditional bonds and its transformation into wage labour, and second, the social and cultural homogenization of wage labour constituting a proletarian life-world. These assumptions explain a first stage in the moderniz-ation of the class structure of society. Further modernization, however, has not generated this transition from the abstract individual worker to a class unity based on a common life-world (class solidarity, class consciousness). It has instead generated the contrary. The cultural reproduction of social class has been decoupled from its structural basis.[12]

Concepts of classes today can no longer be projected upon traditional life-worlds nor can their putative unity be explained by taking recourse to such traditional life-worlds. Culturally, classes have been dissolved. Modern culture in fact stigmatizes them as premodern. With the repudi-ation of old, classbound life-worlds the direct experience of class has been, especially within the working class (Mooser 1983a, 1983b, 1984), destroyed and illegitimized. The eclipse of the visible class distinctions that character-ized class interaction in early modern society also destroyed the illusions that were tied to class concepts. Class as a world of homogeneity, solidarity and communication, as a *Klasse für sich*, has been debunked. The illusion derived from treating the working class as a 'real' class (Bourdieu 1987). The demystification consists in treating it as theoretically constructed.

But the demystification process is still incomplete. The old illusions about 'real' class are replaced by new ones. The theory of class formation has been replaced by the theory of stratification. The new illusion is that classes no longer exist. But this secondary 'substantialization' of the notion of class as status only reproduces the old problem. Status-groups are nothing but theoretically constructed social groups. There is no concrete life-world that stands for a status-group. There are no 'real' status-groups.

A necessary condition for solving the problem of the relationship between theoretical and real classes, between class position and class existence, consists in substituting sociological theories of social inequality for a theory of classes. It requires us first to construct the concept of class outside the notion of inequality. For this notion still presupposes living and concrete social entities, be they classes in the traditional sense or status groups in a more modern sense. Statements about increasing or decreasing social inequality (Haferkamp 1987) are statements that have to do only 'indirectly' (i.e. in a way that has to be clarified theoretically) with changes in the class structure of society. These statements are themselves the product of a class structure. They are the symbolic strategies of social groups trying to change the conditions of class existence and thereby change the given class structure of a society. Descriptions of a class structure as one of inequality are the result of a practice of symbolic classification in which antagonistic social groups in advanced modern societies engage in order to produce and reproduce their social position *vis-à-vis* other groups. It is in such descriptions that we have to look for the

---

[12] This problem can be discussed under the heading 'modernization' of the concept of class. To modernize the concept of class means to take into account the increasing relevance of culture for the objective as well as the subjective side of class.

mechanisms of transforming objective class positions into real classes, which does not, however, imply classes with class consciousness.[13]

A sufficient condition for solving the problem of the relationship between theoretical and 'real' classes in societies in which traditional class cultures no longer exist requires the sociological analysis of subcultural differences that serve as their substitute. The place of traditional class cultures (such as the well-known 'moral economy' of the English working class described by Thompson 1971) is taken by new class cultures. The claim of getting a just income is going to be replaced – and this is a correlate of the thesis of the quantity of competence as the parameter of vertical classification – by claims that are inherent in the idea of a cultural competence. Those who enter such a system of vertical classification (and the modernization of society seems to draw all into it) accept *uno actu* the idea of a highest stage of morality, of a highest stage of taste, of a highest stage of intelligence. The highest class then is the class with the highest competence. Class cultures tend to be differentiated by criteria of lower or higher cultures. Education rather than income marks barriers between social classes. What separates 'real' classes of people is the ability to justify the legitimacy of one's own culture. In a 'disenchanted' social world, those who can better justify have the better chance of prevailing.

Such a formulation points to a fundamental change of the logic of class struggles. Class struggle is transformed into a struggle that uses the medium of claims of competence. In these struggles all reasons are legitimate provided they allow for the rationalization of one's own cultural superiority. This structural transformation of class cultures invalidates the traditional cultures that previously made social classes 'real' classes. Attempts to defend the class culture of the *Bildungsbürger* (Conze and Kocka 1985) and the defence of working class culture (Mooser 1984) are only defensive reactions to their demise. These subcultures are being supplanted, but by what?

## The cultural reproduction of class

What are the class-specific subcultures beyond the traditional ones that allow for the transformation of a potential class into a real class in advanced modern societies? What are the mechanisms that generate genuinely modern class cultures?

One answer to these questions – and this answer is typical for much empirical research on social class – is to correlate 'subjective' variables that indicate cultural orientations with 'objective' variables that indicate class position. Such 'subjective' variables include attitudes toward society and politics, toward one's own person or group (self-classifications), attitudes

---

[13] The problem of class consciousness involves more than what suffices to identify real classes. It addresses the capacity of collective action and is a problem beyond the context of this discussion.

that can easily be taken from opinion polls. This approach is connected with the theoretical assumption that a real class would emerge only through the covariance of objective and subjective aspects of class. A real class would be defined by the homogeneity of objective and subjective conditions of social existence and empirically proved by their statistical covariance. Because tests for such homogeneity usually show that classes in the traditional sense no longer exist in modern society the conclusion is that they no longer exist. Thus, when groups with significant correlations are found they are described as 'milieus' that substitute for traditional real classes (Bolte and Hradil 1984; Hradil 1987).

Such a way of testing for the homogeneity of objective and subjective aspects of class has some serious flaws.[14] For what is called 'subjective class' is itself a theoretical construction of objective class position. What these tests examine is the covariance of two types of theoretical construction, since the attitudes of people indicate nothing but class-specific cultural differences. These cultural differences are generated because people adhere to or oppose norms and values, which in turn differ in their degree of legitimacy because there are more legitimate and less legitimate norms and values and because there are differences in the knowledge of the legitimate norms and values. To prove that one has an opinion (e.g. to tell an interviewer that one knows about the right way to educate children, which is nothing but the way defined by professional educators as the right and legitimate one), is only another dimension of objective class. This merely allows for a more complex theoretical construction of social classes in modern society (Hurrelmann 1985).

How then to identify real classes? An alternative answer to this question consists in describing class cultures on a structural level as generated by *class-specific schemata of experiencing, perceiving and interpreting the world*. Such schemata do not emerge at random; they are rather logically derived from the culture dominating a society. Two examples will help.

First, if we ask anyone in traditional societies, be he a peasant or an aristocrat, about his religious ideas and practices, we get answers verifying the assumption of a unitary and collectively shared religious worldview. Yet we know from actual historical and socio-anthropological research (Leach 1968; Schindler 1984) that there are competing religious subcultures: that of the peasants and that of the lords. The popular religious culture shares the religious worldview defined by the religious high culture. Yet, it lives this religion in a different way. It is the specific use made of the religious culture that generates religious subcultures. The analysis of religious praxis thus allows us to identify religious subcultures.

The second example refers to the modern society. A survey on the

---

[14] Similar problems arise in research on value change. The claim of a change towards postmaterialist values does not take into account changes in class structure that might explain changes in attitudes better than the theory of a general cultural change in society. Such changes might primarily have to do with the emergence of the new petite bourgeoisie. See as an overview of that type of research Klages 1984.

quantity of journals and books consumed would certainly support the assumption of a generalized culture of reading. Everyone reads books and magazines (or at least buys them). Nevertheless, a glance at specific examples shows differences built into this culture of reading. It is a classified culture, divided between *Kickers* and *Scientific American*, between *Quick* and *Freibeuter*, between *Bild* and *Süddeutsche Zeitung*, between the *National Enquirer* and *The New Yorker*. These examples indicate a sharp (and certainly not unique) division between (sub)cultural worlds. What counts is not that people read but what they read. Literary culture is classified objectively by the use made of it. The analysis of the different types of literary praxis allows us to identify literary subcultures.

To grasp subcultural differences the social scientist must investigate the interpretative schemata determining the cultural praxis in a given society. To identify class-specific subcultures the following hypothesis can be formulated: Class-specific subcultures are defined by schemata of experiencing, perceiving and interpreting the social world that thematize the vertical classification of social relations in a society. This hypothesis suggests locating the structure of modern class cultures in schemata thematizing social (in)equality.

The problem of the relationship between practices, interpretative schemes and culture can be clarified using an analogy from Leach 1976. Interpretative schemes are like musical scores. Scores regulate performances as interpretative schemes regulate cultural practices. Scores can be interpreted in this context as systems of rules governing a performance. Thus to understand and explain a performance one must have access to the musical text. Whether the performance is good or bad depends on the circumstances, but the score remains the same. To understand a score it is insufficient to listen to a performance; one also has to know the musical text. One has to be able to read musical texts.

This analogy can be pushed further by specifying that musical scores can be read only by those who know the musical language and can read its notational system. Transporting this analogy back to the social field it becomes clear that the ability to explain cultural practices presupposes the observer's 'reading ability' in cultural specifics. The ability to read modern interpretative schemes implies a reading knowledge of modern culture. We would defend the thesis that the rules for reading modern interpretative schemes can be reconstructed from texts articulating what has been called 'Enlightenment'.[15]

The 'civil society' derived from the Enlightenment has given rise to an interpretative scheme claiming moral universalism and using this interpret-

---

[15] Such structures therefore cannot be observed through direct observation. They have to be analyzed by reconstructive procedures, by a process of distilling the schemata that organize the present-day social world. Thus we have analyzed the political discourse of early modern German society using philosophical texts, pamphlets and statutes in order to identify the cultural logic of the bourgeois classes. The 'score' of these practices is the discourse of enlightenment (Eder 1985).

ative scheme for the legitimation of its praxis.[16] Opposed to the proletarian culture that practised another version of the cultural logic of modernity, civil society – at least in Western societies – has succeeded in dominating the cultural practices. The possessive bourgeois culture, the interpretative scheme of possessive individualism (Macpherson 1967), has become the dominant principle of a genuinely modern social and cultural praxis. In the nineteenth century the intent of the bourgeois class to 'cultivate' the lower classes and teach them the higher civil morality can be explained as an attempt to integrate them into the possessive bourgeois culture. It succeeded quite well (Eder 1985). The idea that the proletarian culture has a higher morality lost all its legitimacy. The discourse on equality characteristic for the possessive version of the logic of modernity destroyed the idea of a proletarian culture while promoting the illusion – typical for this discourse – that acquiring competence will minimize class differences.

Since the nineteenth century the 'scores' regulating the social and cultural practices underlying class struggles have been changed, amended or newly invented. The different performances which have resulted have modified the boundaries between the real social classes, leading to revisions of these social and cultural practices. Once-flourishing practices have become outmoded. The most striking revisions are tied to the rise of the service sector: the new technocratic elites and the new petite bourgeoisie committed to the service industries. The ethos of the aristocracy and the higher bourgeoisie has been revised by the groups of professionals and managers. The ethos of the *Bildungsbürgertum* (the teachers, the professors, the professionals) has been revised by the new intellectual groups (the critics, the journalists). The 'protestant' ethos of the old petite bourgeoisie has been replaced by the narcissistic ethos of the new petite bourgeoisie who bases its 'score' on 'self-fulfilment' and 'self-realization'. The 'proletarian' ethos of the lower classes survives in social groups that are radicalizing the proletarian ethos into an ethos of consumption that imitates the sophisticated consumption patterns of the middle and upper classes.[17] This hedonism is being forcibly restructured by the increase of unqualified workers and of non-workers. In this process, class-specific interpretative schemata emerge that indicate new class-specific practices. New forms of a class-ethos – as Bourdieu (1984) put it – are generated.

The proposition that has been put forth for empirically identifying real classes is to introduce, in the place of tests for the homogeneity of objective and subjective aspects of class, a third level of analysis: namely, differential interpretative schemata of the social world that on the one hand generate

[16] In early modern society the bourgeois class could not yet superimpose its version of the cultural logic of a modern social order, its class-specific practice upon the whole society. It still had to share economic, social and political power with the traditional elites on the one hand and had not yet succeeded in destroying the traditional world of plebeian culture on the other hand.

[17] This difference can be shown in consumption patterns that are organized as imitations of the higher culture. This has been described in detail by Bourdieu (1984).

subjective attitudes and on the other hand are the product of objective class positions. These differential schemata 'transform' objective class positions into subjective class positions. To the extent that this transformation succeeds the theoretical construction of social classes can claim to have identified real classes.

In the following section an attempt will be made to reconstruct such a process of transformation of class positions that have been constructed theoretically as differential amounts of quantity of competence. Three propositions will be defended. First, what distinguishes modern culture from traditional cultures is the ideal of equality. To know the discourse on equality constitutive for modern culture is to dispose of the reading ability of modern cultural interpretations of social reality. When this discourse has to be accommodated to the objective class positions the problem emerges of explaining why social reality deviates from this ideal. Theories of social inequality – and this is the second proposition – try to 'explain' these deviations. The interpretations of social inequality vary with the objective class positions from which one's own position and the position of others are seen. Theories of social inequality – the third and decisive proposition – are class-bound forms of interpreting the ideal of equality between people.[18]

*Class-specific schemata of social experience*

What are some of the characteristic schemata used to justify social class positions? One is that material inequality between actors is the outcome of their differential cognitive competence; their relative social positions are deserved. A complementary idea is that cultural inequality manifests itself as the differential moral-aesthetic competence of actors; their cultural rank is well deserved. Both ideas advance the illusion that those who populate the lower positions and those who populate the higher positions are where they should be. Such arguments are strategies for transforming the factual into something normative. They are – to use a philosophical term – the result of a specific type of a collectively practised naturalistic fallacy: an 'ecological fallacy'. Those using such a fallacy claim for themselves the highest form of moral and aesthetic consciousness, of professional quality and economic value. The specific effect on the subjective level is the interpretation of low social status as the result of incompetence.

This type of a class-specific schema of experiencing and perceiving the social world can be distinguished from that based on an individualistic ethos, where social inequality is seen as the result of differential individual achievements in society. This is a pattern common among those who,

---

[18] This means that the problem of a class-specific worldview – a cognitive schematization of the world – or the problem of judgements of taste – an aesthetic schematization of the world – have to be excluded. This does not imply the assumption of their insignificance concerning the constitution of a real class.

thanks to their economic and cultural wealth, can afford such an ethos. The formal structure underlying this ethos consists in not acknowledging that such individualism and universalism can only be realized by a few, and can only have a particular empirical relevance in society. It therefore can be characterized as another type of a naturalistic fallacy: an 'idealistic fallacy'. By those who share and practise the idealistic fallacy, social inequality is seen as what is functionally necessary to make sure that the best enter the higher positions. The principle of achievement is best suited to fulfill this function. Anyone who has reached a position is there by right.

A third schema is based quite simply on the ethos of consumption. It emerges where material interests dominate everyday life.[19] The imagery of this ethos is also based upon a specific formal structure, one that reduces the representations of status positions in society to the material resources they are tied to. This can be interpreted as a third type of a naturalistic fallacy: a 'materialistic fallacy'. Those who share this fallacy relate social inequality to external forces that cannot be changed by individual will, to pure chance, or to the presence or lack of attention. The lower positions are occupied by those who were hindered from rising: by a bad father, a lack of fertile contacts, or an untimely war or depression. Had the circumstances for obtaining formal education been more favourable, these actors would surely have done better.

These three images of the social world are all based upon the formal structures of *naturalistic fallacies*, deducing what should be from that which is. They can be structurally described in the following three dimensions: the underlying interpretative schema, the cognitive form, and the types of lifeworld (Table 5.1).[20] The three fallacies allow a perception of the social

---

[19] From the perspective of the workers this logic leads to a dichotomic worldview. This worldview differentiates between high and low, between good and bad, between freedom and necessity. This imagery of the lower classes has been described by Bourdieu (1984) as constituting an ethos of 'necessity'.

[20] Behind such fallacies a new type of mechanism that produces a distinctive class culture can be located. It is the prestige tied to belonging to a class that counts. Prestige is concurred, however, only when a group is closed, its quantity limited (maximizing its market value), and its ethos controlled (to integrate the group). Thus it is the prestige usually used to represent social inequality that becomes the most significant indicator of class (Wegener 1985), not only with respect to cultural consumption, but also with respect to some occupations of central importance for modern society. Those occupations that are the more highly classified, that are made more difficult to enter, and are rendered more exclusive through the development of a strict, even eccentric, professional behavioural code (Beck and Brater 1978), become the more prestigious. The mechanism of forming real classes best adapted to the new way of the cultural or symbolic constitution of real classes then is closure of objectively classified groups by attributing prestige to them. This hypothesis of a new mechanism generating class cultures requires concrete analyses of practices that reproduce class-specific interpretative schemes. The aspects enumerated in Table 5.1 give only some general hints. Historical research, especially historical social anthropology, is one field of research that has so far most productively developed this mode of analysis.

Table 5.1  *Types of class-specific cultures*

| Interpretative schema | Cognitive form | Types of life world |
| --- | --- | --- |
| The individualistic ethos of personal identity and of the potential equality among men | Idealistic fallacy: what counts is the quality of culture one has | Predominance of life interests in the cultural, political and public spheres |
| The ethos of achievement; recognition of inequality between men | Ecological fallacy: what counts is the culture one has achieved | Predominance of life interests in the private sphere (family) |
| The ethos of maximizing the chances of consumption; recognition of the division of society into social classes | Materialistic fallacy: what counts as culture is the goods one has | Predominance of life interests in the sphere of work, especially the workplace |

reality such that the discourse of equality can be accommodated to the facts of class position. The result of these strategies of accommodation are class-specific theories of equality that are, in fact, the base of theories that legitimate the social inequality that is the reality of modern society. These theories are thus the key to the analysis of the subjective side of objective class positions in modern society. They are strategies of systematic self-deception. These interpretative schemes of social reality can thus be defined as collectively shared and practised fallacies.

## A social critique of morality

Theories of social inequality are the key to defining real classes in modern societies. They are suited to this task because of their function of representing the class structure and because they are set up to organize the representation of this reality in a class-specific way. Such theories are part of the cultural reproduction of objective class positions. Yet the dominant theoretical discourse on social inequality is nothing but a translation of everyday discourses on social inequality into language that supports and strengthens the everyday discourses. The theoretical discourse on social inequality produces the illusion of its own validity. It is a discourse that reproduces the systematically distorted discourses legitimating factual social inequality (Miller 1987). As long as the theoretical discourse fails to thematize this context of application it contributes to the reproduction of the argumentative fallacies that lie at the base of everyday discourses.

No theoretical discourse on social inequality can escape this dilemma. The normative implications built into the concept of social inequality force integration of the effects of the theory into the theory of social inequality. They also force cognitive reflexivity about how these theories correspond to class-specific schemata of interpreting the world and to what extent they are an expression of the class structure of society.

A possible effect of such a reflexive form of theorizing is the theoretical conclusion that the morality of the upper classes is the highest morality or even the highest-developed morality.[21] One could derive a normative conclusion from this theoretical statement: only those who have reached the highest stages of morality should enter the highest social positions in society. This has a consequence that is fatal to morality, in that the highest morality appears to be the morality of the dominant class. This – as we know – corrupts morality. We would like therefore to propose a different conclusion: the class cultures analyzed above could serve as preconditions for new moral and political learning processes. The dynamics of learning processes would consist in dissolving the specific fallacies at their bases. The conditions for generating 'real' classes would then no longer have to be sought in the philosophical critique of the ideals of modern culture but in the social critique of the ideals modern society claims to represent.

Modern society institutionalized moral universalism as a high culture that was open only to a few. When it started to thematize this reality of modern society it treated it as a manifestation of the 'unfinished project of modernity' (Habermas 1985a). It then hoped that the educational system would correct this problem by triggering moral and political learning processes in the people. In placing hope there it denied its own class structure. The result of the expansion of the educational system was to reproduce the modern class structure not only on the level of material needs but also on the level of culture. Modern moral universalism didn't hinder the reproduction of the class structure. Its philosophical refinement and sophistication as discursive morality has intensified this effect.

Only sociological analysis generating a social critique of modern culture can destroy illusions about the reality of social inequality. A theory of class, formulated without any reflection on its effects and functions, becomes merely another part of the classificatory struggles that regulate the production and reproduction of class differences in modern society. As a theory of social inequality it remains tied to its class-specific base. A way out is moralistic theorizing: be it elitist identification with the upper classes, avantgardistic engagement for the underdogs, or the urge to be a mediator between the two. A sociological theory of inequality can escape such

---

[21] In the sociological analysis of a class-specific morality (and of a class-specific taste and class-specific cognitive qualifications as well) one runs into the problem of which morality is the better one. The form of a moral judgement has normative implications that there are higher or lower forms. This problem has been transformed into a psychological theory by treating the different social forms of morality as steps or stages of a moral learning process. Piaget calls the *telos* of this learning process the competence to produce an autonomous moral judgement. In the same vein, Kohlberg speaks of a postconventional moral judgement being the *telos* of the moral development of human beings. But here we find no way to go beyond the individual to the level of society. Treating such theories of moral development as a medium of the cultural reproduction of society – as tried above – is intended to open up a perspective beyond psychologism.

temptations by relating inequality to the class structure and analyzing the discourse on inequality as a way of perceiving and interpreting this class structure. My proposition is simply to formulate a sociological theory of social inequality as a theory of the cultural reproduction of the class structure of modern society.

# PART III:

# THE THEORY OF NEW SOCIAL MOVEMENTS. A CHALLENGE TO CLASS THEORY?

## 6

## A NEW SOCIAL MOVEMENT?
The Continuing Vitality of the Theory of the 'New Social Movements'[1]

### Preliminary definition

'New social movements' today embrace a vast array of phenomena but can be best divided into at least two types: *cultural* and *political* movements. The first type comprises communal movements such as the youth, the feminist, and the anti-industrial movements seeking alternative relations to nature; the second comprises anti-bureaucratic movements (in environment, housing or psychiatry) and, to a lesser extent, the student movement. They differ in their orientation toward their social environment. Cultural movements oppose present social life. Political movements challenge modern state domination.[2]

---

[1] This chapter was originally published by *Telos* in 1982 under the title 'A new social movement?' (Vol. 52, pp. 5–20). Instead of rewriting it (except for some slight revisions) I commented on its main arguments in new footnotes, adding elements of recent theoretical discussions and literature. In this way, a reconsideration of a text written a decade ago can give an insight into the way the theory of the new social movements has developed, which might be more stimulating regarding the experience of difference (and non-difference!) than writing another article on the same topic.

[2] The countercultures upon which *cultural* movements are based have been analyzed, for example, by Musgrave (1974, pp. 19ff), Misra and Preston (1978, pp. 175ff), and Yinger (1977, 1982). Countercultures are defined by their relation to a dominant culture which distinguishes them systematically from groups that relate to the political sphere. This does not exclude that social movements go through cyclical changes in their relation to their social environment. The social basis of *political* movements is defined by shared concerns that have to do with economic and political oppression and control. It can be called 'populist' protest (in the most general sense). Examples are discussed in Tilly et al. 1975 and Landsberger 1973. See also the

Historically, cultural movements have challenged the process of cultural rationalization by developing anti-rational positions in epistemology, ethics, and aesthetics (Yinger 1977, pp. 838ff). Truth is seen as attainable not through research, but by mystical insight. The good life is seen as the result not of rational moral judgement but of the expression of unrepressed feelings. That which is beautiful is seen as being attained not by artistic experience, but by overturning perceptions. Countercultures, then, are carriers of protest against the overall rationalization of culture and society.[3]

Political movements seeking political power or decentralization have been as common as cultural movements. From the viewpoint of Weber's distinction between formal and substantive rationality, these radical political challenges to formal rationality can be described in terms of a material rationality. Accordingly, economic well-being cannot be attained through abstract and egoistic social relations, but by communal forms of exchange. The leitmotif of political morality is concrete political relations or direct democracy. Similarly, political identity is defined by religious, ethnic or other cultural ties rather than citizenship. Collective mobilization is the context within which this type of social movement can be grasped.[4]

This account of a continual yet fruitless reappearance of political and

contributions to Boyte and Riessman 1986 on the 'new populism' which can be seen as the political mobilization of non-class or trans-class movements. This distinction has also been made by Raschke (1985) in his general treatise on social movements. The difference between both is increasingly vanishing in recent years, because political movements have become cultural entrepreneurs and cultural movements have become politicized. Example of this are conservation movements within the environmental movement and the rise of nationalist and regionalist movements that base their political aims on cultural ideas and identities. One can even speak of a general trend of political movements to become 'cultural pressure groups' (see Part IV).

[3] Roth (1975) has analyzed this other side of rationalization in Weberian terms of charismatic orientations. Examples of this countermovement against rationalization are the English Radicals during the English Revolution. For a good analysis, see Hill 1975. Mysticism, being an important part of this countermovement, is represented not only in the works of the romantic philosophers at the beginning of the nineteenth century, but was already found in the Taborites, who protested against the rationalism of Prague University as early as the fifteenth century. For a definitive statement of Weber's theory of rationalization see Schluchter 1979, 1981.

[4] Political movements draw on a broad diversity of ideas and practices whose common denominator is opposition to the state. The ideas of an economic utopia range from autarchy to communist collectivism. See: Hardy 1979 for England, Peters 1980 and Leineweber 1981 for Germany, and Allan-Michaud 1990 for France. A general analysis is found in Renn 1985 and Sicinski and Wemegah 1983. Religion also plays an important part in the definition of collective identities against the state; see Lewy 1974, for a systematic and historical-comparative account of this phenomenon. Identity has become a central element of social movement theory; see Cohen 1985 and Melucci 1988, 1989. These political ideologies are often tied to a harmonistic ideal of social relations; see Unger 1975, 1987, for example, who argues for harmony and sympathy between men as the foundation of an alternative political morality. A good empirical example is the German 'Greens' and their attempt to build a participatory party structure (Poguntke 1987). A unifying perspective on all these diverse phenomena has been provided by theories of collective mobilization which have started with

cultural protest is challenged today by the ecological movement that seems to crystallize all the aspects of protest into a historically new social movement.[5] This movement is to contemporary political and cultural protest what the labour movement was to various syndicalist, political, or cultural mobilizations of labour. The ecological movement is a new social movement displacing the institutionally integrated labour movement. Whether or not this self-conception is empirically justified remains to be seen. At any rate, a new self-image of a social movement has emerged different from that of the labour movement.

### 'New' movements as neoromantic and neopopulist protest

To designate countercultures and new radical political protest as 'neo-romantic' or 'neopopulist' gives a first hint regarding their historical context: it implies that these new movements have something to do with old ones. Romanticism is an anti-rationalist and subjectivist approach to the social world (Brunschwig 1975), while populism is characterized by hostility to the status quo and anti-intellectualism (Allcock 1971; Canovan 1981; Boyte and Riessman 1986). These designations can be applied to different groups and movements. Those who do so, however, must show that reactions are essentially the same throughout the development of modern society. They follow what can be called a cyclical explanation of collective protest in modernity against a developmental explanation.[6]

Romantic movements result from the identity crises of those strata objectively identified with a mode of social development. These movements are usually apolitical and non-violent and are staffed by members of the ruling classes who have different types of utopian visions. In early modern societies such movements attracted the new nobility.[7] The more radical variants of this romantic flight from reality are utopian movements

---

Tilly's path-breaking analysis (Tilly 1978). See Tilly 1985, 1988 for the further development of this theory and its connection with resource mobilization theory (Zald and McCarthy 1979, 1987).

[5] The literature on the ecological movement abounds. It has turned out to be the most visible and most significant, both culturally and politically, of the new social movements. More recent accounts are found in Galtung 1986; Rüdig 1990, 1991; Müller-Rommel 1989; Pearce 1991.

[6] Cyclical explanations can be found in Bürklin 1987 and have been tested regarding middle class radicalism by Brand 1990. So far there are no historical sociological analyses of the rise and fall of social movements that allow one to go beyond more or less abstract or impressionistic accounts with the exception of Tarrow (1989), who has applied the concept of a cycle to the history of the Italian wave of mobilization in the seventies.

[7] This has been nicely described by Elias (1969, pp. 336ff, 377ff). The characteristic image of this romanticism is the free life of the shepherd, the idyllic representation of a pre-agricultural life.

seeking a republic of love and affection.[8] This romantic backlash against the 'age of reason' tends to occur especially when early modern societies are being transformed into liberal-capitalist ones. This intellectual counter-movement is based on mystical insight and the wish for the extraordinary. Politically, this mentality is ambivalent. Thus, romanticism can encompass both left- and right-wing politics.[9]

Romantic movements in nineteenth-century liberal-capitalist societies were based on a new social group: the *Bildungsbürgertum* (Vondung 1976; Krabbe 1974). Members of newly educated middle classes were reacting to the new phenomenon of industrialization. Thus, it was a new romanticism, focusing on the effects of technology. Its constructive feature was a 'natural' life that generated the idea of a general reform of life. It began with the reaction to modern scientific medicine by opposing to it a natural medicine related to a holistic conception of the person (Krabbe 1974, pp. 78ff). A second phase in this new romantic protest against industrialism was characterized by attempts to seek an alternative to both capitalism and socialism. Its vision was based on rural cooperatives allowing for life with fresh air, the sun, and economic autonomy.[10] Remnants of old religious beliefs were amalgamated into new religions and religious feelings became more important than organization. Ultimately, the old religious base was completely displaced by Germanic religious mythology. Nietzsche and Wagner were central in helping destroy old Christian elements. Consequently, this religious no-man's-land allowed for the introduction of scientific theories about racial inequality. This type of bourgeois middle class romanticism reached turning point with the ideas of 'Volk, Individuum and Land': a system of thought that easily fed into the emerging fascist movements.[11]

After World War II, a new rationalism developed against romanticism and its fascist 'application'. This new rationalism has recently come under

[8] For an analysis of this kind of utopia in modern social and political thought, see Manuel and Manuel 1979. The republic of love and affection has been developed in the most radical way by the Ranters, one of the radical movements of the English Revolution. Deep ecology and those arguing for an environmental ethics have continued these traditions. Sessions (1987) and Nash (1989) give an excellent overview of these discussions, relating these ethical concerns through different historical traditions. See also the contributions to Mesch 1990, which present the broad spectrum of deep ecology positions.

[9] See Brunschwig (1975, p. 292), who shows that in Prussia political romanticism was open for left- and right-wing politics. This phenomenon can be found again in the appeal of ecological ideas to conservative and radical minds. The social composition of the electorate of Green parties in Europe is a good example.

[10] See Vondung (1976, pp. 142ff). This movement also implied the freeing of the body from its artificial distortions, leading to nudism as a cultural movement, and its struggle against corsets, lace-up shoes and other assets of the civilization of the body. See Dreitzel (1981) for the cultural background of these movements.

[11] The destruction of validity claims in Nietzsche's philosophy has been analyzed in Habermas 1968a, pp. 237ff. This destruction allows for a theory of power substituting for the theory of truth.

attack by 'neoromantic' movements to the extent that they raise all the problems of the old romanticism.[12] Thus, recent history can be read as an alternating cycle. The ideas are always the same: rationalism and anti-rationalism constitute the more modern ideological universe of discourse. What supposedly explains their differences is their application: rationalist or romantic ideas have a function in the twentieth-century United States or Germany that differs from the one they had in eighteenth-century England or France. Therefore, it is not a matter of new movements, but only of different contexts within which rationalism and romanticism confront each other.

Populism, contrary to romanticism, is an attempt either to participate in a given institutional structure or to establish a lost institutional context that guarantees the autonomy of the people. The term 'populism' was first coined to describe nineteenth-century peasant protest in Russia.[13] This was an ideological movement claiming that political revolution and the moral regeneration of Russian society could only come from the 'people' by rejuvenating peasant values: the future was to be constructed in the image of the past. In this sense, populism vindicated peasant autonomy and self-determination in a changing social context (the commercial transformation of agriculture).

The coming of industrialization and parliamentarianism changed the cultural, social and political context for populism. Entrepreneurs and state officials who controlled and regulated industrialization came to threaten various social groups.[14] These groups reacted to these threats by attempts to achieve a moral regeneration of old, cherished values, the old 'American' virtues. The ideological orientation of middle class populism has a strong rationalist component. Within this populist context, the egalitarian

---

[12] See Greverus (1979) for an analysis of this new romanticism in Germany; a critical analysis of neoromantic attitudes can be found in Peters 1980, pp. 327ff. See also Weiß (1986), who sees a return of romanticism in the postmodern cultural critique. The term 'neoromanticism' is justified because the old *topoi* of romanticism, such as affectivity, communalism, naturalistic life-forms, and mysticism, return in the new religious and psychotherapeutic movements, as well as in esoteric worldviews that have gained a widespread reading public. For a good theoretical and empirical analysis of these phenomena see Wuthnow 1976, 1986 and Beckford and Levasseur 1986. A connection of this neoromanticism with fascism within the environmental movement has been established by Bramwell 1989. Beyond the provocative aspect of this argument one can draw the conclusion that the left–right difference is no longer sufficient to classify the new social movements.

[13] See the article on Populism in the *Encyclopedia of Social Sciences* (1935). For systematic historical accounts of populism see Venturi 1960; Puhle 1975; Holdermeier 1979; Destler 1966. See also the contributions to Dubiel 1986, which give a good description of the ideological ambivalence of populism.

[14] The central groups are the small farmers in the Midwest in the nineteenth century and the small-town bourgeoisie in the twentieth century; for the latter phenomenon, see Lipset 1959 and Trow 1958. A classic is Goodwyn (1976), who sees populist demands as a basically democratic phenomenon. Populism can even be regarded as the American version of radical democracy. See McKenna 1974; Boyte et al. 1986; Boyte and Riessman 1986; Kann 1986; McNall 1988.

dimension of nationalism, i.e. the idea of being one nation among many others,[15] is lost in a particularistic defence of 'universal values'. Moreover, this protest generates moral rigidity concerning social behaviour: the world that is perceived as threatened is also that of a moral asceticism related to the 'Great Tradition'. In Europe these phenomena were only slightly more complicated (Symmons-Symonolewicz 1965). This process threatened those middle classes bound structurally to the bourgeois movements for political or economic freedom, for national unification and for bourgeois morality against the authoritarian morality of absolutism. Industrialization produced the typical ideological conversion of the petite bourgeoisie trying to live in an industrialized world that had no place for it. The most extreme form of this defence was twentieth-century fascism.

The collective behaviour of peasant and industrial populism is identical. It defends social-structural autonomy against encroachment from above; seeks particularistic collective identity; demands more participation in existing institutions; and generates a reactionary ideology. Today these orientations again emerge in the movements directed against the formal rationality of modern political life contained, for example, in parliamentary, administrative and judicial procedures. Modern regional movements, tax revolts or citizens' initiatives join the old populist orientations. Challenges to the modern welfare state or bureaucratic socialism such as demands for participation on all institutional levels, from neighbourhood, school, workplace to local and regional administration are seen as attempts to reintegrate the people's material interests back into formal-rational institutions.[16] This 'neopopulism' is a further backlash against formal rationality in modern politics.[17]

---

[15] For a differentiated view of nationalism, see Smith 1972, 1981, 1986. Anderson 1983, who pointed out the constructed character of national community, has given a new and fruitful direction to this research area. For a theoretical account in terms of rational-choice theory see Rogowski 1985. See also the contributions and discussions in Tiryakian and Rogowski 1985 and in Melucci and Diani 1992.

[16] These movements have expanded rapidly, ranging from small group mobilization to diverse forms of ethnic revival. In this respect, the theory of the 'new social movements' can in fact help to differentiate between those forms of mobilization that are based on traditional issues (such as the search for collective identity based on historical experiences) and those that are based on new issues. The difference lies in that the new issues are constructed (including collective identities) and not given. Analogous to the Weberian distinction between traditional and legal bases of domination, we could distinguish between traditional and voluntaristic forms of mobilization. New social movements then are those which construct and define an issue out of a generalized concern in the process of mobilization. Ethnic revival (Smith 1981) would be a manifestation of the former, regionalist movements such as the Italian Lombard League a manifestation of the latter. The environmental movement certainly would have to be considered (with few exceptions regarding its 'wings') as a manifestation of a voluntaristic form of mobilization. Its historical construction cannot be separated from events such as the Club-of-Rome report or the Brundtland report.

[17] The discussion on the new populism has been expanding over the last years. See Boyte 1980; Boyte and Riessman 1986; Boyte et al. 1986; Kann 1983, 1986; and Feagin and Çapek 1991. Feagin and Çapek argue that populist 'movements are not disconnected from class, but neither do they explicitly carry the banner of class' (p. 48). Here the distinction between an

This explanatory model is based on the idea of two cultures, one of formal rationality, always accompanied by its counterculture of material rationality. Depending on the social location of the countertypes, they are either reactionary (i.e. carried by political elites) or revolutionary (i.e. carried by those excluded from power).

This cyclic explanation presupposes a rigid separation of formal and material rationality. The formal aspect is seen as the core of modernity and the material aspects as its context. Thus a rational bureaucracy is seen driven by material interests into different directions, always in danger of losing its constitutive formal rationality and of dissolving into anarchy. Therefore, populist and countercultural challenges have to be controlled. The core institutional structure has one primary function: to extend its ability to control. In effect, this explanatory model assumes that movements complement social control. They inform the system about the social reality to be controlled, and they also guarantee the adaptability of the institutional system. Thus, movements are nothing but indicators for modernizing elites. Formal rationality goes hand in hand with a functionalist logic that treats social actors and their interests as 'problems'. The weakness of this objectivist conception is its inability to identify historical actors creating society.

Thus, it cuts off the most interesting questions. Whether there is something new in contemporary movements can be answered only by looking at these movements as part of a process by which society is created (Touraine 1978, 1981). From this perspective, political and cultural movements are alternative forms of social integration. Supporting that, these collective actions are preliminary attempts to create a new society and clear the way for raising the question of whether in these collective actions new forms of social integration are being developed.

## A developmental explanation of new movements

To answer this question, it is necessary to distinguish several different types of social protest. Not every form of protest is a social movement. Fascist movements, for example, are forms of collective mobilization, but they are not social movements. They may indirectly contribute to the modernization of society; but this is not their explicit goal – on the contrary. *Social* movements are those directly and intentionally related to modernization from the seventeenth century on. In this sense, there are only two: the first one appeared during the transition from traditional domination to the early modern state and involved primarily the middle

objective determination and a subjective relevance of class is made. The bridge proposed between non-class populist theory and class theory is to look more closely at the cultural texture of class and collective action!

classes but also some plebeian groups;[18] the second is the labour movement, which challenged the restriction of emancipation to political emancipation. Here the main emphasis shifted from political emancipation to distributive justice.[19] This notion of 'social movements' clearly requires a reconstruction of their relation to modernity. Social movements are genuinely modern phenomena. Only in modern society have social movements played a constitutive role in social development.

In premodern societies, the dynamics of change are the prerogative of those in power, and are directed by processes of domination (Eisenstadt 1973). In primitive societies, social dynamics are even further removed from social practices. Change is largely determined by material conditions such as natural events or population pressures (Gluckman 1963; Eder 1976). Unlike social protest in premodern societies, which is institutionally bound, social movements in modern societies are located precisely where change takes place. Thus, for the first time, they can play a historical role in the historical creation of society (Touraine 1981). That cultural orientations can be challenged is constitutive for modernity. This is not so in traditional societies, where disputes occur only on the social level; the cultural system is simply given. This pattern changes with modernity, where cultural traditions can be challenged by conflicting values and norms. The process of challenging cultural orientations rather than the reliance on cultural traditions is characteristic of modernity.

Both the movement for political emancipation and the labour movement challenged cultural traditions and provided a normative direction to social development. Both sought to redirect social evolution and have created a new society, although they have not succeeded in transforming state structures. Thus, it is necessary to ask whether they prefigure a new social movement trying to rebuild society. Early populist and countercultural claims of millenarian movements have been utopian. The experience of most people in welfare-corporatist or socialist-bureaucratic states, however, forces one to redefine autonomy, self-determination, and discursive procedures of decision-making. It is this new social meaning that allows for the transformation of populist and counterculture protest into a social movement.

This approach presupposes a specific theory of modernity as a process seeking to fulfil the potentials of its constitutive structures (Habermas 1985a). In this regard, new movements are new only because they bear new hope for the collective realization of the predicaments of modernity.

---

[18] Moore (1966) has implicitly dealt with this social movement. There is no general and comprehensive work on the early modern social movement.

[19] The labour movement has been analyzed mainly in historical treatises (Conze 1973), but there is none that gives a good systematic treatment of this movement. For a general overview, see Kendall 1975 and Grebing 1986. Social-historical analyses of the labour movement in Germany have been provided by Conze and Groh (1966), Conze (1973), Kocka (1983) and for the early twentieth century by Winkler (1985, 1986, 1987). For a sociological analysis of worker opposition movements see Friedman 1985.

Thus, developmental theory of modernity is not a theoretical no-man's-land. On the contrary, there have been theoretical attempts towards a developmental explanation for changing normative and cultural orientations. There are theories postulating changes in modes of social integration that range from economic to psychological ones. Accordingly, the new protest movements tap integrative problems located on the motivational level. What is problematic is not political emancipation or economic justice, but subjective individual happiness and 'the good life'. In this sense, the 'paradigm of the life-world'[20] becomes the new movement's focus. This model still leaves the question of whether this paradigm is a new model of collective action and a developmental step in the history of collective action. Whether the new movements amount to social movements depends on how conceptions of happiness and the good life are related to normative ideas about the social order and the resources of action available. This perspective thus focuses on the capacity of actors to translate ideas about the good life into historical action.

The task then is to reintroduce historical actors into a theory of social development by starting with the constitution of collective action and not with its ideological correlates.[21] This approach to social movements relies on two things: a reconstruction of the cultural and normative orientations of modern social movements; and an analysis of how protesting social groups order these elements structurally and thereby constitute collective action. There are three criteria for defining collective action characterizing a social movement. A social movement must have a self-image and a clear idea of who are those against whom it defends a way of life. Furthermore, it is necessary to relate the antagonistic relations between a collective *ego* and a collective *alter* to a common field of action, namely the control of the development of a socio-cultural life-world.

## Towards a theory of modernity

When cultural traditions can be questioned in terms of action theory, all components of social action – values, norms, motives and facilities – can be challenged. The evolutionary potential of modernity is in its opening the possibility of criticizing the value component of an action system. This potential is developed by two theories dealing historically with systems of

---

[20] A first version of this explanatory approach can already be found in Mannheim 1936; this has been taken up by Turner (1969) and Habermas (1987). As an application of the concept of 'life-world' to the study of social movements see Raschke 1985.

[21] On a more abstract level, the relation of the form and the content of collective action is at stake. The approach to be proposed starts with the assumption that it is the structure of collective action that counts.

social action: Smelser's theory of collective behaviour (Smelser 1962) and Touraine's theory of the self-production of society (Touraine 1978).[22]

Smelser accepts straightforwardly the hierarchy of the four functions as Parsons has conceptualized it, putting 'values' on top, and 'situational faculties' at the bottom of the hierarchy. 'Norms' and 'motives' occupy the intermediate levels.[23] This hierarchy implies some logical relations: changes on top necessarily involve changes at the bottom, but changes at the bottom do not necessarily involve changes at the top of the hierarchy. By constructing the system of social action in this manner, Parsons and Smelser have tried to give a general sociological answer to the old Hobbesian problem. The theory of the structure of action systems is conceived as a solution to the problem of establishing a social order. This theory can be applied historically (as Smelser himself has shown), but it does not explain the process of the definition and redefinition of an action system. It can be applied to history but it does not explain historicity, the process by which a social order is being created.

This is the point where Touraine tries to push the Parsonian approach one step further. Touraine's Marxist heritage lies in his concept of a 'cultural model', which determines the action system and which articulates the material process of reproduction in the spheres of consumption, distribution, organization of production, and production as a cultural activity. Leaving aside a consumption-oriented cultural model, the cultural orientation of distribution gives rise to a society characterized by struggles over state power. A cultural orientation based on the organization of production gives rise to different social struggles. Society is to be created on the basis of control over the forces of production. The cultural orientation of the activity of production again changes the action system. Instead, the *telos* of production is the object of social struggles. The power to define what should be produced constitutes a new field of historical action. This assumption allows Touraine to distinguish between different types of societies, each representing different types of systems of historical action. Besides premodern subsistence societies, this account differentiates

[22] It is true that both authors, even mentioning the four dimensions of an action space, primarily deal with the normative and the evaluative aspects of it. The dimensions that deal with resources and the organization of action remain rather empty categories. This explains why resource mobilization theory (Zald and McCarthy 1979, 1987) has been so successful: it filled the empty space left by the dominating paradigms in social movement theory and analysis. The macro-bias of these theories is also a reason for the later rise of micro-analyses of mobilization and social movement histories. See McAdam 1988 among many others.

[23] This level has become the favourite field of rational-choice approaches in social movement theory. See the work of Oliver (1980), Oliver and Marwell (1988), Oliver et al. (1985), or Klanderman's motivational theories (Klandermans 1984, 1988). This has led to two competing ideas of social networks: that networks are held together either by interest coalitions or by a socially created consensus. Neither theory is exclusive. Self-interest and norms are the two variables that cannot be reduced to each other (Elster 1989) and thus have to be taken as complementary and interacting factors in creating and reproducing social interaction networks.

between commercial, industrial, and postindustrial societies. Commercial societies focus on the problem of distribution, industrial societies on the mobilization of the forces of production, and postindustrial societies on the cultural direction of social development.

Both Smelser's functionalist and Touraine's historicist account cannot effectively deal with historical time. There is much well-ordered difference, but no dynamic in both theories. Whereas Smelser introduces time only at a descriptive level, Touraine does so by means of a hierarchy of economic functions with production on top and consumption at the bottom. This leads to the question of how the hierarchy of economic functions is constituted and of whether it is a social universal. Touraine is afraid to cross the barriers raised by his arguments against an evolutionary interpretation. His approach, however, implies an evolutionary logic of social development: the articulation of production as a cultural activity on the level of cultural historical action. In this context, cultural models based on organization, distribution, or consumption appear as less evolved forms of systems for historical action. When the organization of production defines the cultural model for social action, questions concerning 'use value' become subordinate. The same is true for the other types of historical action.

What is this implicit *evolutionary logic*?[24] If modernity is characterized by having all its composing elements open to challenge, then their historical meaning can be established as the outcome of collective discourse.[25] Consequently, changes in systems of historical action are regulated by changes in the universe of discourse, and these changing universes of discourse form a logical sequence. Of course, cultural models organize not social relations but a life-world, which subsequently generates conceptions of the relation of man to nature. The conception of work is a special case of this evolutionary process.

Aside from peasant society, where work is seen as interaction with nature, there are three structurally different *cultural models* based on an organic, a mechanical, and a cybernetic relation of man to nature (Moscovici 1968). In the first case, man creates nature by transforming it through knowledge and organically adapting to it (as in the artisan world of the Renaissance); in the second case, nature is exploited by man instrumentally (industrialization since the end of the eighteenth century); and in

---

[24] The term 'logic' is used here in the weak sense of a developmental sequence of stages. For a use of this concept relevant to the purpose of this chapter, see Kohlberg 1981. For its application within sociological theory see Habermas 1984, 1987. An application to historical processes (nineteenth-century political evolution in Germany) can be found in Eder 1985.

[25] This claim is based on the premise that the elements of action systems are related to each other through communication. Discourse is taken as the kind of communication within which all elements of the action space can be thematized and made the medium for communication. This theoretical perspective obviously presupposes Habermas's theory of communicative action and practical discourse (Habermas 1984, 1987). For its sociological application, see Eder 1985 and Habermas 1989b.

the third case, there is a realization of the limits of human and outer nature leading to the search for a reflexive form of relations between the two.

These cultural models correspond to normative orders that regulate social relations and endow them with a moral quality. Changes in normative orders are the result of changes in their moral construction. They are the result of moral evolution, and the stages of moral evolution constitute different concepts of a just moral order. Again, neglecting the case of peasant society, types of a just moral order can be distinguished in modernity: moral orders based on the functional differentiation of professional roles; on possessive individualism; and on collective efforts to create justice and happiness for all. In the first case, rationality is based on the king's sovereignty as the unity of particular social orders; in the second, on the principle of negative liberties, everyone becomes his own sovereign, and only slight empirical differences are used for creating social orderings. Attempts to institutionalize these orderings, however, have produced considerable problems. Attempts to correct this through welfare politics or socialist transformation have not been successful. Today the task is to construct a moral order able to generate 'a just and good life'. The logic underlying these changes is characterized by the growth of discursive ways of handling conflicts and thereby guaranteeing individual autonomy. These changes may overcome the authoritarian form of non-procedural law regarding conflicting parties.[26]

### A theory of social movements

Having described the different structures of systems of collective action in modernity, it is now necessary to explain how they are embodied in social movements. The two already discussed theories have laid the ground for dealing with social action on the collective level. Smelser distinguishes different types of collective behaviour. The highest form of collective action is embodied in value-oriented movements that try to 'restore, modify or create values in the name of generalized belief. Such a belief necessarily involves all components of action, that is, it envisions a reconstitution of values, a redefinition of norms, a reorganization of the motivation of individuals and a redefinition of situational facilities'

---

[26] The first step was to bind the prince as the supreme judge to natural law; the second step was to bind everyone to the rule of law; a further step should establish nothing but procedures for handling conflicts. This is a very short summary of a theory of the development of modernity unfolded in Eder 1985. It is an attempt to project the evolution of social and political thought onto the institutional make-up of modernity which manifests itself mainly within the legal framework. The idea of a procedural law and a procedural rationality are the logical outcomes of this way of reconstructing the evolution of modernity. For this discussion see Eder 1988c. This procedural conception of the rationality of the institutions of modern societies is a necessary condition for bringing back social movements into the theory of society from which they have been excluded by models of formal rationality as the characteristic element of modern institutions. This Weberian notion of modernity is thus put into question.

(Smelser 1962, p. 313). Value-oriented movements thus challenge the entire action system. Touraine's account is very similar: a social struggle generates a social movement when it tries to direct social development, thus defining the central organizing aspect of a system of historical action.

Both theories diverge in explaining social movements. Smelser accounts for social movements through a 'value-oriented theory', and lists the following variables: adaptability, social structures, structural strain, growth and spread of generalized belief, precipitating factors, mobilization of participants for action, and social control (Smelser 1962, pp. 15ff). These variables account for the emergence of a social movement only within the previously mentioned logical order. Collective behaviour is a reaction to structural strains resulting in a generalized belief subject to external variables which control its emergence as collective action. The central problem of this theory is the behavioural perspective: collective action is not creative activity, but behaviour determined by external conditions. Nothing within a social movement can explain why some reactions take place rather than others. There is no connection between belief and action other than an empirical one outside collective behaviour.

Touraine's concept of social movement provides an alternative to this. He considers collective behaviour as the activity of a collective actor governed by its own laws. As is true for individuality, a social movement is defined by a collective identity, an antagonistic relation to an opposed group, and a common field of action. The only difference is that the actor is displaced by the social movement as a collective actor. This allows for a solution to Smelser's problem. Here the constitution of a social movement as a collective actor can be analyzed as the integration of the three above-mentioned dimensions. Similarly, the constitution of a collective actor implies a particular kind of collective action which Touraine considers historical. The fundamental difference between the two theories is that Smelser looks at the social system producing collective action, while Touraine looks at collective action producing society. To the extent that Smelser's approach does not deal with historical action but remains restricted to 'reactive violence', it cannot explain the rise and fall of modern social movements. In this sense, Touraine's approach is much more adequate.[27]

---

[27] At least regarding the rise of social movements. The possible fall of social movements is not foreseen in a theory of society that equates society with movement-based action systems except as possible cases of 'pathogenic' developments of modernity. See Touraine's attempt to handle this problem by opposing a view of a society created by movements to the liberal-conservative view of endless and self-organizing reproduction (Touraine 1992). See also, from different points of view, the arguments for a continuing centrality of social movements in Zald 1988 and Melucci 1984, 1989. The end of social movement literature is partially also a reaction to disappointed hopes linked to the rise of the new social movements. See, among many others, Oberschall 1978.

Social movements move society by providing an alternative cultural model, and a moral order that contributes to institutionalizing it, in that sequence. A case in point is the clash between the old labour movement in its trade unionist form and the new ecological movements. This is the clash between a productivist and an ecological model of development. Furthermore, this new cultural model is not advocated only by social movements but also by modernizing elites. This is manifest in the conflict between old and new technocrats – the first concerned with growth and the second with ecological problems. Even within such a common orientation between the new ecological movements and the new technocrats, there is divergence concerning the way to reach the goal or the social relations to direct social development after the institutionalization of a new cultural model. Social movements thus take the form of an opposition defined by principled moral standard. Thus, in the nineteenth century, two classes competed to direct industrialization. Capitalist entrepreneurs were the modernizers who regarded the outcome of market relations as just. Workers were tied to the same model, but regarded the capitalist path as unjust. Consequently, they developed a socialist alternative to the capitalist model. Both classes referred to the same industrial society. The social models within which their antagonism took place were not different evolutionary stages, but diverging evolutionary paths. Conflicting moral orderings emerged independently of a stage sequence, but as part of an antagonistic interpretation of the normative ordering of society. The common ground in the moral dimension is the individualistic concept of man underlying different images of social relations.

The introduction of the moral variable adds a second criterion to define social movements (the first was relation to a cultural model); a social movement is a collective action trying to defend intrinsic normative standards against their strategic-utilitarian instrumentalization by modernizing elites. Each stage of modernity has its specific social movement and its specific dominant elite (social classes). Antagonistic interpretations of a moral order constitute class antagonisms.

The learning processes normatively constituting a social movement can be clarified through historical examples of social movements during early modern society, industrial society, and the emerging new society. The key problem for the early modern state was the organization of a new mode of development characterized by a stratified town economy (Mousnier 1974, 1980) and a bourgeois lifestyle. In order to direct this new mode of development, it was necessary to influence the social distribution of rights that defined access to land as well as to political titles. The modernizers of early modern Europe were the princes and the urban patricians trying to direct this 'legalization' of society (Poggi 1978). The opposing movement was constituted by plebeians who challenged the absolutist state or the patricians (Bendix 1978). Examples are the Puritans in England, the Jacobins in France, the radical democrats in nineteenth-century Germany, and the Jeffersonians and Madisonians in the United States. Both modernizing absolutist princes and democratic movements defined a new system of historical action and marked the beginning of the history of modernity.

As a new mode of development based on a new social goal and a new moral order became dominant with industrialization, the social goal was the maximization of the forces of production. This was tied to another type of social order not connected with the distribution of rights but with the social organization of production. What was at stake was not the political but the economic order as a moral order. The modernizing elites behind this new social order were capitalist entrepreneurs and state functionaries. They propagated the new mode of development based on the industrial development of the forces of production and the market economy (Polanyi 1957). This economic system was structurally compatible with the new social goal: everyone takes as much as he can. Questions of justice were reduced to questions of maximizing wealth. The labour movement emerged in reaction to this. It sought a different way of developing the productive forces, defined by an alternative economic organization more just than that of capitalist modernizers. This movement contained the radical-democratic features of its historical predecessor and added the vision of a just organization of work in a democratic society.

Today the mode of development starts to change again.[28] The development of industrial productive forces no longer generates antagonistic social relations. Rather, the development of applied science and information technologies provides new potentials. This is not just a 'third industrial revolution'. It is a new cultural orientation articulated in a new type of social antagonism between technocratic modernizers and the clients of bureaucracies (Touraine 1981). This state of affairs redefines the principles of social organization, in that it implies a model of society grounded in a new normative concept. There is no extra-social reference as there is in the political model (a moral order based on a legal order) or in the economic model (moral order based on negative liberties). The grounds of the moral order are now collective needs and wants. A new society emerges, within which social movements develop who try to oppose those who administer needs and wants, while defending 'their' needs. These movements are characterized by a different cultural orientation of social development; by a new type of antagonistic social relation between technocracy and its

---

[28] There are many attempts to conceptualize this transformation as to the emergence of postindustrial society, programmed society, or communication society. An interesting concept is offered by Luke (1989) who describes the emerging society as an 'informational society'. He also directly links the rise of new social movements with the 'informationalizing of postindustrial societies'. The term *postindustrial* seems to be the one which catches best the changes in class structures, working conditions and the institutional framework within which the welfare state itself is being transformed. It has only to be stripped from connotations of an emerging service sector or even self-servicing society which have turned out to be overstating the case.

clients; and by a new collective identity that cuts across traditional lines and is ultimately based on the equal consideration of every particularity. Therefore, the movements emerging today can be seen as the successors of the old movement tied to an earlier society. In this sense, they can be called 'new social movements'.[29]


## A 'new' social movement?


Do the scattered new social movements constitute a new social movement trying to create a postindustrial society? Are the new movements that have emerged since the late sixties part of a system of historical action within which a new type of society is being constructed? If they are not part of it, how can they be brought into a social movement trying to control new cultural and social models of social development? Do these new movements constitute a 'social movement' that is oriented against the prevailing normative order? How do they deviate from the given normative concept of collective identity? Do they know who it is they oppose or the cultural and social models they advocate?

Against the claim that counterculture and radical political movements are a normal collective deviance, nothing more than neoromantic and neopopulist protest, the counterculture and radical political movements should be seen as distorted manifestations of a new social movement. What constitutes these 'distortions'? Counterculture movements have a collective identity, but no social relation to an opposing collective actor, so that their normative orientation to social action becomes utopian. Radical political movements are aware of an antagonistic relation but have no collective identity which would allow for conflictual strategies of action. Thus, their normative orientation becomes particularistic. These utopian modes of normative orientation relate to a new direction for social development, while particularistic orientations relate to a new social order waiting to be constructed.

Political radicalism was historically tied to a millenarianism seeking to restore the order of a just and holy state. Today it struggles for participation in political decision-making. As such it is committed to 'radical democracy' in all social spheres. This normative orientation takes a populist form when struggles are organized from particularistic viewpoints without an image of social antagonists. Hence, these movements are ambivalent. They can be channelled into a social movement such as

---

[29] The term 'new social movements', coined by Touraine, created an intensive discussion in the eighties. See as important contributions to this discussion Melucci 1980; Offe 1985c; Kitschelt 1985; Kriesi 1987; Tilly 1988; Klandermans 1991; Klandermans and Tarrow 1988.

yesterday's labour movement or today's institutional groups and integrate racist theories as well as nationalist and imperialist ideologies.[30]

In a different sense, countercultural movements are also an ambivalent form of collective action. They seek new individual and collective identities with a romantic twist. Thus, the central question of political identity is reduced to mere cultural identity. By retreating from homogeneous culture, romantic movements became objectively opposed to official culture, but subjectively this antagonism remains extraneous to their self-image. Romantics escape capitalism or bureaucracy simply by not relating to them: they behave as if they were irrelevant. This subjective denial of antagonistic relations is at the source of their ambivalence.

Early romanticism was a protest against formalized absolutist politics. It was an elite's protest against its own lifestyle. A more radical romanticism appeared in eighteenth-century utopian writings, prefiguring ideal forms of life more or less compatible with the general thrust of the early radical-democrat movements.[31] Nineteenth-century romanticism was also a retreat from industrial life, seeking either a restoration of pre-industrial life or a new vision of the union of work and love. Philosophical romanticism began with the critique of formal rationalism and ended with an organic, reactionary thought. While this emerging philosophical irrationalism was open to every kind of pseudo-scientific belief, especially racism, it also had a more progressive side in the socialist movement.[32] Neoromanticism is as ambivalent as the original romanticism. It contains elements of a counter-knowledge opposing the dominant knowledge. The ambivalence is clear in two opposing forms of this counterknowledge: it either perfects the technical world with behavioural utopias or denies it through Freudo-Marxist utopias of unrepressed wants and needs. The latter comes nearest to a collective action seeking new forms of social life without being in the centre of the social movement responsible for this creation.

As for the question of whether the new movements are potentially part of an emerging new social movement, the normative potential of the new movements is determined not only by its ability to act collectively but also by its ability to relate to a new way of developing society. This poses the question of a historically adequate reference to a new logic for creating society. The integration of these aspects into a new social movement has

---

[30] There are clear theoretical options how to handle this phenomenon. Laclau (1977) tries to embed the new populist movements in the old labour movement, whilst Touraine et al. (1980) try to embed these movements in a new anti-technocratic movement. The populist literature (see above) offers a third variant, building upon radical-democratic traditions of the nineteenth century.

[31] Examples are Rousseau's *monde idéal* and the radical utopias from Mably and Morelly to Saint-Just and Robespierre.

[32] One can think of the socialist utopias such as those of Saint-Simon, Fourier or Owen, which have been realized in social experiments such as the socialist community of New Harmony in Indiana or the Fabian Society.

yet to happen.[33] But what can be done with collective actions that are not yet a social movement? One answer is to intervene in these collective actions and to crystallize them into a new social movement. There is no way of knowing in advance what the emerging new movement will look like. Yet, it is difficult to stop taking part in the learning processes constituting a new social movement. Thus, sociological intervention begins where theorizing about a new social movement must end.

[33] The answer to the question of whether there is one new social movement representing *the* new social movement which is replacing the old labour movement as a historical actor, has been left open by Touraine. A good candidate for this has been the environmentalist (or ecological) movement. Olofsson (1988) argues in favour of such a theory. The basic idea is that the relationship of man to nature is the basic common theme unifying differing demands (from gender through animals to the non-organic world). I also argued this way in Eder 1988a. Therefore, instead of continuing to talk of 'new' social movements, the time has come to give these new social movements a name. Any term from environmentalism, ecological movement, life politics movements might serve as a possible candidate for name giving. They all denote the same problem: the nature–society relationship, or 'the question of nature' (Moscovici 1990).

# 7

# COUNTERCULTURE MOVEMENTS AGAINST MODERNITY
## Nature as a New Field of Class Struggle?[1]

## Introduction

We are experiencing today a flowering of counterculture movements ranging from psycho-culture to deep ecology (Jerome 1974; Luke 1988). Attacks on modern culture based on its rationalism have always been commonplace. But something has changed. The protest has gained a political dimension that disturbs the institutional reproduction of modern societies through its attacks on the model of social development particular to advanced Western industrial societies.[2] There is a general tendency leading to a central conflict in the modern world much more pervasive than that of the nineteenth century. The conflict in question centres on what type of development modern societies should engage in. The new counterculture movements are trying to stall and even reverse what they regard as the self-defeating process of modernization (Yinger 1977).

One manifestation of the self-defeating process of modernization is the increasing environmental crisis. This crisis has begun to mobilize counterculture movements all over the world. Increasingly it seems that the less counterculture movements against modernity are mobilized, the more the negative consequences of modernization will be felt. These movements, moreover, also change the cultural definition of the relation of men to nature in the way that they define the relation of men to nature as one of *exploitation*.

The following analysis of the confrontation between counterculture

[1] This is a revised version of an article that appeared first in *Theory, Culture and Society*, 1990, Vol. 7, pp. 21–47.

[2] This challenge appeared first outside modernized societies in those countries that emulated the cultural model of modernization. The religious movements in the non-Western world are an example of this first challenge. It then invaded modernized societies, thus giving a global dimension to protest against modernity. The counterculture movements which had so far been treated as an exotic phenomenon in the modern world have become the key in determining the fate of the modern world. For some of the more important discussion and research in this area see Musgrave 1974; Abrams and McCulloch 1976; and Case and Taylor 1979. For a treatment of these countercultures as part of the evolution of religious culture see Wilson 1967; Glock and Bellah 1976; Bellah et al. 1985. An empirical study of counterculture in developmental terms is to be found in Wuthnow 1976.

movements and advanced modern societies in environmental crisis will be focused on Europe (without reference to the American, Russian and Third World arenas). To understand the conditions and implications of this phenomenon we can start with three propositions:

1.  The exploitation of nature is, like the exploitation of the workforce, part of a global process of modernization and rationalization – of which capitalist development is only one aspect. No country escapes the dynamic of this process. A rule of differentiation maintains, however, that the more dependent the country, the more nature is exploited, or the other way around: the less dependent the country, the more the problem of exploitation of nature is thematized.
2.  The ongoing differentiation and intensification of the exploitation of nature is changing the class structure of advanced modern societies. The dominance of the working class in determining cultural directions is being usurped. This process fosters the making of a new social class.
3.  The emerging new class structure replaces the model of industrialism constitutive for capitalist and socialist societies and gives counterculture movements a central role in determining the direction of further 'modernization'. A new type of society is emerging in which class conflict will be centred on the problem of the exploitation of nature.

To support these propositions we will first demonstrate how the rationalist tradition in modern culture, including the Marxian critique of modern society, is insensitive to the relation of man to nature and then locate the counterculture movements within what we can call the 'purity perspective'. We will then examine a historical reconstruction of counterculture traditions that shows how these movements and their carriers are intimately tied to the 'problem of nature'. This background will allow us to describe the emergence of new counterculture movements as indicators of a new class struggle and a new class structure concerned with the exploitation of nature. Finally, some theoretical and methodological consequences of these changes for a renewal of critical theory will be discussed.

## A cultural critique of modernism

### Marx's concept of nature

A look at Marx is justified on the ground that Marx's theory of history explicitly takes the relationship with nature into account to explain what triggers progress in modern societies (Cohen 1978, pp. 96ff). This explanation assumes two contradictions as mechanisms of progress: that between the relations of production and the forces of production and that among social classes. How these contradictions relate to each other and to social development is one of the most difficult problems in the interpretation of Marx's theoretical thinking (Godelier 1978; Habermas 1979;

Elster 1982, 1985b). Instead of going into this in detail,[3] I would rather concentrate on the problems of conceptualizing the forces of production within the first and basic contradiction and their implication for the theory of class conflict.

This 'productive' side of the contradiction is interesting because it takes into account the relation of man to nature as it affects the progress of mankind. Marx gives the productive forces the role of a pacemaker. He sees the way a society relates to its natural environmental as decisive for its development. The key to Marx's understanding of nature and its cultural use is in this conception that the natural environment is something to be besieged by man. Marx – at least in the later stages of his thinking (Schmidt 1971, pp. 210ff) – sees the natural environment as a mere object of human activity.

The conception of a relation to nature has been 'naturalized' by Marx. Sahlins (1976) made this point in his critique of Marx's conception of culture and nature. Nature is not, Sahlins argues, a mere object to be appropriated. It is socially constituted and culturally defined. There is no natural environment. Rather, it is society which creates nature as a cultural environment (Moscovici 1968). In criticizing Marx because of his naturalism concerning nature, we arrive at the conclusion that relating to nature is culturally variable and that the relation taken by Marx as the natural one is just a special case to be explained by his cultural milieu. Today it has become apparent that modern society can no longer integrate this culturally defined environment into its own reproduction. It has produced a form of nature whose effects it can no longer control. The cultural model of nature defended by Marx has led us directly into what we call now the environmental crisis.

Marx could not foresee the effects of the specifically modern form of a relation to nature and the effects of releasing the forces of production. He saw only that the relations of production were factors blocking the progress built into the forces of production. Class struggle was necessary to dissolve these social relations of production. The relationship with nature embodied in the forces of production is not affected by this class struggle, for the direction of the development of the forces of production is 'naturally' defined given the premise that the increasing domination over nature is contributing to progress of mankind. Changing the social relations of production through class struggle would only lead to optimizing the domination of nature. The class struggle as conceived by Marx enables men to increase the domination of nature. This might explain why Marx sees no reason to perceive the relationship with nature as an object or field of class struggle.

Meanwhile, the domination of nature has been perceived as inextricable from its exploitation. The forces of production, in incorporating an

---

[3] See above Part I, Chapter 2 for an extensive discussion.

exploitative relationship with nature, have generated a new basis for class conflict in modern society. Besides the social relations of production the social relations with nature have become an arena of class conflict in modern society. A new class conflict is emerging that mobilizes a type of movement different from that typical for nineteenth-century class conflicts over wages, and that integrates counterculture movements into the class struggle. These counterculture movements happen to be carriers of cultural traditions that thematize the social relations of nature. In so far as social relations with nature are becoming the central problem of the reproduction of modern society, these counterculture traditions are becoming the determinants of the cultural model that is at stake in the new type of class conflict. Thematizing nature as a field of class struggle forces us to overcome the cultural restrictions typical for Marx's view of modern society. We have to rebuild our theoretical conceptions to reflect the cultural logic of the relation of men to nature in modern society.

Marx provides no framework for the cultural traditions within which modern society organizes its relationship with nature. Instead of analyzing cultural traditions he relies on the Hegelian belief in the 'objective spirit'. This objective spirit turns out to be a very subjective one: the spirit of the dominant European cultural tradition. Marx thus ends up producing euphemisms for the outgrowth of a specific type of Enlightenment optimism prevalent in the beginning of modern society. Practically speaking, he endorses the belief in progress by science and the belief in *homo faber* shaping his natural (and social!) environment at will.

Thus the type of thought constitutive for modern social criticism turns out to be uncritical in a decisive respect. It is significant to note that the theory most critical of modern society shares with the competing systems of social and political thought – the liberal and conservative – the basic assumptions that nature is subject to man and that nature has to be conquered by man to further the progress of mankind.

### Alternatives to Marxism

Disputing Marx is the reality of two competing cultural traditions in European history that thematize the relation to nature. Their basic antagonism can be traced back to traditions prior to the beginning of modernity in Europe. The cultural roots of the modern counterculture can be found in the Greek and Jewish cultural heritage that constitute its cultural history through the Christianization of Europe (Eder 1990). This double tradition continued even though traditional society faltered and modern society emerged. Marx adheres to the first tradition, which he represents as an integral part of the process of rationalizing social and political thought tied to the modernization of society. The other tradition is embodied in the history of the counterculture movements that have accompanied modernization since its beginning. Marx's theoretical perspective on the cultural tradition he lives in relativizes his contribution to the understanding of modern society: it appears to be a culturally very specific one. However, this type of thinking has dominated modern intellectual thought – from conservative to radical. Marx is only the most interesting figure in this tradition because he bases his most devastating critique of modern society, his analysis of capital, on a very specific reading of the cultural context from within which he argues.

To transcend this particularistic restriction, sociological thinking needs to distance itself more radically from its own traditions. It has to radicalize its emancipation from social and political thought and constitute itself as a science able to analyze and criticize this cultural tradition instead of simply adhering to it. Only such a radicalism will help us to escape restricting the critical role which is the only legitimation of sociological analysis.

Bringing other cultural traditions back into the social analysis and explanation of modern societies requires an even more radical critique. The self-ascribed rationalism of modern culture was criticized by Marx as being insensitive to social differences, an argument that stimulates a 'social critique of practical reason'.[4] Today we can further extend this critique with a 'cultural critique of practical reason' (Eder 1988a). This cultural critique identifies not only the different usages of practical reason among social classes, as Bourdieu (1984) proposes, thus continuing the Marxian argument, but differentiates among meanings of practical reason that result from different cultural traditions within modern culture. Such a 'cultural critique' of the dominant rationalism of modern culture, of 'modernism', thematizes the problem of nature in a new way. This will enable us to view nature as a field of cultural struggles and lead us to a theoretical explanation of the objective meaning of the so-called environmental crisis.

Going beyond Marx means that sociological analysis has to relinquish the predominant modes of social and political thought dominating modern culture. We have to develop an adequate sociological critique of the intellectual rationalizations shaping modern culture, its 'modernism'. To do so, it is no longer enough to simply rely on the intellectual history as the reference history for an understanding of the modern cultural world. We have to examine the non-rational foundations of rationality and see how the intellectual history itself develops from this source.

Thus, from a sociological point of view, this intellectual history (i.e. 'modernism') must be made an *object* of analysis. We have to *objectify* this

---

[4] This social critique is not yet fully developed, since it involves tracing how social and political thought as well as counterculture thought are the product of social processes. To relate such thinking to class positions is only the beginning. We can also look at the social processes that constitute such systems (and antisystems) of thought. Theories of a social production of thinking and learning are the most promising developments in actual theoretical discussions. Nevertheless we cannot stop at such a critique. We have to proceed to a cultural critique and all the difficult methodological problems it entails. See, above all, the works of Bourdieu and Habermas as two complementary and competing solutions. For further developments starting from a Habermasian position see Miller 1986 and Eder 1985.

history. Reconstructing it will show us what kind of symbolism lies beneath the claims of rationality in modern culture. The rationalizing factors that are built into the intellectual history of modernity will become clearer. We will above all be able to undermine the naturalistic assumptions within this intellectual history and to relate them to the underlying symbolic structure defining the relation of man to nature.

To approach such non-rational foundations of rationality we can start with the fact that no modern intellectual system of thought escapes the problem of defining some basic set of principles or values. These systems of thought differ to the extent they make use of such 'anthropological' assumptions. We could state the following 'law of rationality': the fewer anthropological assumptions there are, the more advanced the formal structure of social and political thought. By taking the point of view of a historical sociologist the decisive problem lies with that of identifying the basic assumptions on which these intellectual systems are built. In relating such assumptions to a basic symbolic code (Geertz 1966, 1973; Douglas 1975), we will be able to objectify this rationalist tradition and to grasp modernism as a specific cultural tradition within modern society.

The basic assumptions which define the symbolic code of 'modernism' can be described in two respects: first, as an attempt to distance it from all previous cultural traditions and second, as an attempt to constitute society beyond nature. Modernism's characteristics are thus negative attitudes towards the *cultural tradition* from which it comes and towards *nature* within which it lives. This is the basic premise of modernism: to locate itself outside nature and culture as the context of thinking and action. Modernism negates the impact of culture and nature upon its own form of thinking. In terms of social and political thought this negation leads to ethnocentrism (in the worst case) or to anthropocentrism (in the best case).

The last critique thematizes the basic anthropological assumptions of the rationalism of systems of thought in modern society. We find the symbolic universe underlying modern rational philosophical systems within such anthropological assumptions. The premise of these systems of thought is a general anthropocentrism: the model of human action and interaction is the standard of comparison for the model of the interaction between men and nature. Thus the symbolic code of a relationship that subordinates nature to man is built.

Analyzing the relation of man to nature leads us to ask how, for example, modern philosophical systems give a coherent and consistent justification to the relationship with nature. We could, for example, use the Kantian moral ethic, reading it as applying exclusively to man, who is thought of as acting according to the a priori principles of practical reason. Nature is then clearly inferior. But this hierarchy is not a logically necessary outcome of rational reflection. It is an outcome of a cultural tradition that has turned on its head the subordination of man to supernature. Anthropocentrism is as much a cultural institution as theocentrism traditionally was. Modernism rests on a symbolic code that is

Table 7.1

| | Culture | |
| Nature | + | − |
| --- | --- | --- |
| + | postmodernism | primitivism |
| − | traditionalism | modernism |

ultimately hierarchical, based on models of higher and lower levels of consciousness, stages of development, and rights of being.

*Alternatives to modernism*

This modernism, however, has lost its monopolistic position in advanced modern societies. Modern culture offers us at least three alternatives to modernism: *postmodernism, primitivism,* and *traditionalism* (Friedman 1988). Modernism as discussed above is the form contained in intellectual systems. The other three offer 'non-modernist' approaches that differ from 'modernism' in so far as they give up the idea of a society disembedded from its cultural tradition and from nature. These four ideal types of cultural tradition can be schematized as combinations of a positive or negative view on nature and culture (Table 7.1).

Modernism is only one of the four possibilities. It is based on a practical reason that gives a negative symbolic value to both culture and nature. Postmodernism on the other hand generates a practical reason within a symbolic world that puts positive emphasis upon nature and culture. Primitivism and traditionalism radicalize the one or the other symbolic value. Even if the latter are fashionable they are excluded from further discussion as symbolic contexts that only aggravate the problems which afflict modern society. Neither a return to nature nor a return to the old virtues will help. Thus we are left with 'postmodernism' as the only viable alternative to 'modernism'.[5]

The difference between the remaining two can be used to analyze

---

[5] The term 'postmodernism' has been used in such different ways that its use has to be defended and specified. Postmodernism is normally seen as a negative mode of thinking, opposed to the dominating rationalism. This description, however, is insufficient. It lacks a sociological perspective which takes postmodernism as a way to reappropriate cultural traditions that are based on grounding a different relation of nature to society. With increasing ecological damage and the increasing problem of meaning in modern life, postmodernism fulfils an important social function which explains its present-day conjuncture. Cultures which are on the verge of modernization and/or industrialization are looking for ways to achieve these goals in a way different from that pioneered by European culture. But Europeans are not confined to importing this global phenomenon from the outside. It is possible for them to develop this globalizing view within their own national cultures, for all modern cultures contain the possibilities for that which is realized elsewhere. What I am pleading for is the 'globalizing view from within'. For an excellent discussion of the implications of the idea of 'postmodernism' see Featherstone 1988, 1989; Lash 1990.

systematically dominant and counterculture traditions in modern culture. This perspective allows us to see the two sides of modernity (Schäfer 1985) without a priori assumptions concerning their rationality or irrationality. I see modernism and postmodernism as nothing but the intellectual surfaces of the deeper cultural streams, of two ways of relating to our cultural traditions and of two ways of relating to nature. Both are, as we will see, closely related. On a structural level we can say that we have to go behind these competing systems of thought to different constructions of the culture–nature relationship, to different ideas of the dividing line between nature and culture. This dividing line is, as cultural anthropologists can tell us, the basis of civilization and its development.

Sociological analysis has to name the illusion of being outside of and apart from any cultural and natural context. It must also be sensitive to countercurrents, for alternatives to the dominating modes of thought. This does not mean that it has to side with these countercurrents or alternatives. On the contrary, it has to 'objectify' both sides of modern culture.

## Modern counterculture traditions

### The other image of nature in early modern Europe

It is not necessary to look to a distant past or to faraway societies to find social forces other than those characteristic of modern European societies that can be seen as carriers of a genuinely social relation to nature. European cultural history also contains currents of thought and action committed to a more sensitive relation to nature. However, they have so far remained undercurrents, not taken very seriously either by the dominating social forces and social movements in modern society or by its theorists – and Marx is only one of the more important ones.

The following is intended to show how a double cultural tradition has developed in the course of European history. The increase in knowledge that allowed for the rationalization and, ultimately, instrumentalization of our relation to nature also produced a parallel sensitivity to the nature being objectified. Historical research undertaken by Thomas (1983) summarizes the alternatives of the relation of men to nature in modern society in the following four dichotomies (1983, pp. 242ff): town or country, cultivation or wilderness, conquest or conservation, and meat or mercy.

At least after the experience of the great urban epidemics, the country became sentimentally the locus of a better life, one closer to nature. The wilderness was where the old virtues of men, their natural forces, were still useful, even necessary. Conservation principles developed as an attempt to save the natural world from the destructive effects of civilization. And an attitude of mercy developed toward beasts as being not prey or food but fellow creatures. These ideas lay at the base of all the cultural movements that have emerged since the eighteenth century. They idealize the country life, seek a better life in the wilderness, call for the conservation of nature and a right to life for threatened creatures, and plead for an end to killing animals simply for the sake of human consumption.

Thus we cannot accept the idea of a sharp division between an early 'medieval' and a later 'modern' stage in European history, where the early stage is characterized as a time when poetry and concrete imagery governed the relations between man and nature and the later period as one when abstract understanding and rational/scientific treatment of nature triumphed. There are crosscurrents in this history which must be given due respect for its complexities. We propose, however, to reduce the complexity to two ideal crosscurrents: to a culture that sees nature as something to be dominated by man and to a counterculture embodying a natural piety toward nature. These two crosscurrents disagree over whether absolute human superiority over nature is universally shared or not.

It has been long established Christian doctrine that man can justifiably do what he wants with the animals and plants put into the world for his use and delectation. There have, however, always been some practices that split this doctrine, one of which has been hunting. Thomas More thought hunting the most abject form of butchery, whereas others thought it to be a ritual form of struggle with nature allowing man (male man) to find himself within the universe. During the sixteenth and seventeenth centuries a new refinement of sentiment toward the natural world, at least in the middle classes, could be felt throughout European countries (Harwood 1928; Salt 1980, 1886). Thus even before the romantic movement there were trends that made nature venerable. All this happens before Bentham found in mere sentience the basis of morality that included each being capable of sentiments (thus pulling man down from his metaphysical pedestal!).

In this sense we can trace a line from the Greek Cynics, Sceptics and Epicureans, who denied that mankind was the centre of the universe, to modern counterculture movements (Sloterdijk 1983; Niehues-Pröbsting 1988). This line of philosophical reasoning ended in a naturalism that did not offer a moral foundation of a non-instrumental attitude to the natural world. To look for a moral foundation – as Bentham thought – in utilitarian philosophy is a difficult course to accept. This would imply using utilitarian philosophy to ground a non-utilitarian attitude towards the natural world (Singer 1976, 1979). It would mean enlisting the devil to attack himself. A possible solution might lie in some principled rejection of anthropocentrism (Spinoza could be an example) or a Kantian practical reason that mediates between man and nature rather than makes him the master of the universe (Böhme and Böhme 1983).

In the modern past, the intellectual representation of these countermovements within 'Romanticism' (Weiß 1986) was the first intellectual endeavour that had long-standing effects upon the intellectual rationalization of man's relation to the natural world within European cultural history. It produced the first intellectual rationalization of counterculture traditions.

## The romantic model

The early modern development of sentiments toward nature can, as Thomas (1983) has argued, be seen as the beginning of a non-utilitarian attitude to nature. This 'development' is probably nothing more than a more public manifestation of attitudes prevalent throughout early modern history (and before). Increasing communication is certainly responsible for this unveiling. It has led to the thematization of those things outside official culture such as animal liberation and the encouragement of a gentle relation to nature that first culminated in the Romantic movement.

The model of an alternative relationship with nature can be reconstructed from what has been called the Romantic movement. The Romantic movement extended the universality of moral rules beyond the human sphere to beasts, plants, and nature as such. Nature was thought of as representing life and therefore required the application of moral principles. The universalism of the Enlightenment was thus radicalized to apply not only to human beings but to all life. Nature was enshrined as the real world beyond the artificial world of society and politics.

The Romantic movement was primarily an intellectual and artistic one (Timm 1978; Weiß 1986). It manifested itself in philosophy, literature and music. The Romantic idea of nature is therefore still primarily an intellectual/cognitive one. It is contained in ideas about a natural cosmos beyond what we can rationally grasp. Nature becomes the basis of a modernized religion for intellectuals and artists. It is also therefore opposed to modern science which reduces nature to an object of theoretical reason.

Underneath the intellectual surface was a broad stream of a more popular thought. Regarding their effect on everyday life, two types of cultural movements were the most important ones: the communal and the vegetarian movements (Krabbe 1974; Frecot 1976; Sprondel 1986). The nineteenth-century experiments in country communal living were created to foster a closer relationship with nature. They mobilized people into leaving the cities. The concern with health dominated their relation to nature and practising horticulture gave them 'healthy' non-animal food. The movements for animal rights and the vegetarian movements promoted a genuinely social relationship with nature. The dialogue with nature that the romantics were dreaming of was practised and put into practice in these movements.

The embodiment of the romantic moral can be found at the turn of nineteenth century in the agrarian romanticism and in the agrarian communes which flowered, for example, in Germany between 1890 and 1933 and again after 1970 (Eder 1988a, pp. 256ff). The most famous early agrarian commune became the vegetarian horticultural colony 'Eden' that called for a new community of genuine pure life as opposed to the life in the cities (Linse 1983b, pp. 37ff). This colony is part of what have been called the bourgeois fugitive movements, which have to be understood within the context of the *fin de siècle* feeling of the late nineteenth century (Hepp 1987). After World War I, during and after the November Revolution, this movement expanded rapidly (Linse 1983a). We find communist communes, women's communes, populist and anarcho-religious communes, evangelical and Quaker communes, and Jewish communes, all seeking a 'third way' between capitalism and communism (Linse 1983b, pp. 89ff). The life-reform movement, the heading under which these movements were later subsumed, was seen as the carrier toward another society. The communes of the second half of the twentieth century have continued this tradition (Abrams and McCulloch 1976; Case and Taylor 1979; Hollstein 1981; Eder 1988a).[6]

The discussion of the Romantic movement and its derivatives shows that nature has since the beginning of modernity been the latent field of social and cultural struggles. Two factors have changed this latency. The ecological crisis has made nature the arena of public disputes. And, an increasing reflexivity in dealing with cultural traditions has led us to thematize competing notions of relating to nature. Both have made nature a manifest and increasingly central field of social struggles in modern society (Schimank 1983). There are reasons to see it as becoming the field of a new type of class struggle replacing the old one, which only focused on the just distribution of goods in society. Such an emerging new class struggle would centre on another idea: on the idea of a more 'pure' nature, of an unpolluted environment (Eder 1988a).

To prove such an assumption, a more stringent theoretical account of the two cultural traditions that modern culture carries must be developed. The dominant tradition is tied to what I will call the 'justice perspective', the counterculture tradition to the 'purity perspective'. Both perspectives are historically complementary, but analytically distinctive. Whereas the first tradition assumes a civilized culture as a given to develop a form of rationality, the second tradition thematizes the symbolic (non-rational) foundations of any claim of social rationality. In taking this second perspective we will arrive at the symbolic level beneath the level of intellectual rationalizations that allows us to compare and to confront both traditions. Thus the ground for our last hypothesis is laid: the symbolic

---

[6] Fascism instrumentalized this tradition. It succeeded in mobilizing the bloody by using the unbloody tradition, thereby destroying the unbloody tradition by the bloody one. This explains phenomena such as the SS in the concentration camps caring for dogs and little gardens or SS doctors playing Schubert string quartets and Hitler being a vegetarian. The bloody tradition thus proved again to be the stronger one.

order is where the new class conflict in advanced modern societies is located.

## Purity as the key to counterculture traditions

### The two sides of modern culture

It is not easy to find a common denominator for all the cultural movements that thematize a different relationship with nature. The differences are striking. A list of them includes, as we have seen, movements for animal rights, vegetarian movements, communitarian movements, and movements for a more healthy and natural form of life. My sense of the common denominator is of a relationship to nature that gives it a symbolic meaning other than that institutionalized by society. Counterculture traditions carry with them an alternative cultural code of relating to nature. This alternative code embodies a symbolic form of the relationship of men with nature, a sensibility toward nature as embodied in the Romantic model. It is a relationship with nature opposed to the institutionalized, dominant relationship defined by the idea that man should conquer nature. Having experienced the negative consequences of this attitude toward nature, this dominant cultural code has started to be critical of itself. It has become commonplace to speak of man's 'exploitation of nature'. This self-critical description has not changed the symbolic form underlying the relation to nature. It has put into question its negative consequences and tried to re-establish an equilibrium with nature that allows leaving the dominant symbolic form of relating to nature unchanged.

Both cultural codes are part of one culture; they can be seen as the two sides of one coin (Schäfer 1985). Let's simply arrange these two sides as a series of opposing pairs. The dimensions referred to in these pairings are the cognitive, the affective and the normative. To give this scheme a substantive base I will use some of the categories used to describe nineteenth- and twentieth-century modernity.

Such a binary analysis of modern culture can be represented in the following pairings:

| | | |
|---|---|---|
| *cognitive* | rationalism | romanticism |
| | science | religion |
| *normative* | possessivism | communalism |
| | participation | self-determination |
| *affective* | disenchantment | reenchantment |
| | civilization | naturalism |

These pairings confront the dominant culture and the counterculture on the level of their different rationalities. They explain the two ways in which the relationship with nature has been conceived. Nature is either treated as an object to be used or as a person to interact with. The first meaning is unambiguous. Within the dominant rationality nature has no chance to defend itself. Even assuming a utilitarian ethic to defend nature, it restricts itself using the principle of minimizing suffering to living beings. The second meaning is less clear-cut, since nature cannot act. This problem can be solved by acting on behalf of, or as a proxy for, nature. Taking the perspective of beaten and exploited nature man acts as if he interacts and even communicates with nature.

The dominant culture, from conservative to radical, based on the idea of an instrumental relationship with nature and backed up by an ideology of domination, characterizes most of modern thought. The second tradition has, however, gained new importance in present-day societies. The ecological crisis has provoked a relation to nature that draws on the 'other' cultural tradition on which modern society is built. This cultural dissent separates not only intellectual traditions; it separates moral worlds. These moral differences between the two cultures lead us to the very roots underlying their real antagonism.

*Justice versus purity*

To give a theoretical account of the moral basis of the two cultural traditions that are implicit in modern culture, I will distinguish between the *justice* and the *purity* perspectives. These perspectives refer to two competing moral conceptions of the world. Taking the former as our point of departure, we will show that it cannot grasp what the second tradition thematizes: a moral perspective upon nature going beyond its being a means for human well-being. I will claim that the purity perspective contains the justice perspective as a special case of looking at nature. Therefore, the second perspective introduces aspects of man's relationship with nature systematically excluded in the justice perspective.

Within the justice perspective, the *instrumentalist* tradition of the relation of man to nature has dominated modern culture. An alternative relationship with nature was sacrificed and surrendered to this 'morality', and has become equivalent to self-destruction, because it only aggravates the current crisis in the relationship between man and nature. The most important type of morality has been the utilitarian justification of the relationship between man and nature, an idea that links Bentham to modern environmental economists and has spread – paradoxically – with our greater awareness of the environmental crisis. This utilitarian model of morality can be understood – as Weber (1956) did – as a manifestation of 'material' or 'substantive' rationality.[7] This means applying criteria of

---

[7] This model has become the starting point of a new discussion of how to conceive a just society whilst maximizing the individual freedom of everybody; see Rawls (1971) regarding the idea of a just society and Lukes (1991) for its political and moral implications.

justice to our relation with nature. The formulation of an 'exploitation of nature' derives from this 'justice perspective'.

But the justice perspective does not take into account the real and basic difference between the dominant culture and the counterculture. The justice that would like to see an end to the exploitation of nature is a type of justice that only minimizes this exploitation in order to be able to continue it further. There is nothing in nature to support a 'just' treatment by which to interrupt this logic. The justice perspective runs into the problem of pinpointing the beginning of exploitation. Is there exploitation when man can no longer exploit nature? And is exploitation more than the damage the exploiter suffers by exhausting his resources? Exploitation evidently is a fuzzy concept. Injustice to nature is an insufficient motivation for people to question the basic premises of their relation to it. It only mobilizes animal liberators who see equal treatment of all beings as the fundamental premise of human moral action, a premise characteristic of the utilitarian ethics of animal liberation (Singer 1976). However, the liberation of animals will not challenge the basic symbolic structure within which we organize our relation with nature. It will only alleviate some of the consequences implied by this deep-seated symbolic usage. It will help to minimize the suffering of beasts used for experimental purposes, but it will not change the relationship of men to beasts. It will not remove men from their moral pedestal.

Therefore the problem of nature, as conceived within counterculture traditions, has to be handled as a problem beyond the scope of justice. It has to do with decency, with sentience, with attitudes that cannot be grasped adequately via the notion of justice. We have to look for another model of 'morality' to describe man's relationship with nature. This other model can best be described as the purity model (Douglas 1966, 1975). The 'purity perspective' is more than an alternative to the 'justice perspective', because it thematizes another moral foundation of man's relationship with nature. The 'purity perspective' codes the difference between nature and culture in a way that allows for an alternative moral definition of that difference. This is evident when we look at some symbolic values attributed to the notion of purity: health, body and soul. The complementary concept is impurity; its analytical dimensions can be described as: pollution, force and discipline. The notions of purity and impurity refer to a level of culture, where its moral foundations are at stake. The complementary values thematize the symbolic basis of culture. This value system is seen as the key to understanding the relation of man to nature not only in premodern but also in modern societies.

The purity perspective shows us that behind the cognitive aspect of moral consciousness, as embodied in the idea of justice, is a strong affective element that shapes the meaning of justice. This level of analysis removes us from the cognitivist discourse and its sociological description as part of a rationalization process. We can start to reconstruct cultural traditions regulating the relation of man to nature on a more elementary symbolic level. Moving our focus from justice to purity gives us a better understanding of the differences underlying the emerging modern European spirit of environmentalism.

But there is still more to such a change toward the purity perspective. It offers us a new cognitive perspective on the basic antagonisms in modern society. To the extent that the symbolic infrastructure of our culture is put into question by the problematization of our relationship with nature, conflicts on the level of the symbolic order emerge. By identifying different cultural codes based on competing symbolic orders within modern society we can go beyond Marx's notion of the dynamic of modern society. He ultimately reproduced the instrumentalist tradition that has dominated the relation of man to nature in modern culture. An alternative relationship with nature was sacrificed and surrendered to the idea of 'rationality'.[8] But modern society's rigid and heroic adherence to this rationality has become equivalent to self-destruction. Therefore, this rationality has to be 'embedded', has to be civilized by what has been called an alternative relationship of man with nature.

## Society, nature and culture

### Nature as the new field of class struggle

Such an analysis not only broadens our theoretical notion of the cultural 'code' underlying European culture, it also forces us to see the carriers of countercultural traditions as more than movements of protest against modernity and modernization (Eisenstadt 1981). I claim that the two competing models relating man to nature have become the field of a new emerging type of historical struggle over two types of modernity in advanced modern societies. We will try to show that the competing models of modernization have become the object of a new type of class struggle in advanced modern societies.

But will this struggle change our relation to nature and, if so, how? To answer such questions we have to look at the social forces now trying to redefine the relation of modern society to nature. Nature has become a field of collective action within which new social groups are engaged. The groups have never belonged to either the dominated or the dominating

---

[8] For a systematic reconstruction and critique of the modern concept of rationality see Habermas (1984, 1987). His reconstructions of Weber's concept of rationality and its relation to the critique of rationality in classical Critical Theory, i.e. in Horkeimer's and Adorno's *Dialectic of Enlightenment* (Horkheimer and Adorno 1947) and in Horkheimer's *Critique of Instrumental Reason* (Horkheimer 1967), are attempts to anchor the critique of modern rationality in a counterfactual discursive (and therefore implicit) form of rationality that is seen as constitutive for modern culture. Whether this model is sufficient to serve this function is open to debate.

class. They belong to the 'middle class' (a concept which is more a black box than a substantially defined category).[9]

The groups comprising an emerging 'new middle class' in advanced modern societies differ from their historical precursors. They appear as carriers of a new type of society – doubly opposed to the class structure of industrial society: opposed to its dominant classes and opposed to its dominated classes. The new middle class is the potential carrier of counterculture traditions. This new class, however, is still tied to a specific class habitus: the petit-bourgeois. This habitus is part of a middle-class-based cultural tradition that has been expanded and developed since the second half of nineteenth century. A historical reconstruction of the development of this mentality shows that it is in fact a distorted form of counterculture traditions. Counterculture traditions, the thesis states, have so far has been embodied in a distorted form in the middle class. The middle class is a class 'in the making', substituting the old petit-bourgeois outlook for a new 'ecological' consciousness (see also Part IV in this volume).

The new middle class groups are not only potential carriers of counter-culture protest, they are also potentially a new social class. This is due to the expansion of middle class groups into the service sector, which is apparently becoming the key sector of the emerging postindustrial society. The petty shopkeepers and artisans defining the middle class of the nineteenth century have been complemented in the twentieth century by white-collar workers and, since the sixties, by service sector workers (the new middle class groups). These groups are the potential carriers of movements that mobilize counterculture traditions against the dominant culture. The petit-bourgeois mentality that carries with it counterculture traditions in a distorted form thus gains a new significance to the extent that the new middle class is shaping an emerging new class structure.

The ecological crisis contributes to the further socio-cultural crystalliz-ation of this new class because it is this class that it affects most directly. The relationship with nature has always had a central significance for the petit-bourgeois lifestyle. Its leisure patterns, wandering, climbing, excur-sions into the countryside, all forms of tourism, make this clear. The ecological crisis threatens the life-world of middle class groups more than

[9] The term 'middle class' is a historical as well as a systematic category. Historically, it refers to the emergence and increase of a class of 'workers' who either own some means of production or control to some extent the means of reproduction beyond the sphere of work. Here the work of Bourdieu is of major relevance (Bourdieu 1984). Systematically, this class location has been called by Wright a contradictory one (Wright 1985, 1986). This is the result of the traditional perspective on the class structure of modern societies. When taking middle class groups as the reference point for an emerging new class structure, then the principles of social classification have to be changed. To identify new principles of social classification we have to construct new antagonistic social relations. Such antagonisms are, the hypothesis runs, to be found in nature as a new field of class conflict. See for an extensive discussion of the theoretical problems and possibilities of such an approach the chapters in part IV of this volume. See also Eder 1989.

that of any other. These middle class groups are emotionally tied not only to a just world but to a good world to live in and they react much more intensely to the effects of exploiting (pollution) the natural environment. The increasing menace to the natural base of this life-world contributes to the increasing 'alienation' of the new middle class. This 'alienation' manifests itself in middle-class-specific practices such as organizing individual action against systemic processes to protect the life-world from pollution (a necessarily frustrating and thus self-defeating strategy) or relying on psychological treatment in order to cope both psychically and physically in this menacing environment.

We can conclude then that the new middle classes are the potential carriers of a new relationship with nature. They are subjectively prone to a non-utilitarian relation to nature and objectively tied to its problems. Middle class groups will therefore play a major role in the new field of class struggle now opening up. The struggle may transform an until now hidden cultural undercurrent into a cultural model orienting a new type of historical action. Thus nature will become the new arena. The way the natural world is symbolized will become the new cultural model organizing class action in the emerging middle class society.

## Counterculture movements and the new class struggle

The ecological crisis has not only changed the field of class struggle; it has also changed its logic. The idea that *social* movements are the carriers of progress has vanished, along with the idea of that progress itself. Instead, social movements are being openly confronted by *cultural* movements (Raschke 1985, pp. 110ff) that have since the beginning of modern society been their antagonists. The problem of nature has engendered a division between mobilized classes of actors as carriers of modern development: between the social movements constitutive for the dominant modernity and the cultural movements claiming 'another modernity'. Social movements have defined and still define the dominant visions of modernity: individual rights and material well-being. Counterculture movements have claimed and continued to claim something beyond such visions: a society that, to be sure, secures individual rights and material well-being, but embedded in nature, not beyond it, and in harmony with nature, not in spite of it.

The history of social movements continues today. For example, they have taken up the problem of nature. The ecological movement is concerned with a more rational relation to nature. Its concern is utilitarian. Its message is to optimize the relation to nature, to establish a cybernetic state of nature in society. This vision is opposed to that of the cultural movements that are interested not in rationalizing the relationship to nature, but in giving it a new meaning: to establish a social relation with nature. This makes cultural movements counterculture movements.

Counterculture movements have existed since the beginning of modernity. The social movements that created civil society have always been accompanied by sectarian groups looking for a more spiritual form of life in civil society. Some examples are the 'fugitive movements (*bürger-liche Fluchtbewegungen*) widespread in nineteenth-century Germany, and aesthetic movements distancing themselves from the normal forms of bourgeois life (Linse 1983a, 1983b; Sprondel 1986; Weiß 1986; Hepp 1987), both countermovements to the bourgeois movement of the eighteenth and nineteenth centuries. Similarly the labour movement has had its collateral groups. Typical examples are communitarian movements which tried to establish utopias of social equality and solidarity beyond mere socialism (Schäfer 1985). Cultural movements are also inextricably tied to the present-day ecological movement (Galtung 1986; Luhmann 1989). In Germany such collateral groups call themselves an 'alternative movement', thereby marking the distinction from the 'realists'. This self-definition should be understood in two ways: as an alternative to society and as an alternative to the dominant social movement trying to define the 'historicity' (Touraine 1981) of this society.

Identifying cultural movements as carriers of a social relation with nature does not only add another type of movement to the social movements generating modern societies. These cultural movements are potentially opposed to the social movements they have accompanied in the course of modernizing society. This potential opposition between social and cultural movements becomes a real opposition when the central conflict built into modern society is no longer the relationship of social movements to modernizing elites, but the struggle between social movements and cultural countermovements claiming competing visions of modernity. This difference between visions of modernity is not new; it has been going on since the beginning of modern society. It has become, for the first time in modern history, more than a difference. It has become a real social conflict and struggle, and thus a historical force.

This new conflict challenges modern society's central and self-given attribute. It questions the old idea of progress through the conquest of nature, through technological development. The idea of technological progress achieved by conquering nature is constitutive of the social struggles of the bourgeois and labour movements, and also for the present-day ecological movement. These movements differ only in their ideas of the path technological progress should take. Depending on some calculations on the future of nature, some urge that it should be slowed down and others urge the opposite.[10] They do, however, all plead for a more 'rational' path of modernization. The ecological movements are simply

[10] An interesting recent example for this phenomenon is the discussion of 'sustainable development' that has begun to dominate the ecological discourse; see in Milbrath 1989; O'Riordan 1990; Turner, R.K. 1990. For an 'official' follow-up to the Brundtland report see the contributions to Goodland 1991, sponsored by UNESCO.

trying to do a better job than the old, both the bourgeois and the labour, movements.

The cultural movements, on the other hand, do something very different. They see the relationship towards nature as a moral, not an instrumental one. They focus not on technological development in the realm of nature, but on a moral development in this realm, putting the dominant relationship with nature directly into question. The major contribution of these movements that continue historical counterculture traditions in modern society is an alternative to the idea of technological progress. It consists of the idea of a moral progress in our relation to nature.

My working hypothesis is therefore: in a deviation from the pattern of previous cultural movements in modern society, present-day cultural movements have the potential to realize the vision of another modernity. Through the development of modern society, cultural movements that are trying to revise the relationship to nature have been put into the centre of its dynamic. The ecological crisis of advanced modern society establishes these countermovements in the role of a new historical actor. This new role is to oppose the dominating vision of nature in modern society and establish a new relationship towards it. The new scenario for a new role has just begun. Contemporary ecological movements have only acted as the midwife for this new historical actor.

## Some consequences for post-Marxist social theory

### The changing role of the concept of modernity

What conclusions, theoretical as well as methodological, can be drawn from the emergence of a new field of class struggle, a new type of class conflict, a new idea of progress in advanced modern societies?

The first conclusion affects the theory of modernization. This theory is dead. The classical discussions about modernity share, despite far-reaching dissent on concrete issues, a consensus concerning one principle: that it is equality that separates modern society from traditional society (Dumont 1977). Used to rationalize and legitimate the model of equality, justice has become the key idea of modernity. Modernization is conceptualized as a process leading toward more equality in the different spheres of social life. From a political point of view, equality is the basic premise of a system whose elements are specified as equal rights. From an economic point of view, it shapes a system whose elements are specified as wage labour. Both equal rights and the wage-labour relations have been institutionalized. The idea of equal rights has been institutionalized in the form of citizenship (Marshall 1950). The idea of equal economic opportunity has been institutionalized in the form of wage labour. Modernization can be seen as a process of institutionalizing equality in the political and economic sphere which thereby increasingly realizes justice.

But these key issues of modernization theory are increasingly being replaced by other issues. The discourse on modernization is confronted with the phenomenon of religious movements trying to impose modernization in non-Western societies, with the anti-modernist attacks on the signposts of modern political and social thinking. These issues, however, are secondary compared with the new key issue, the *problem of nature*. This problem feeds the new crisis currently faced by advanced industrial societies, the ecological crisis which challenges some of our core assumptions of modernity. It has two main effects.

The first impact is that the discourse on modernization changes its locus of discussion. The reproduction of society in nature, the social way of dealing with nature, becomes a central concern in the discourse of modernity. In the classical approach to modernization the main problems lay in controlling the political and economic reproduction of modern social systems. We must now deal with problems of ecological reproduction. The forces of production, the idea of a self-propelling technological progress, has become a theoretical problem in theorizing about modernization.

The second arena of impact is the cultural implications of the ecological crisis. The problem of nature is not only a technical one of adapting the system of modern society to its natural environment. It is also a cultural problem that challenges the moral basis of modern society. The idea of moral progress made possible by the culture of modernity, an idea previously touted as one of the convincing strengths of modernity, begins to look empty; for the outcome of this moral progress can be seen to threaten the basis of life. Therefore, our theoretical notion of the morality specific to a modern ethic is at stake.

The ecological crisis that characterizes all modern societies, the advanced industrial societies as well as the industrializing societies, the capitalist as well as the socialist societies, leaves us with an alternate version of modernity, one that does not wage war with nature, but makes peace with it. The current crisis requires more than a critique of the ethnocentrism of modernization theory. The critique has already been made and it is devastating. It shows that modern society is nothing but another – and ultimately the most disgusting – attack on human sociality. The assault on ethnocentrism contained in the idea of modernity has been radicalized and disputes over the claim of progress credited to the culture of modernity. Thus we probably have to rebuild – above all – the moral foundations of modernization theory in order to grasp the changes going on in these societies. The recourse to old theories will be more futile the more these changes gain ground. We need a new theory of moral progress.

## The changing role of social critique

A methodological conclusion can also be drawn from this discussion since our theoretical reformulation of the theory of rationalization in modern society entails a new model of social critique. This new model is quite different from that characteristic of the enlightened philosopher who knew what was good for society. We are not formulating a political theory about the right way to organize a society. This old model of critique, the so-called practical philosophy of the eighteenth century, need not be revived, nor does the nineteenth-century model of critique as exemplified by the Marxian programme of immanent critique. This programme postulates objective historical trends (or laws) out of which normative conclusions concerning oppositional action can be drawn. This model still presupposes an intellectual elite that determines and proclaims what right action is backing up its position with some objectivistic theory of historical laws.

Neither critique is adequate any more. You can neither presuppose a consensus on philosophical constructions of what the good city is nor a consensus on the objective laws of society. Both possibilities have been nullified by the *de facto* development of modern society itself: the emerging form of collective self-organization is incompatible with these forms of critique. A new type of critique is called for. Social theory has lost its claim to objective validity. It is only one possible way of interpreting the social world, only one attempt to decipher the objective meaning of a historical situation. But as such, it is part of the collective learning processes it reconstructs historically. Social theory as critical theory is an intervention into the interpretations of those trying to shape the course and direction of collective learning processes. Such a conception of critique is of a 'therapeutic' nature. What this means is that professional socio-scientific analysis has the task of dissolving all rationalizations that pervade social action.

As sociologists, we know that we are not the ideological masters of social and cultural movements that Marx and his contemporaries thought themselves to be. We are only specialists in interpretations – and we have to push new interpretations beyond those to which we have become accustomed, beyond what I have called 'modernism'. We can fulfil the critical task only by deconstructing the illusions of the rationality, or its substitutes, ascribed to a society or to a social class or to a social group. This is the only way sociological analysis can intervene into the processes creating another (and even new) modernity, a society that is able to question not only its social relations of production and the institutions endorsing them but also its relation with nature. Only then will the idea of a postindustrial or a postmodern society really make sense.

## Conclusion

Counterculture movements have reframed the modern relationship of man with nature as one of exploitation. This framing gives these movements a new historical role within the present-day environmental crisis. This hypothesis is based upon three assumptions: (1) that this crisis is part of a general process of modernization; (2) that it fosters the formation of new class lines; and (3) that the exhaustion of the industrial model of development gives counterculture movements the possibility to foster another model of man's relationship with nature. This has allowed us to criticize the idea of modernity (using Marx as a reference) as a particularistic cultural tradition (as 'modernism'), that coexists with alternative models of modernism. It has been argued that modern culture is based upon a double cultural tradition containing two models of culture and two models of man relating to nature. It is shown that this double cultural tradition can be traced back to early modern Europe (and even back to the beginnings of European culture); the dominant tradition is the one tied to industrialism; the other one is a dominated tradition that has manifested itself in the Romantic model (which was reacting to Enlightenment as its better alternative) and that has been feeding counterculture movements throughout the last two centuries. Ultimately, an attempt has been made to describe this counterculture structurally as a specific model of understanding man and his relation to other human beings as well as to nature. These two cultures can be described as being bound either to the justice perspective (its apotheosis is to be found in the welfare state), or to the purity perspective which emphasizes cultural integrity and difference and thematizes health, the body and the soul as something that cannot be distributed and shared equally but rather must be embedded in a meaningful life-form. Thus we have today two (rather old) cultures that clash and constitute a new field of social conflicts in modern societies. These conflicts do not only serve to mobilize people but they also lead to a social-structural crystallization of actors as classes, thus constituting new forms of class conflict, the central class in it being the old and new middle classes. In its course the traditional petit-bourgeois culture is transformed from its historically distorted form that it found in the last century into a historically new form that enables this class to play the role of a new historical actor in modern society.

PART IV:

# NEW CLASS CONFLICTS? THE THEORY OF MIDDLE CLASS RADICALISM

## 8

## THE 'NEW SOCIAL MOVEMENTS'
Moral Crusades, Political Pressure Groups, or a Social Movement?[1]

### Introduction

The view the new social movements have of themselves is that they are both a 'new' movement and a 'social' movement. The following thoughts are an attempt to objectify this subjective view they have of themselves, to examine the empirical assumptions and normative premises on which it is based.

This analysis is composed of three separate parts. First, I would like to deal with the problems inherent in the traditional attempts to explain collective action in terms of class theory and to suggest a genuinely sociological explanation. Next, I want to sketch a phenomenology of the new social movements, which will identify both the social-structural basis and the collective identity of the groups mobilized in them. Finally, I would like to deal with the normative problems connected with an explanation of the new social movements (are they 'new' movements, are they 'movements' at all, indeed are they the harbingers of a new social formation?) and then discuss the rationalistic premises which are at the basis of any attempt to explain the new social movements.[2]

---

[1] This is a revised version of a paper that was first published in *Social Research*, Vol. 52, pp. 869–90. Footnotes have been added and the text has been shortened to make it easier reading.

[2] An overview of the literature can be found in three recent volumes on social movement theory and research, i.e. in Rucht 1991; Dalton and Kuechler 1990; Diani and Eyerman 1992.

## Class position, class consciousness and collective action

One of the contexts within which the theory of collective action can be located (when it is not reduced to a psychological theory) is *class*.[3] In the debates about the relation of collective action and class, two mutually exclusive theories of class have been used: the theory of the objective and the theory of the subjective class position to which correspond two models of explanation: the social-structural and the cultural. In the first case, collective action is seen as the result of the structure of class position; in the second, it is the result of the consciousness actors have of their class position. These approaches are again encountered in analysis of the new social movements, albeit in somewhat different terminology (which is due to the changes in social circumstances). The idea of collective action determined by the objective class position is at the basis of the theory which sustains that those affected by bureaucratic decisions are the privileged actors (Offe 1985c). The idea of collective action determined by collective changes in consciousness can be found – with an empirical twist – in the theory of postmaterialism (Inglehart 1977, 1981, 1990a). These two variants could also be combined in the form of a two-variables theory: as soon as the actors have become conscious of the objective position, collective action automatically follows. However – and this is the first point I should like to make – this does not happen.

The first explanation (the social-structural model) takes as its explanatory variables the political regulation and control of economic contradictions and the conflicts related to it, and takes the welfare state as the basis of its interpretation of the new social movements.[4] In doing so, it lists the following problems: the division of the burden of the consequences of the political regulation among different groups; the expansion of state power into the private sphere; the excessive demands on the capacity of the state to regulate the social system. What is new from an evolutionary point of view is that after the political harnessing of the old class conflict, the problems which arise as a result of this have now themselves to be harnessed. The social conflicts are shifted from the economic to the political level.

In this theoretical approach, the old problem of the objective determi-

---

[3] See also the more extensive discussion on the relationship between class and social movements in the next chapter. The main point made is that the new social movements are manifestations of middle-class-based collective mobilizations. See Offe 1985c for a systematic account of this assumption. Important contributors to this debate since have been Pakulski (1990), who pleads for a coexistence of class analysis with other types of analysis of social movements, Kriesi (1989) with a negative conclusion regarding the link between class and new social movements, and Luke (1989), who argues for an new class emerging in the wave of mobilization we call new social movements.

[4] See Offe 1985c and Habermas 1985b as the classic examples, and Hirsch 1988 and Roth 1989 relating the discussion to the theory of fordism and postfordism.

nation of a class actor is moved to the institutional level; instead of one central collective actor (the proletariat), several different collective actors can be identified. The institutional harnessing of the class conflict bases collective actions upon issues which are of a necessarily particular nature. The assumption that modern society no longer has one central conflict, but that the latter is, on the contrary, segmented and fragmented into specific problems, and the concomitant theory that one individual class actor is transformed into several protest actors, does nothing to change the objectivism of this model of explanation, which consists in the premise that collective action results from the objective position itself. However, since historical experience tells us that it was often precisely those affected objectively who did not revolt, we must have recourse to other variables: in this case to problems of the 'consciousness'.

The second type of explanation, the theory of a new postmaterialistic consciousness in society, is based on the hypothesis that new postmaterialistic values are the cause of new collective protest. Thus the subjective (or cultural) dimension of the protest actor is played off against the objective (or social-structural) dimension. The new class consciousness becomes constitutive of the new protest actor. However, this explanation fails to take into account the repercussions which these new values themselves have on the reproduction of objective structures. A collective actor can admittedly justify his actions by professing to want nothing more than a better world. Yet this implies a failure on the part of the actor to recognize his own institutional effects.

At this point it is necessary to return to the objectivistic model of explanation, which introduces, behind the cultural changes, the institutional context of reproduction as the central prerequisite of collective protest. However, this results in something akin to a mutual stabilization of two conflicting models of explanation of protest action, in which whatever remains unexplained by one can always be ascribed to the other variable. In the first case, social movements result from social-structural changes, in the second, from cultural changes. From the analysis of the institutional capacity for dealing with problems, social-structural determinism infers issues, to which the new social movements are more or less rational answers. Cultural determinism sees changes in values as results of a new class consciousness, which then requires external incentives to be put into motion. In both cases, social movements are taken to be social phenomena brought into being by external forces. Thus the well-worn path of objectivism and subjectivism, which characterizes the explanations of collective action in traditional class theory, has merely been trodden once again.

How to go beyond the old division between subjective and objective class position, beyond the concomitant social-structural and cultural determinism in the explanation of collective protest? Is there something beyond objective social structure and subjective consciousness? For a social system to be reproduced, it is necessary that the social actors have the possibility of 'improvising' within the objective structure that determines their actions. This capacity is historically and socially determined. Bourdieu (1980, 1984) describes it as a *habitus* (a collective disposition) which guarantees the reproduction of objective and subjective structures. A habitus, through reproducing its subjective conditions, makes the reproduction of its underlying objective structures possible.[5] A habitus thus mediates objective and subjective social realities.

The idea of a habitus as put forward by Bourdieu explains the reproduction of class positions and subjective dispositions, but it runs short of explaining its dynamic of self-transformation.[6] The problem that can be solved by an explanation of collective action is the process of the collective construction of a habitus beyond its double reproductive function, which is to reproduce itself and the social positions to which it is linked. One is not born with a habitus; on the contrary, it is something which one acquires through interaction with other individuals. Its acquisition can be regulated by traditional norms; in that case a traditional life-form becomes the starting point for the acquisition of a habitus, which, in turn, can become the starting point for collective action. However, the acquisition of a habitus can also be the result of the dynamics of a post-traditional social order; in this case the acquisition of a new habitus becomes the starting point of an innovative collective protest. In the first case it is ascribed group affiliations which count, in the second it is achieved group affiliations (both of these play a central role in the new social movements, particularly in the Women's Movement). Tilly put forward the theory, on the basis of historical research, that primitive and reactionary forms of collective action have their basis in the traditional life-form (in a communal base), whereas modern forms have developed from an associational base (Tilly 1977).

A collectively shared habitus can thus be linked to varying historical contexts. It turns out not only to serve as a reproductive mechanism for class positions and dispositions, but also as a central explanatory variable in the explanation of the dynamics of collective protest. Thus we have reached a genuinely sociological perspective for the explanation of collective protest situating it in between objective and subjective conditions of existence. The double function of habitus, to reproduce its conditions of existence and to serve as a medium of collective action, provides a new nexus of class and collective action where class is linked to the reproductive and collective action to the constructionist side of the same process. In order to grasp the mechanism of construction, one must be able to discern

---

[5] A good discussion of the habitus concept is found in Matthiesen 1989. Its basic limit is its non-dynamic character. A habitus is – by definition – a relatively stable collective disposition, anchored in a position whose change has to be explained by factors external to it.

[6] This point has been accepted as a criticism by Bourdieu. See his comments on criticisms in Eder 1989, reprinted in Bourdieu 1990.

its creative mechanism.[7] Such a constructionist sociological perspective beyond social-structural objectivism and cultural subjectivism provides a general frame of reference which will underlie the following discussion of the theory that ascribes a petit-bourgeois habitus to the new social movements.[8]

## The phenomenology of the new social movements

### The petit-bourgeois basis of the new social movements

It is the petite bourgeoisie that expresses the collective protest of the new social movements. The new social movements are – historically speaking – a second wave of the protest of the 'honest man' and petit-bourgeois radical democrats who managed to have a significant and ambivalent moral, political and social influence in the nineteenth century.[9] A phenomenology of the new social movements must start from the assumption that they are part of the history of the petit-bourgeois protest which has from the outset accompanied the modernization of society.

This type of collective protest is based on an objective structure which is characteristic of the petite bourgeoisie. Metaphorically speaking, it falls between all stools. It is not the upper class, neither the cultural upper class which represents the 'high' society nor the economic upper class. It is objectively locked out from the top, because it does not have the power to make its needs socially accepted and legitimate. In the development of the bourgeois class, the petite bourgeoisie is that part of the bourgeoisie which never succeeded in becoming really bourgeois. On the other hand, thanks to its control over the means of production and its state-guaranteed jobs, it did not become part of the proletariat. On the contrary, it can set itself apart from the bottom end of the class scale by condemning the instrumentalism of the lower classes and establishing its own needs as the true needs. The petite bourgeoisie never made history – neither as lords nor as serfs. On the contrary, their fate is dependent on the conflict between both.

With the social advancement of the middle class (which is bound up with

[7] Luhmann's systems theory especially has attracted scholars to develop a constructionist perspective in its conceptual frame. The concept of self-creation or self-organization of collective protest (Japp 1984) aims to develop a theory of the social constitution of collective protest. Social movements as systems of action which create themselves can be understood as systems which make the capacity of communicative conflict resolution the mechanism of their self-organization. See also Japp 1986, Bergmann 1987 and Ahlemeyer 1989. This has remained, due to its complex terminology, a German discussion so far. The underlying constructivist perspective is discussed in Luhmann (1990a, 1990b).

[8] This theory has been first explicitly formulated in Bourdieu 1984. Earlier versions are Parkin's theory of middle class radicalism, based on an analysis of the British peace movement (Parkin 1968). Another interesting piece on middle class unrest in Britain, regarding protest of self-employed groups, is Elliott et al. 1982. This topic is treated in more depth in the next chapter of this book.

[9] An excellent discussion of the protest of these groups is found in Gusfield's analysis of the American Temperance movement (Gusfield 1966).

the development of the service society), the petite bourgeoisie has achieved a new significance. The reclassification of the social groups resulting from this development has produced a new middle class with specific internal differentiations (Bourdieu 1984):

- The executive petite bourgeoisie is found among the lower and middle white-collar workers whose functions are merely executive; they comprise those who have attained 'better' positions in the status system thanks to their academic and professional titles. However, since they have only academic and professional titles (i.e. cultural power) at their disposal, and not the means of production, they are obliged to symbolically set themselves apart from the lower classes.
- The declining petite bourgeoisie belongs to those directly affected by processes of social reclassification and declassification: the peripheral staff in the service sector. It represents, in other words, the old petite bourgeoisie directly affected by structural changes in production.
- The new petite bourgeoisie belongs to a group which comprises the administrators of the new clients of the welfare state, i.e. those who provide 'social repair' services (e.g. social workers, psychologists, teachers etc.). This group comprises those who do not speak as, but on behalf of a social class. They are thus the people whose task it is to look after the disadvantaged, but they are not disadvantaged themselves.

What these various groups have in common is their specific social-structural position.[10] This position deprives the old and new middle classes of any possibilities of collective defence against the market (and bureaucracy): their social-structural position makes their members perfect consumers, who have to fight for status on the diverse markets. They are compelled by their position – in contrast to the groups which belong to the lower class and the upper class – to 'individualization'.[11] The plasticity and

[10] The discussion on social-structural homogeneity of participants in collective action and protest supporters is still open. On the basis of electoral data, class lines are no longer visible (Bürklin 1984). This data, however, does not measure the effects of class. It only shows that the link between class and voting preferences has weakened. Serious answers to this question afford first two separate types of analyses, analyses of social-structural configurations and analyses of collective action patterns. How both phenomena interact and whether there is a systematic relationship between them is then to be studied and analyzed within an adequate theoretical framework. See for this problem the Introduction to this volume.

[11] Individualization has a double meaning. It refers to the objective individualization in the sense of being cut off from traditional socio-cultural bonds and becoming a free-floating individual with an open option space. It also stands for the chance to become a person with a highly individualized identity, capable of generating an autonomous identity formation. Beck (1983, 1992) is pertinent to this discussion. See also Giddens, whose notion of individualization has more to do with the idea of autonomy (Giddens 1991). Both meanings are certainly related. However, the same problem that vexes the link of class and collective action comes up again. Both vary rather independently, and it has to be determined whether there are rules (which are more than correlations!) underlying their interaction. This implies, for example, that objective individualization does not necessarily lead to subjective individualization. It can even block it. This is important for the interpretation of middle class radicalism below.

the variability of their needs ('you can only show that you are different from the others through your taste') determine the action space of the petit bourgeois within the social status system. This enables the petit bourgeois to set himself apart from the relatively stable needs of those who are subject to the constraints of daily life. He can at the same time look towards those for whom the connection between their needs and 'good' taste is the most natural thing in the world.

The *petit-bourgeois consciousness* corresponds to its objective position. It can be interpreted as a mixture of bourgeois universalism and plebeian particularism. Torn between these two directions, the petit bourgeois looks for norms and values which are hard to justify within the model of universalistic reasoning and which at the same time are not merely the outcome of the constraints of daily life.[12] Postmaterialistic values fit the bill perfectly: not to be materialistic and at the same time to compete with the norms and values of the bourgeois high culture. They are not part of the moral economy of the lower classes; at the same time they set themselves apart from the time-honoured bourgeois ethic by 'refusing to participate in the rational discourse of understanding'. They appear to be less susceptible to theorizing, and they do not have (in contrast to questions of distribution, for instance) any criteria which can be made equally binding for everyone. Nobody can be forced into happiness.

Historical analogies to this petit-bourgeois collective consciousness can be found in the (petit-)bourgeois Commune Movements of the nineteenth century. It contains the elements which were then in the first half of the twentieth century used to sustain new romanticism (the emphasis on nationalistic traditions, the opposition to intellectualism and progressivist optimism) and neo-Darwinism (theories of racial purity, the metaphysics of national redemption). The morality of the new petit bourgeois continues this tradition: the return to direct experience, to anthropomorphous nature and the old dream of eternal peace, liberation by the group and within the group are common goals which reformulate old petit-bourgeois thinking.

This collective consciousness can be further differentiated along the lines of the internal social-structural differentiation within the petite bourgeoisie. The 'doxy' of the petit-bourgeois collective consciousness is defined by the executive petite bourgeoisie, to which the form of consciousness of the declining petite bourgeoisie is as orthodoxy, while that of the new petite bourgeoisie is as heterodoxy. These variants of petit-bourgeois consciousness can be characterized as follows, depending on the social-structural

---

[12] This description draws heavily on Bourdieu (1984). The lead set by him has been taken up in some of the work on postmodernist culture (Featherstone 1989, 1990, 1992a). The argument points out a close relationship between consumption styles, middle class locations and a postmodern culture. This argument is based on the contention that the postmodern strata of cultural intermediaries (a new middle class!) pursue a postmodern lifestyle because they have the necessary sensibilities and dispositions. It is a matter of adequate interpretation to see this postmodern culture as a continuation of petit-bourgeois culture.

position of the petit-bourgeois moralist: (1) the doxy of intimacy, peace and ecology (the new moral issues); (2) the orthodoxy of the classical ideal of the family, of deterrence and economic growth; (3) and the heterodoxy of the ideals of new sensitivity, of eternal peace and of man's harmony with nature.

The paradigm of a life-world, the hallmark of the executive petite bourgeoisie, is on the one hand redefined defensively, as a defensive paradigm of the 'life-world' (what is particularly striking about this is that the declining petits bourgeois owe their consciousness to a language 'borrowed' from the executive petite bourgeoisie); on the other hand, the paradigm of the life-world is redefined by the new petite bourgeoisie as an offensive paradigm of the 'life-world', as a 'new' morality. This paradigm of a life-world specifies and redefines the old petit-bourgeois individualistic ethos. Happiness becomes the new key to a petit-bourgeois consciousness.

These descriptions still beg the question why the new middle classes and the forms of consciousness found among them can be deciphered as 'petit-bourgeois'. Only a 'phenomenology' of middle class positions and dispositions has been presented so far, much in line with current interpretations, scientific and literary, of the (old and new) middle class. The association of the label petit-bourgeois is not yet justified on such grounds. What this label does, however, is to create a link between different fractions of the middle classes, especially of its new fractions, on the one hand, and forms of consciousness. The concept that provides for such a mediation is that of *habitus*. If there is such a thing as a *petit-bourgeois habitus*, then we can conclude that even for the emerging new fractions of the middle class, the 'new middle classes', the petit-bourgeois habitus is the medium by which their objective and subjective existence are coupled. The habitus of the new middle class is – this is the proposition – a *petit-bourgeois habitus*.[13]

The habitus of the new middle class is determined by its situation in between the upper and the lower classes. The habitus of the new petit bourgeois is objectively determined by the defence of individualization, which is imposed upon him by the status system. In this defence, the dilemma of the petit bourgeois is reproduced: he defends a life-world that is at the same time traditional and modern; and he identifies himself at the same time with both the rulers and the ruled. He has recourse to the old world of the artisan as well as to the world of the peasant, to the forms of solidarity of an (idealized) working class as well as to the forms of communicative association of an (idealized) bourgeois class. The tension between universalism and particularism, which is determined by the objective position, can be resolved by recourse to a life-world which is less

[13] An early analysis in these terms can be found in the work of Lederer, a German sociologist and historian, working at the beginning of the twentieth century. See his work written between 1913 and 1919 on the 'habitus of the non-self-employed', which refers to the habitus of the white-collar workers emerging since the turn of the century (Lederer 1979). This description already contains the elements of a petit-bourgeois habitus that we use today for their description.

than moral discourse and more than moral economy: a form of life resulting from objective individualization and referring to an individualistic idea of happiness. This petit-bourgeois habitus manifests a concordance in its objective and subjective structure. The dilemma of the petit-bourgeois habitus consists in his being unable to identify with either the objective position or the collective identity of the (upper) bourgeoisie; nor is he able to identify with the objective position or the collective identity of the proletariat. The *petit-bourgeois protest* remains tied up within the constraints of this dilemma. This can be seen in the ideal types of petit-bourgeois protest, which will be described in the following section.

### Forms of petit-bourgeois radicalism

A first form of the new petit-bourgeois protest is based on the central position they give to moral issues. Morality becomes the subject of collective protest. This moralization of the world is aimed at fulfilling a postulated moral standard. The difference between moral ideal and social reality becomes the motivating force of collective protest which characterizes *moral crusades*.[14] These moral battles lead to a restructuring of the collective moral consciousness; in place of the old bourgeois ethics (in its acquisitive, upper bourgeois and proletarian variations), a new moralism arises. The motives underlying this moral protest reflect the internal structural division of the petite bourgeoisie. One can identify three variants of this moralism: (1) individualistic optimism; (2) puritanical moralism, which is primarily antifeminist and antipornographic; (3) and ethical doctrines of salvation.

The forms of collective action or protest typical of this field of symbolical (moral) battles are primarily ritual. The collective moral protest follows the logic of the ritual reversal of official reality. Protest action is simply the reversal of institutional action: not to be centralized, but decentralized; not to be legal, but legitimate; not formal, but informal; not to act strategically, but expressively. The protest action is a continuation of an old logic of collective protest, the logic of moral indignation. In traditional societies this action is borne by Messianic movements; the customs of carnival are the last remnants of this tradition. In modern societies this protest is secularized, and it is institutionalized in the form of various, more or less stable countercultures. Empirical examples are:

---

[14] This term is taken from Gusfield (1966). The description of the new social movements and their supporting strata in terms of moralists has become widespread. See Giesen (1983), who generalizes this idea in an analysis of the 'moral entrepreneurs' as a central element of modern public discourse. Moralizing protest issues has become a central element today in environmentalist discourse. The use of public relations in communicating environmental topics has become a dominant feature of ecological communication, thereby changing the form of mass mobilization for environmental themes dramatically. This is the central theme of a research project on the making of environmental issues in five European countries (Eder 1992a).

- the peace movement: it explicitly adheres to ritual forms of expression which can be interpreted as the reversal of the official representation of society (sit-ins as the reversal of parliamentary sittings; occupation as the reversal of policing);
- the women's movement: the world of the woman is the reversal of the world of the man; thus the 'feminat' (exclusive female leadership) of the parliamentary party of the Greens, for example, can be interpreted as a reversal of the official model of the organization of a political party.

A second form of the new petit-bourgeois protest stems from problems connected with the crisis of the welfare state, the frustration and dis-illusionment with the party system and with bureaucratization. This is the starting point for a different type of collective protest, for a new type of *political pressure group*. It is based on political issues which are not dealt with by the dominant political culture; in this sense this collective protest is aimed at the selectivity of political institutions. This form of protest is characterized by the following elements: problems hitherto ignored are made into subjects of discussion, the necessary knowledge about the subject is provided by experts and brought to the attention of the public by public relations professionals.[15] This makes an increase in institutional adaptability possible in the sense that more information is processed within the political system.

The internal structure of the petite bourgeoisie is articulated in the form of this type of protest: it is transformed into the mixture of realists, conservatives and fundamentalists typical of 'green politics'. This is reflected in particular in the treatment of ecological problems, which oscillates between rustic romanticism, the politics of alternative energy and a new policy of growth. The forms of action with which the petit-bourgeois habitus is politically mobilized are citizens' action groups, alternative hearings and the participation in the political system with an 'alternative' interpretation of the rules of the game. This petit-bourgeois radicalism is articulated in the form of an 'alternative' public opinion that is able to set itself apart from the mass public opinion which has become part of the culture of the lower classes. At the same time it seeks to compete with the elitist public of the ruling political culture. It is above all the ecological movement that offers empirical examples of this type of movement, in that

---

[15] As an example of an analysis of the debate on nuclear energy see Kitschelt 1984. The role of professionals has become even more widespread in the development of the environmental-ist movement in the eighties, creating tensions between constituency and movement organizations. This phenomenon has been a major topic in the resource mobilization approach (Zald and McCarthy 1987, pp. 97ff). The European discussion on intellectuals in movements, relying mainly on Gramscian notions, has not added much to elucidate this phenomenon.

it contains the diverse forms of political protest and makes a new type of pressure group of them within the political system.[16]

A third form of the new petit-bourgeois protest results from problems connected with the crisis within the industrial society and its 'production-oriented' logic. The new issues are forms of social production which are more life-world oriented, and alternatives to labour in return for payment become the subject of collective protest. Such a collective protest no longer merely applies to what has been 'ignored' or 'suppressed', to a new 'cultural model' of the organization of social relationships. It is not a question of justice or happiness (as is typical of moral crusades), but of a different form of producing justice and happiness. Admittedly, these cultural models remain bound to the objective position of the petite bourgeoisie: they vary from ideas of a (postindustrial) service society freed from the problems of shortages, via ideas of a society of small business-men, to ideas of an expressive form of organization of social relations. In this case we can speak of a petit-bourgeois *social movement*.

On this level, parallels to the labour movement of the nineteenth century can be found. In the first instance, the analogy is made possible by the fact that in parts of the new middle classes downgrading processes are taking place, which are bringing the status position of these groups closer to that of the proletariat: to have nothing but one's own labour to sell in order to reproduce oneself, and at the same time to have to offer this commodity on the external labour market or even outside this labour market where it is paid under cost. On the other hand, the labour movement embraced the utopian model of other forms of social relations (bourgeois intellectuals thinking 'on behalf of' the proletariat were particularly fond of pursuing such objectives), as well as models of a form of socialism without the costs of industrialization.

The forms of action typical for dealing with these issues are differentiated from forms of action which are geared towards political effectiveness in so far as the former consciously fulfil an innovative social role: forms of action such as self-help or cooperation, i.e. new forms of solidarity, determine their approach to social reality. The key word 'association', which the labour movement itself adopted in its own way, is readopted and reinterpreted: as an association regulated by communicative and affective relationships. Empirical illustrations of this type of petit-bourgeois protest are found in the alternative movement and the self-help movement. Alternatives present themselves to those who are able to set themselves apart from the rest of society (the utopias in which the new petite bourgeoisie take refuge). Self-help remains the watchword of the declining

[16] See the contributions to the collection of studies edited by Dalton and Kuechler (1990) for this. The unifying theoretical concept for this phenomenon is 'institutionalization'. Movements become a normal aspect of political life. Obviously, a favourite object of such a perspective has been the transformation of environmentalist movements into green parties. For this see Bürklin 1987, Rüdig 1991, and the contributions to Müller-Rommel 1989.

petite bourgeoisie. The executive petite bourgeoisie has an ambivalent attitude towards these two forms of protest.[17]

The new social movements manifest a form of middle class protest which oscillates from moral crusade to political pressure group to social movement. Hence the problem to be explained presents itself as follows: what is the logic underlying the transformation of a habitus into a protest, and what are the specific mobilizing conditions which determine the form of this protest?[18] This question of the transformation of a habitus into protest cannot be reduced to the analysis of mobilizing conditions. An explanation must start with the reproduction of the mobilization and identify the logic of transformation that is built into the specific mobilization of the petite bourgeoisie. However, this cannot be separated from assumptions of the rationality of the protest action. One can resolve such problems by way of definition. Thus Touraine (1981), for example, maintains that the form of protest that can be classified as a social movement is rational *per se*. This argument is based on a naturalistic fallacy. The same applies to the idea that what is new represents an increase in rationality, because what is new can equally be easily irrational. The problem then arises of how to establish criteria of rationality that allow one to grasp theoretically the normative implications of a phenomenology of protests in the new social movements. For this purpose, I shall first discuss the theories of collective behaviour or action, theories which interpret the particular form of collective protest either as a reaction to the malfunctioning of the social system, or as an attempt to maximize the potential power resources for the actors' own interest. Both theories are, according to my hypotheses, inadequate. I will therefore suggest that collective protest should be understood as a *collective learning process*. By systematically reconstructing these approaches, I shall then explicate the various 'rationalities' of collective protest action in the new social movements.

## Explaining collective protest in the new social movements

### The three logics of collective protest action

The question of the rationality of collective protest action has been answered in two different ways. As long as one bases one's arguments on the assumption that collective protest is the result of *subjective dissatisfaction*, the problem of the rationality of collective protest does not arise. Collective protest then takes on the appearance of a more or less rational

[17] This kind of difference has also been found in one of the few empirical studies on this topic; see Kriesi 1989.

[18] This process has been discussed under the heading of consensus formation and consensus mobilization by Klandermans (1988). A habitus is based on an implicit shared consensus, whereas a movement consensus presupposes additional action to generate it. There the transformation of a habitus into a disposition to participate in movement action is a question of specifying an implicit consensus shared by social groups or classes.

answer to social problems (the classical theories from LeBon to Smelser have worked on this assumption). The 'highest' form of collective protest is in Smelser's theory of collective behaviour, 'value oriented' movements, i.e. movements which make final moral questions the subject of discussion.[19] This form of collective protest has been described above as a moral crusade. A moral crusade is directed against cultural imperialism (whether real or imagined), which is combated by moral mobilization, with recourse to a different, and – so it is assumed – better morality. This protest is rational in so far as the difference between theory and reality is the subject of the protest. It becomes irrational when (as is shown for example in the moral majority movement or other new religious movements) the ideal against which reality is measured is the morality of the movement, which is assumed and claimed to be right.

These theories of collective protest have been challenged by more recent theories, which declare collective protest to be a form of *rational behaviour*. These rationalistic interpretations are based on 'rational-actor theories', which are complemented by organization theory (which stresses questions of internal and external resource mobilization) or systems theory (in which protest is then seen as a political resource in the conflict with the political authorities, a resource which in turn is dependent on the structure of the political system). In more recent times these rationalistic theories have enjoyed a great deal of popularity (this is presumably connected with the increasing significance of protest action for the political process, and also with the euphemistic treatment of protest action as unconventional political behaviour). These theories have led to a 'more political' interpretation of collective protest action (Tilly 1978, 1985), and in particular have served as a corrective for the irrationalistic explanations of collective protest. In this way, a difference between the logic of collective protest and the logic of political factions no longer exists.[20] The only difference is that they have different resources at their disposal, which they can employ in the battle for political influence and political power. For this reason they are only a special form of pressure group.

Admittedly, this assumption of rationality is very restrictive. It reduces the rationality of protest to the rationality of interest groups, to the ability to maximize (or at least guarantee) the strategic accomplishment of interests in the given opportunity structure. Thus normative motives – for instance the establishment of a good and just society (which could conceivably run counter to the actor's own interests) – are systematically underrated as a possible explanatory factor. The idea of rational objectives is not susceptible of explanation by an assumption of rationality which

[19] This theory still attracts attention, especially in attempts aiming at a psychological explanation of mobilization and movement action. It is used to complement resource mobilization theory (Klandermans 1984; Klandermans and Oegema 1987)

[20] The best example for this approach is found in the work of Opp; see Opp 1989.

restricts the rationality to the mobilization of resources for given objectives.

A second criticism of the rationalistic theories refers to their individualistic premises. Collective action is a result of the 'objective' (or external) coordination of individual decisions. The given opportunity structure determines the conditions of cooperation. These theories thus presuppose discrete, socially unrelated individuals. However, the 'more social' the actors are, the less can be explained by a theory which presupposes such discrete, unsocial individuals. This makes it necessary to make use of non-individualist theories of rationality.

The third – and decisive – objection to the rationalistic theories refers to the systematic self-deception which is built into the logic of such protest behaviour. It is not the aim of political pressure groups – in contrast to moral crusades – to moralize society, but to establish the social conditions necessary for accomplishing their own moral objectives. The rationality of pressure groups consists in the dissociation of moral and empirical reality: they deal with empirical reality strategically, whilst they reduce morality to the objectives they want to achieve. But the strategic use of means contains a central element of irrationality, because it leads to the systematic exclusion, for strategic reasons, of empirical information which could result in a change in moral points of view. The empirical reality of the normative demands is manipulated – but then the protest action becomes indistinguishable from institutional action, which, by definition, is related to the upholding of the normative structures on which it is based.

A fruitful approach to an explanation of collective protest which does justice to these three criticisms is found in the interpretation of collective protest as a *collective learning process*.[21] Collective learning processes are concerned not only with particular interests, but also with principalistic moral considerations. A soon as moral questions arise, however, people have to talk with each other in order to be able to cooperate. The rationality of collective learning consists in the fact that, in principle, all questions can become the subject of argumentative debate. This characterizes a social movement in contrast to a moral crusade or a pressure group. There is already a tradition of interpretation of collective protest as a collective learning process. Among the theorists of the history of the labour movement (Vester 1970; Na'aman 1978), the idea of a social movement as a collective learning process is common, although the theoretical implications of this concept have not yet been clarified. A systematic attempt to explain the conditions and rules of collective learning processes has been undertaken by Miller (1986, 1992). In his theoretical framework, he begins with the sociological assumption that the preconditions of the possibility of collective action are based on the ability of social actors to participate in argumentative debate. This is at the same

---

[21] For this concept see Miller 1986, 1987; Eder 1985, 1987a. For a discussion of these approaches see Strydom 1987.

time the point of departure for the ontogenetic development of this ability and for the construction and reconstruction of social reality.

From this point of view, the problem of the rationality and irrationality of collective protest is shifted from the individual to the relationships between individuals, to the form of sociality. This could be called the theory of the social constitution of the rationality or irrationality of collective protest. It allows us to reformulate the question of the rationality of collective protest. In so far as the sociality which is implicit in the collective protest makes collective learning processes possible, it is 'rational'; in so far as it impedes these learning processes, it is 'irrational'.

Applying the differentiation (mentioned above) between 'communal-base' collective protest and 'associational-base' collective protest, one can differentiate between two forms of sociality, each of which results in a specific form of protest action:

• The given social context determines the form of sociality; collective protest consists in the mere defence of this social world; thus learning processes cannot take place.
• A social world which is to be constructed by means of communicative conflict resolution determines the form of sociality; thus the necessary preconditions for collective learning processes are given.

The first type of sociality leads to irrational social movements: they prevent innovative solutions to the self-organization of collective action. The irrationality of this type consists in its having recourse to traditional forms of social relationships and thereby rejecting the possibility of communicative conflict resolution. The second type of sociality leads to rational social movements; social conditions are established which force those involved into learning. Its rationality consists in being a form of associative practice which is based upon communicative social relations.

### Collective protest in the new social movements

It is, however, a long way from an analysis of the constitution to the analysis of the result of collective protest. To what extent rationality and irrationality in the new social movements reach the level of a 'social movement' or remain restricted to the level of the 'moral crusade', is the point of departure of a genuinely social analysis of collective protest, which will be dealt with below in the form of several hypotheses. Connected to this is an attempt to transform the descriptive phenomenology of the new social movements into a social analysis. The collective protest of the petit bourgeois in the new social movements is expressed – as described above – in three ways. It is (1) a symbolic crusade fighting for the recognition of their own culture as the legitimate culture and thus against the prevalent morality; (2) a political pressure group fighting against the euphemistic treatment of or complete disregard for social problems, thus against its own decline in the status system; and (3) a social movement fighting for a radical democratization of social relationships as such (not only social relationships in production!).

The *moral crusade* is the form most favoured by the petite bourgeoisie. Petit-bourgeois radicalism is of a primarily moral nature. This group is predestined by its social position to mobilize moralists. Historical movements as well as current ones suggest such an interpretation (the peace movement as a revivalist movement). The point of reference of this protest is the set of moral principles which have become the basis of modernity. The moral crusades of the new social movements are collective reactions to the cultural modernization which has increasingly widened the gap between morality and the life-world. Universal moral concepts such as peace, justice or a good life are not susceptible of fulfilment in the immediacy of the world we live in, in empirical reality. Fear and the overcoming of it in forms of collective protest are a reaction to this cultural modernization. In this situation the petite bourgeoisie fills a role which it has rehearsed throughout history: it is the guardian of the moral virtues of modernity, a role which it has learned how to play since its birth (Martens 1968).

The *political pressure group*, on the other hand, is a provocation for the petite bourgeoisie. It would not like to be a pressure group but nevertheless tends to organize its interests in this form. A particularly apt illustration of this is to be found in its dealings with the law. On the one hand using the law as a medium to push through its own interests, it at the same time refuses to identify itself with the law as an expression of institutionalized violence. The debate on civil disobedience points in one direction (Frankenberg 1984; Rucht 1984); the legal contesting of planning decisions and the concomitant juridification of conflicts of interest point in another direction. The collective protest which is institutionally organized follows the imperatives of legitimacy to the same extent as the imperatives of legality.

The form which is most alien of all to the petit bourgeois is the *social movement*. It is not part of the petit-bourgeois habitus to reflect on his own social-structural position and on his own consciousness, on the empirical and normative conditions of his existence. The cultural model of social development which forces itself upon the petit bourgeois because of his social position is distorted in an individualistic manner. A collectively shared world is always something external for the petit bourgeois, something imposed upon him (after all, it is precisely the petit bourgeois who becomes enthusiastic about the market, first the labour market, and nowadays the market for educational and professional titles, and is then bewildered by the social consequences they produce). Even today the petit bourgeois fails to recognize the social conditions of his cultural models: the element of self-exploitation which is built into the new forms of solidarity is an indication of how empirical reality is systematically excluded from the petit-bourgeois project of a life-world-oriented form of social production, distribution and consumption. This misjudgement on the part of the petite bourgeoisie becomes regressive the moment it is affected by unemployment and downgrading and is at the same time forced by its habitus to misjudge the social condition of this situation. The petit bourgeois then seeks the new society in the past: in a mythical and mystical past, the reestablishment of which is intended to prevent the impending downgrading. The social movement degenerates into a mere countermovement, which is able to produce nothing more than a fictitious communality. But that is synonymous with social conditions which no longer make any collective learning processes possible.

A 'rational' social movement in the new social movements can be found – if at all – only in niches, and even in niches within niches. In the Communes and 'alternative' forms of work, which take up the old communitarian traditions, the radical democratic project of the petit bourgeois is preserved. These projects contain the conditions required for collective learning processes which envisage a genuinely new form of social relations beyond moralism and power. Thus the forms of protest peculiar to the new social movements show that the social position of the petit bourgeois opens up the possibility of becoming a radical democratic movement as well as the possibility of Biedermeier moralism. In this way a historical situation repeats itself here: a mobilization of the petite bourgeoisie is taking place, a mobilization which drives this petite bourgeoisie back and forth between fear and utopia. The outcome of this is probably as uncertain today as it was then.

# 9

# DOES SOCIAL CLASS MATTER IN THE STUDY OF SOCIAL MOVEMENTS?
## A New Theory of Middle Class Radicalism

## Does social class matter?

### Why should class matter at all?

The concern with class in social movement theory and analysis seems to raise old questions that have been surpassed by the evolution of modern society. Class no longer plays a role in the diagnostic discourses of advanced modern societies. It has even become fashionable to perform critical diagnoses of modern societies beyond and against the discourse of class. The fall of communist regimes and the rise of nationalism have given an additional impetus to argue against the obsoleteness of class analysis regarding modern societies. Class has to do with industrial society and its ideologies, and since these societies and their ideologies no longer exist, we should free ourselves from the old conceptions and analytical tools to understand modern society.

We will follow a strategy that is altogether opposite. The reason for this has to do with the idea that we are interested in the question of to what extent the new social movements are indicators of new and deep social cleavages or antagonisms in modern society. The new social movements have been given credit for introducing new issues, being carriers of a new paradigm of social existence, and pointing toward new social cleavages in modern societies besides the traditional religious and ethnic cleavages. The new cleavages introduced by these groups are then perceived as substituting the old cleavage based on class, the cleavage between capital and labour. This argument usually implies that with the institutionalization of class conflict, the notion of class no longer applies. This argument confounds a historical and a structural explanation. The historical argument of institutionalization can be true; but this does not necessarily imply that we have to accept the structural argument. It may be that industrial class conflict no longer dominates class conflicts. We even accept the idea that this type of class conflict is diminishing in importance, but we will argue against the idea that class conflict is vanishing with the disappearance of its first embodiment, namely class conflict organized around the contradiction of capital and labour.

Why then do we stick to class as a structural element in explaining social movements? The conceptual and theoretical option for the concept of class has to do with the way modern society is organized. When analyzing the arenas of social movements in societies based upon an egalitarian and libertarian culture, we are left with two arenas: political rights and industrial relations. We then analyze either the struggle for the extension of universal rights or the struggle between classes of people whose interests, norms and values are incommensurable.[1] The logic of political rights is universal inclusion of every human being into structures that guarantee these rights. The logic of industrial relations is relating antagonistic classes of people to each other. Which of the two is chosen in constituting collective action varies empirically. The labour movement combined both aspects. Whether the new social movements do so as well, or whether they are predominantly collective actions of the first type is also an empirical question. We assume that like the old movement the new social movements contain both elements. They are movements which strive for more justice, for more rights and freedom; and they are simultaneously movements which oppose categories of people to other categories,[2] thus creating a conflict arena over issues in which the gains of some are necessarily coupled with the losses of others.[3]

Thus the rationale for sticking to the concept of class has to do, firstly, with the assumption that the new social movements cannot be reduced to movements demanding universal inclusion. We want to find out whether these movements (defined as issue-movements) reveal antagonistic and even incommensurable interests, norms and values at stake in an issue. The second rationale is that we want to conceptualize new social movements in a way that does not exclude beforehand the possibility of their being part of emerging new social antagonisms.

---

[1] This term of incommensurability, taken from recent discussions in political theory, means not only 'incompatibility'; it also means that conflicts are *unvermittelbar*, that they represent a social difference that can only be resolved by power and domination or by changing basic principles of social organization and social order.

[2] The term 'category' has still to answer the question of whether we are dealing with classes or not. To be able to identify categories of people is not a sufficient, but it is a necessary condition for the existence of class. The second condition to be introduced is the symbolic world within which a society interprets the categorical differences existing in a society. This second element is historically variable, and this is the reason why the idea of 'economically' determined classes is a culturally and historically specific interpretation of categorical differences among people.

[3] The environmental movement is a good example. Its universality consists of the plea for an integration of nature into society, for a gradual extension of rights of men to rights of nature. Its class character is grounded in the fact that environmentalist action will produce categories of people with gains (those with an interest in an ecologically modernized economy) and categories of people with losses (those who are excluded from nature as an aesthetically rewarding life-world). The environment is a field of class struggle as well as a field of demands for more political rights up to rights for animals or nature as a whole.

*Conceptual clarifications*

The question of whether social classes matter in the analysis of social movements cannot be answered without discussing the problems that underlie class analysis and movement analysis. Within class analysis there is the problem of whether classes, in the sense of shared characteristics of their social existence, still do exist, whereas within social movement analysis, the problem lies in whether movements can still be seen as mobilized classes in the sense of class-conscious historical actors. In taking the extremist versions of each, we have class analysis as an analysis of objective conditions of existence of social groups on the one hand, and movement analysis as an analysis of the collective and creative practices of groups of social actors on the other. How can both perspectives be brought together?

It could, for example, be asked to what extent social class is an independent variable that explains the rise and fall of social movements. Such a question presupposes that we have an idea of what a *class* is. We must define some criteria that constitute class as an independent variable. We could ask to what extent the concept of class can be applied to characterize specific social groups in modern societies, and we could then analyze the economic, political or cultural status of such groups.[4] Class is thus seen as external to the collective practice of social movement actors, and this is what makes it an independent variable in the explanation of mobilizing practices. Such a perspective also implies that we can define *social movements* as independent of class, and conceptualize them in terms of a theory of collective action. Social movements are defined as collective practices within which rational interests, norms and values determine the outcome of collective action. These criteria are not imposed as structural constraints upon action, but as options in the course of collective action.

The theoretical construction of the two variables leaves out, by the very conceptualization, the problem of their interrelationship. We could solve this question – as it is usually done – through methodological considerations of probability. For instance, we would ask how probable it is that indicators of class have to do with indicators of mobilization, and conclude some interrelationship between the phenomena observed from the probability of covariance. The question of whether mobilization can be attributed to class is thus resolved by looking at co-occurrences in space or time.

But such co-occurrences do not allow for a causal explanation. One of

---

[4] This also excludes that we reduce classes to groups sharing a specific 'habitus'. By defining classes in relational and not in substantial terms, we will be better equipped to see the antagonisms that separate social classes. Our theory, like that of Bourdieu, puts the emphasis on the difference between theoretical construction of class in terms of social antagonisms, and the empirical reality of class (Bourdieu 1987). However, it deviates from his proposition regarding the empirical indicators of class which in Bourdieu are ultimately identical with socio-psychological traits of status groups.

the reasons is simply that to the extent that a causal explanation would work, the grounds for further causality of the same set of conditions are destroyed. The idea of a structural determination of courses of action has a paradoxical effect: the more social structures produce courses of action that have effects upon structures, that even create structures, the less this structure has a determining effect. The paradoxical property of class theory is that its empirical realization destroys the conditions of its empirical adequacy. To resolve this paradox by simply giving up any structural analysis and explanation leads to an individualistic agency theory and to a return to the principles of methodological individualism. We will defend, in opposition to such reductionist strategies, a 'structuralist' theory of agency. The idea is that we must analyze collective action as a type of action whose collective nature is constituted by structural features of society. Class is such a feature. Collective action is embedded not only politically, but also socially. Therefore the general question is: *To what extent does collective action reproduce traditional forms of class conflict, and to what extent does collective action contribute to its reorganization and eventually to new forms of class conflict?*

This basic question allows us to differentiate between two types of effects that emerge in the interplay of class and collective action. The first effect is the traditional one of class 'determining' collective action. The second is the effect of collective action upon class. This latter effect is less visible because it only becomes manifest when (traditional!) class no longer has effects on collective action. If we show that the first effect does not exist, we are not yet allowed to conclude that class does not play a role. There is still the possibility that social movements give collective action a new meaning that not only manifests itself in, but even contributes to, the redefinition of the class structure and the traditional class conflict tied to it.

As long as we only look for an answer to the first part of the above question, we do not have to take into account the structural conditions of the 'creative' aspect of social movement analysis. But as soon as we do, a second structural feature has to be introduced: culture as the repertoire of making sense of collective action. In a historical situation where an old class structure loses its meaning for collective action, redefinitions of the social situation become a central part of movement action. Collective action has to make sense of itself, has to invent a meaning, but is restricted in such sense-making by the cultural repertoire of possible meanings. The first effect, as described above, works without culture; culture can be reduced to an ideology reproducing a given class structure. The second effect cannot be described without reference to culture. Our interest then shifts toward the possibilities contained in these new meanings of identifying and referring to a new class conflict beyond political or religious or cultural cleavages that abound in any society. Class, we conclude, matters in the study of social movements in two very different ways and it is the second effect that is our main concern. Therefore, we have to look at the 'new' cultural meanings ascribed to collective actions which lead to diverse

social conflicts, to 'mobilization' and 'countermobilization' outside traditional class relationship. Whether these new meanings dissolve it by
reducing it to mere political cleavages that can be handled by institutionalizing procedures of conflict resolution, is the subject matter of a
controversial debate. Our hypothesis is that the new social movements,
seen from the 'creative' side of collective action, create meanings that no
longer relate to traditional class conflict.

We take this theoretical proposition as a starting point to reinterpret the
link between class and movement. We conceptualize the 'creative' activity
in the new social movements as an interaction between action and culture
and will grapple the 'creative' character of collective action through
analyzing interests, norms and values that orient it. To include class as a
variable we postulate that there are different ways of relating movements
with social class: either class-character of collective action or cultural
definition of class relationships. The model for explaining these different
links of class and the generation and reproduction of movement mobilization can be represented as follows:

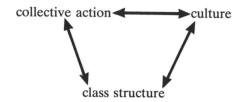

The theoretical implication for class theory is that class has two effects. It
has a determining effect which is the 'conservative' test of the role of class.
It has explanatory relevance and power because we claim that anchoring
protest practices in class-specific social positions allow for explaining the
specific strength and durability of these practices. The first effect of class
then is to serve as a 'social opportunity structure' for collective action. This
is what we described as the first type of relationship between class and
movement. However, the class structure is not invariant; it can be
redefined by collective action. This second effect implies that given class
structures no longer determine collective action and that culture can no
longer be reduced to a class-specific ideology. Collective action thus gains a
'creative' aspect. It creates an arena of social conflicts within which the
principles of separating and opposing classes of people are redefined. Our
model therefore contains a feedback loop within which culture works as
the mediating variable between collective action and class, allowing for a
dynamics of the class structure in the course of collective action itself.

From this arises a simple and basic question: do the social movements
produce practices and meanings of these practices that allow us to describe
them as part of a new class cleavage in modern societies? Or do these
practices produce meanings that can be dealt with within the system of
institutionalized dispute resolution? To test such a big question, two

general hypotheses can be formulated. The first is that the new social movements carry *identity projects* with them that cannot be made the object of political forms of conflict resolution. The second is that the new social movements are concerned with *issues that are non-negotiable* within existing institutional frameworks. These indicators provide a superb possibility to test the theory that the new social movements are forms of middle class radicalism and middle class protest. These theories contain assumptions about the class character of the new social movements that can be confronted with hypotheses developed within a non-historicist and formal theory of class. In the following we will show how a formal and non-historicist conception of class can shed light on the relationship between middle classes and social movements. The discussion will concentrate first on the problematic notion of a middle class in traditional class theory, and then discuss the history of middle class radicalism and contemporary middle class protest, relating them to their ambivalent class character.

## Social movements and the middle classes

### The middle classes and class theory

The traditional notion of class has been used to realize two different normative intentions. The first has been to identify those who are exploited as a class. Class in this sense has become nearly synonymous with exploitation.[5] The other normative interest has been the identification of the exploiters, of people who are in a structurally advantaged position or who possess direct personal power over others such as the capitalist class as the embodiment of the structurally advantaged. This class model has been generalized into a model of power. Classes are related to each other in terms of power or lack of it; the powerless are those who have no control of the material conditions of their existence; they are simply the poor people. On the other hand, we have classes of people with economic, social or even cultural power; the so-called 'new class'[6] is the embodiment of such political and cultural domination.

Between both normative motivations for identifying classes, there has

---

[5] This is basic to the Marxist conception of class, above all in its socialist variant. The Communist variant was oriented more toward the structural determination of the powerful (which by the way might explain the real effects of this type of thinking!).

[6] This generalized notion of class underlies the analyses of the poor as a powerless class (Piven and Cloward 1972). The interest in class as a power elite has been put forward by Mills (1956). There are also conservative versions of class as a power elite. Not only are the classic theories of dominant classes (Mosca and others) good examples, but so are the more recent theories on the 'new class' (Schelsky 1975; Gouldner 1979). For a good discussion of such assumptions see McAdams 1987.

never been a systematic place for the *middle classes*.[7] They simply could not mobilize theoretical attention except in derogatory formulas such as 'petit-bourgeois classes', 'labour aristocracy' or 'small property owners'.[8] There has been no normative concern to deal with these groups, who only posed difficulties for traditional class theories (which did not contribute to an adequate understanding of them). The first systematic concern has also been motivated by a negative experience: the role of the middle classes in the rise of fascism. It was only in the seventies that the middle classes again gained theoretical attention,[9] and this is the first time that they have been seen in a non-derogatory light – the reason is the role of the middle classes in the rise of what has been called the new social movements. The middle classes were seen as a social class that has become a historical actor, thereby developing a consciousness that had innovating effects upon society and significant effects upon the institutional framework of modern societies.[10] This explains the renaissance of an interest in the middle classes, which, of course, has given support to the assumption that lower class and its embeddedness in industrial class conflict can no longer serve as the model to understand the emerging middle class.

We will argue that the term 'middle class' makes sense historically within the context of a class relationship defined by the working class and the capitalist class.[11] Their intermediate position explains the specific reaction and movements of social groups that have not become a class. It is the exclusion from a class relationship, the non-class existence of the middle

---

[7] The middle classes are composed of at least three different groups: the old and new self-employed, the office employees and the new middle class (those working in the culture industry and in the health business). For this distinction see Bourdieu 1984. Data on the new self-employed (the least known among these three groups) are given by Steinmetz and Wright (1989). For data on Germany see Bögenhold 1985, and with a more historical perspective, Winkler 1983. For an empirical analysis of old and new middle class in Germany see Pappi 1981.

[8] These terms can already be found in Marx, where they also had a political function. This ideological and political loading is another indicator of the troubling effect these groups have had for the traditional class theory. A good overview over the discussion on the middle class with special reference to the new middle class is given by Burris (1986).

[9] This is due mainly to Bourdieu, whose work is sometimes seen as a treatise on the middle class. This is at least true for his most famous book *The Distinction* (Bourdieu 1984), even given the fact that he sticks to the traditional negative image of the middle class. The reference to a more positive view of middle class radicalism has played an important role within the discussion of the environmental movement and the peace movement. See Parkin (1968) as an early figure, as well as the work of Cotgrove and Duff (1980, 1981), Kann (1986), Brand (1990) and Offe (1985c). See also on this the foregoing chapter.

[10] This 'new class' version of this hypothesis can be found in ideas expressed by Ehrenreich (1989). She argues that those who 'discover' other classes – professionals, media personnel, managers, and intellectuals – are a middle class with an enormous power over our culture and our very self-image as a people. Her analysis does not deal with class relations, but with the inner life of this class, with the class cues that make this class recognizable for its members.

[11] We speak of middle classes in spite of the fact that they are social groups defined by their exclusion from a class relationship. This is terminologically inconsequent, but we stick to it

classes, which proves to have explanatory power regarding collective action: middle class radicalism can be explained by its tendency to avoid being identified with the lower classes and their failure to become a dominant class. This situation of the middle classes, however, changes with the rise of the 'new' middle class. To clarify this new situation we will turn to the controversial assumption of the 'new middle class' as the class base of the 'new social movements'.

The concept of a 'new middle class' raises the problem of whether it can be seen in continuity or in discontinuity with the old middle classes. The central argument for discontinuity has been that the loss of a working class culture has led to a non-class culture of protest and private retreatism; there are two versions of this, one claiming the emergence of a universal mass culture, another claiming the emergence of cultural differences that dissolve culture into highly individualized cultures.[12] Both developments, contradictory as they are, have one thing in common: they deny the possibility of a culture that is related to class conflicts and class relationships as had been characteristic for the working class. The new middle class has – like its historical predecessor, the old middle class – developed its culture outside the dominating class relationship; the emergence of a new middle class dominated culture is in continuity with the history of middle class culture, with the petit-bourgeois habitus, as Bourdieu (1984) has called it.

However, we will modify the thesis of a cultural continuity in one respect and argue that with the new social movements the middle classes have become for the first time a constitutive element of an emerging new class structure. This presupposes the idea that class structure has changed. The 'old' class structure has excluded the middle classes systematically and viewed them as borderline groups. We see the new social movements as the mechanism creating a new class structure in modern societies, giving

because we have become used to describe these groups as middle classes. The use of the plural is thought to be sufficient to indicate the specific nature of the middle classes being a class.

[12] A sophisticated version of the latter explanation can be found in Pakulski 1990. He argues for a non-class interpretation using the concepts of 'generation', 'situs' and 'mobility' to account for the social basis of the new social movements. But such variables do not replace a class analysis; they simply indicate that there is a time dimension, an institutional dimension and a social dimension to the phenomenon of new social movements. Not every generation is equally affected and this therefore points to historical conjunctures. Not every autonomous situs in an institutional environment leads to mobilization; the *rentier* class of the nineteenth and early twentieth centuries lived without being mobilized in their institutional niches. And mobility toward the city does not necessarily lead to movement action; deviant action is obviously a functional equivalent. The interesting question is under what conditions such factors really lead to movement action. The claim is that these conditions have to do with their role and function within class relationships.

these middle classes a central role in the restructuring of class relationships in modern societies.

## A historical perspective on the middle classes

Since the beginning of modern society, the middle classes have played a decisive role in political and cultural modernization. The carriers of the enlightenment have been teachers, intellectuals, and functionaries, grouped into associations (egalitarian groups opposed to the traditional form of corporations that were hierarchically organized and a central part of the Old Regime) against absolutist rule. Often described as a bourgeois class, these social categories never gained real economic, social and political power. They were powerless people, but conscious of their powerlessness and able to use it to change the traditional world.

The mobilization of this group in the nineteenth century (the petit-bourgeois radicals of the Revolutions in the thirties and the fifties of the nineteenth century) have been the object of both ideological attacks by Marx as well as real attacks by the established authorities. These radicals used strategies of mobilization ranging from pragmatic political mobilization for party politics to terrorism. In social-structural terms this group has not been very numerous, but it has had key roles in the social structure in that it belonged to those who controlled the flow of everyday communication in society. Merchants and artisans offered social settings where people met and exchanged ideas. Teachers and functionaries whose socializing function is constitutive of their professional role had everyday contact with people.[13] Structurally, the middle classes have been defined by their structural location in the service sector. This sector has increased since then, to include the non-proletarianized craftsmen and tradesmen, the emerging white-collar groups since the beginning of the twentieth century and ultimately professional groups in the social service industries that have increased in number over the last four decades.[14]

The development of the middle classes as a culture shows, however, an erratic profile. These groups have been defined in recent discussions as sharing the habitus of the 'petit bourgeois'. This label originally referred more to the culture of small property owners (in opposition to the large property holders, the capitalists and traditional land-owning classes) than to their exact class position. This term, originally restricted to small

---

[13] This phenomenon is extensively treated in Eder 1985. The literature on the emerging public space in the late eighteenth and nineteenth centuries is pertinent here.

[14] This has been the object of studies of an emerging service sector and even service class society. The discussion ranges from Touraine 1969 to Gershuny 1978, 1983, and – summarizing German data – Mutz 1987. For an analysis of the service sector proletariat see also Blossfeld et al. 1991 and Esping-Andersen 1992.

property owners (craftsmen and tradesmen), has been extended to other non-production groups, and ultimately to middle class groups in general. Between the World Wars these groups had been described as a class based on conspicuous consumption[15] and as being politically reactionary.[16] They were held responsible for the rise of fascism. There is controversial literature on the question of to what extent fascism was a mobilization of middle classes and a manifestation of middle class culture.[17]

It suffices to note that, regarding the term 'middle classes', we have definitions which signal the non-classifiability of these groups within the class relationship tied to the industrial capitalist society, and that we must, as concerns the petit-bourgeois character of these groups, attribute characteristics tied to this specific structural location between social classes. This analysis has made it abundantly clear that they are alien to traditional class theory. Moreover, this discussion shows that the description of the middle classes in class terms contains a fundamental ambivalence. There is no consensus in the discussion of whether the middle classes should be seen as a dominating or a dominated class. Interpretations on the new middle class diverge radically: for some they are the new proletariat, for others a new dominating class.[18] This basic ambivalence is not due to a bad theory, but to the phenomenon itself. Instead of motivating us to give up the use of class as an explanatory concept, we claim that both conceptualizations are correct. The middle classes are made up – *within* the traditional class structure – of both dominant and dominated classes; they contain in themselves relationships of domination as a latent social relationship. The theoretical ambivalence can be taken as an indicator of an unresolved puzzle, the puzzle being that the theoretical construction of middle classes tries to assimilate the phenomenon of the

---

[15] See, for example, Kracauer 1985. Similar arguments can be found in Lederer 1912, 1979 and Dreyfuss 1933.

[16] See Winkler (1971, 1978, 1979), who has done extensive research on these groups. He argues that this group has become – at least in Germany – the carrier of what has been called the 'refeudalization' of the bourgeois classes that explains their specific social and political habitus. Countervailing tendencies, having to do with processes of trade unionization, are analyzed by Prinz (1981) and Kocka and Prinz (1983).

[17] This argument has been put forward by Speier (1977) and by Hamilton (1982). This thesis has been heavily criticized by Falter (1982, 1984).

[18] The new middle class is often regarded as a new technological and cultural elite because of its greater conceptual ability, better knowledge, and increased opportunity to become involved in politics (Baker et al. 1981, pp. 10–11; Alber 1985). Lipset (1988) also argues in favour of the latter. For more sweeping claims see Schelsky 1975, Gouldner 1979 and Konrad and Szelenyi 1979. A well-argued point in favour of such a position is found in Lash and Urry 1987, pp. 161ff. See also Abercrombie and Urry 1988 and Carter 1985. For the alternative interpretation referring to a new service proletariat see Esping-Andersen 1992.

middle classes to the model of class characteristic of traditional class relationships.[19]

Today, it is necessary to change our perception of the middle classes because of two reasons: first, it is no longer possible to use a model of class analysis where the majority of the population falls in between the classes[20] – this obviously undermines the relevance of the traditional class structure; second, the middle classes have become the most dynamic element in the modernization of modern society – they have proved to be an important carrier of collective mobilization, thereby fulfilling a social role ascribed to the lower classes by traditional theory. Both reasons leave us with two options: either give up class-theoretical explanations, or revise the class-theoretical approach. Our proposal is a 'revisionist' one: to take into account the change in modern society that has shifted the locus of class relationships from industrial relations to other fields.

To argue in favour of such a case we will have a closer look at the 'new' middle class. We suspect that the new middle class has attracted attention primarily not because of its class location, but because of its specific culture. We see in this predominance of cultural analysis an implicit way of dealing with what we have called the creative effect of culture upon class. But the middle classes, neither socially anchored within class relationships nor within a culture of universal inclusion (a civil society), have so far been unsuccessful in defining their role and their identity in these terms. Their culture has been one of permanent failure. They failed when engaging in the conflicts over universal inclusion, and when joining class conflicts, they ended up on the side of the dominant class.[21]

However, the history of the middle classes can also be read as an attempt to create arenas where new forms of universal inclusion and new forms of class relationships are being constructed. Re-reading the history of the

---

[19] The term 'middle class' is already revealing: it implies the attempt to find a location for social groups in a class relationship which is no location at all. The paradox that is produced by the term 'middle class' is that there are classes and that there are groups that are not part of the class relationship defined by these classes and at the same time defined in terms of exactly this relationship. Important in this context is the Marxist discussion on middle classes. See Bechhofer et al. 1978; Bechhofer and Elliott 1981, 1985. For a critique see Goldthorpe 1978. Further accounts in a Marxist framework are found in Burris 1980; Wright 1985, 1986, 1990; Johnson 1982; Abercrombie and Urry 1988.

[20] Hamilton and Wright even simply talk of the 'masses' (Hamilton and Wright 1986). For the vagaries of the discourse on the middle class in America see DeMott 1990.

[21] Especially in this respect, the middle classes have not only failed, they contributed to the modern pathology of universalism. Being the carrier of modern forms of anti-universalist forms of citizenship (i.e. nationalistic, populist or even racist forms) they blocked themselves from becoming a historical force in realizing a civil society. This experience seems to find a repetition in the actual mobilization of the middle classes in Eastern Europe!

middle classes in this way finds its rationale in the phenomenon of the 'new middle class'. This class, joining the social and cultural history of the middle classes, can be perceived as a key to new forms of universal inclusion of differences and to new forms of class conflicts arising in postindustrial societies. It is from the perspective of the new middle class that we can interpret the history of the middle class as a failure in the attempt to define its own meaning. It is from this perspective that we can identify the two basic problems confronting postindustrial societies: the inclusion of cultural differences into a universalistic political and social order (in a democratically organized civil society), and the fundamental conflict between economy and ecology that points toward a new field of class conflict beyond industrial relations as the field of class conflict.[22]

The historical analysis of the middle classes lays the ground for a discussion on the changes that have been brought about by the emergence of the new middle class and by the mobilization of the new middle class in the new social movements. However, it has left out a systematic methodological questioning. The advancement of a revised theory of class in general, and of the middle class in particular, obviously forces us to avoid the methodological procedure generally used to prove a class base in social movements. Therefore it is imperative to lay some methodological ground for the theory to advance.

## Operationalizing class

In the search for measures of a class base, some researchers have resorted to analyzing the social composition of the activists of a given movement. These researchers have literally taken the idea that a class consists of activists. The same strategy has been followed regarding the social composition of supporters (defined in terms of identifying with goals taken up by a movement), but neither are indicators of a class character of mobilizations. What would happen if we applied this argument to the working class? Labour activists or supporters of the labour movement would have become the criterion of the existence of a working class. It is obvious: there is much more to the labour movement than its activists or its supporters. They are – and this is the systematic place of such analyses – parts of what has been called the 'social opportunity structure' for the

---

[22] An interesting approach for identifying such basic conflicts in and beyond the classic conflict between capital and labour can be found in O'Connor 1990. He argues in a basically Marxist framework to extend the idea of contradictions of capitalism, adding to the classic first contradiction a second and third which are meant to account for new social movements in relation to the state. Given the preliminary nature of such ideas, it still remains to be seen whether the argument for an emerging new class relationship and the theoretical notion of a second and third contradiction of capitalism can be integrated at some point in the future.

making of a class. They tell where the people who engage in protest action come from, but they do not tell why the actions of these people should be regarded as being an element of class. One's class origin is no guarantee that one's action is class action.

A second step in the analysis would be to investigate more intensely the dimensions of the protest culture emerging among mobilized middle class people. Shared symbolic properties add to the social-structural characteristics the dimension of a cultural unity of middle class radicalism. This is not yet a measure of class; it allows, however, the addition of a second series of necessary conditions for class to emerge.[23] The criterion is a certain cultural unity emerging from collective action that can be generalized across and beyond mobilized groups. Within the classic Marxian and Weberian perspective, such shared characteristics can be divided into *interests*, *norms* and *values*.

Shared interests are an elementary definitional criterion of movement culture. This criterion is itself variable, depending upon interpretations of what one's interests are. Historically, the interests of the proletarians shared the frame of injustice,[24] and within these frames they have been able to define their interests. Whether this frame is universal is an open question (except for hard-core rational-choice theorists). Given the dominance of the injustice frame, at least for modern Western societies up to the present, we can define shared interests as the calculation that we get less than we should. This frame has been dominant so far in the transition from traditional to modern society and modernization.[25]

Shared norms are a second aspect of a movement culture. Thus the definitional criterion of class becomes dependent upon given institutional frameworks. This applies to notions of 'blue' and 'white' collar, which is primarily a legal definition. Norms differentiate between different types of citizens and create a sense of community based upon norms which define a citizen's status. Such normative definitions do not necessarily coincide with the criterion of shared interests. But the normative definition of what belongs together has certainly an effect of creating a wider circle of cultural

---

[23] They, by the way, also allow to embed group formation in a cultural history. This is important in the case of middle class radicalism that can only be understood within historical contexts.

[24] Here the much neglected historical work of Moore (1978) on injustice frames as a basis of disobedience and revolt is pertinent.

[25] This does not mean that further modernization will still rely upon such interest. At least the ecological discussion, for example, raises doubts concerning the continuing dominance of this interest. For the classic discussion see Hirschman 1977, 1982. A revival of these discussions takes place in what has been called 'Analytical Marxism' (Roemer 1986). The point throughout these discussions remains the same: interests play an important role, but without contextualizing interests in norms and values, they do not work. For a plea to introduce norms in an interest-based theoretical framework see Elster 1989. For an analogous attempt to do so with values see Hechter 1989, 1990, 1991.

belonging, thus transforming the culture of protest into a more encompassing group culture.[26]

A third mechanism for transforming and normalizing a movement
culture is shared values. This has been the object of the 'social psychology
of class' and has been used in traditional stratification research to prove
and disprove the existence of classes in terms of shared values.[27] This
criterion again measures to what degree people have been socialized into a
culture, something that is not necessarily an aspect of class. It gives us
information about the degree to which people classify in evaluative terms
social reality and in which they are capable of giving answers within this
classification system. Thus we may get data on classes of people that might
crosscut important cleavages; we are ultimately left with an indicator of the
degree to which society is integrated on the level of value orientations.

Attempts to construct a notion of class simply by adding the social-
structural and cultural dimension of constituting social groups of actors
have proven to be meaningless. The procedure of looking for correlations
between occupational positions and attitudes, of correlating the new a-
rational, non-rational or neo-rational forms of life to traditional class
differences (mainly measured by father's occupation) does not measure
what it is supposed to, which is class. In order to identify the effects of
emerging protest cultures on redefining the field of class conflict, we have
to define class in a way that goes beyond demographic and cultural
criteria.[28] Thus one of the difficulties in operationalizing the relationship
between movement and class is methodological: the procedure chosen for
its proof can easily be made representative and reliable, but it is not
necessarily valid. It measures the extent to which this culture is able to

[26] We avoid 'term' of class in this context which is reserved to a level of analysis beyond real
groups of people. But in the literature the term 'class' is loosely used. The institutional
definitions discussed above have normally discussed in the context of class (see the
contributions in Clegg 1989). An interesting example of the role of institutional norms in
defining occupational groups as a class is the study of the formation of the 'cadres' in France
(Boltanski 1982). An application of normative regulations of citizenship and its effects upon
the differentiation of 'classes' of citizens can be found in Lockwood 1987.

[27] The classic piece of work is that of Centers (1949), who discussed class in terms of
attitudes and value orientations. Values have become prominent in sociology during the
dominance of Parsonian sociology. See as an important work in this tradition Kluckhohn and
Strodtbeck 1961. Since then it has only been with Inglehart (1977, 1990a) that the role of
values has received renewed attention. See also the negative answer to the question 'Should
values be written out of the social scientists' lexicon?' given by Hechter (1991).

[28] The demographic reduction of the concept of class is characteristic for most stratification
and mobility research. For a recent discussion on the role of class theory in quantitative
stratification research, see Sørensen (1991). He maintains that we do not need class theory in
order to explain inequality in the labour market or income differences. Such an irrelevance
would even support our claim for a class-theoretical perspective. Class theory is not a theory
of the working of the labour market, but of the social construction of conflictual fields of
action. The argument in the following will be that the demographic dimensions are presocial
categories, that occupation, educational level, household characteristics gain their structuring
force not in themselves, but by the meaning given to them by the actors, the institutions and
the existing culture.

extend to other classes. This turns the way of measuring class action upside down: what has been taken as manifesting class is nothing more than a measure of the degree to which a class culture can produce the image of its classlessness. Sociology has the task of showing the limits of the imperialism of class cultures, whatever they are (including the revived rational working class and labour movements culture). How then to prove the existence of a class? What are the data necessary for such proof?

The types of data needed are, firstly, on the social opportunity structure for collective action. This opportunity structure is defined by the social-structural effects of traditional forms of class conflict; they are those of industrial society. This justifies the use of occupational statistics and demographic data for describing the 'reservoir' on which collective mobilization draws. This is the legitimate place of social-structural analysis in social movement research – but it should not replace a class analysis of social movements which is something different. Secondly, we need data on the cultural orientations of mobilized groups which can show their continuity with specific interests, normative belief systems and value orientations. But we should not rely in this respect solely upon survey data. Since culture has a textual nature, we should take texts more seriously. Literary texts are a first approximation, but nothing more. Analyzing interviews as texts and not as a list of words that indicate answers is a further step. We don't need simply the opinion of actors – we need data on the semantic space within which actors locate themselves. Opinion research barely fulfils this need. Such data could provide the cultural links with traditional classes (as is implied in the theory of middle class radicalism). This second type of data already broadens the social space within which we locate movement events. It is a second step toward a class analysis of social movements.

Class analysis itself requires a different methodological, mainly reconstructive, strategy. As such, it is dependent upon the character and quality of the data gathered in the first two steps. It implies performing a structural analysis of cultural data in the sense of identifying mutually exclusive ways of defining social reality. It is only through such a structural analysis that the possible field of class conflict can be identified. This ultimate step is to find out to what extent traditional categories of people can be reclassified in such a way that they can be grouped around cultural dichotomies at stake in collective mobilizations. As far as we succeed in regrouping traditional categories of people in a way consistent with the cultural definitions of the issues at stake we succeed in identifying a real class that fits our theoretical construction of class derived from the cultural definitions of the situation. Class analysis is – contrary to the inflationary use of the term 'class' in theory and research – a methodology that has still to be developed.

Methodological problems can only be solved by applying theories. Therefore, we will propose a framework that lays the ground for an explanation of the new social movements in terms of a class theory within which the middle class has taken over the role the working class had in the class theory of industrial society, namely to define the field of class conflict the new middle class is engaged in.

## A theory of the new middle class radicalism

### A theoretical construction of the new middle class

The theory of class upon which we will base our theory of middle class radicalism is basically a constructivist version of class theory.[29] This constructivism presupposes two elements: *agency* and *context* within which and upon which agency is situated. There is a third element, the *structural outcome* of acting within and upon a culturally defined situation, which ranges from the internalization of conflict into the subject through the institutionalization of social and political cleavages to class conflict. This third element is the variable that must still be explained.

Agency has to do with the capacity of social groups to define and redefine the interests, norms and values that separate themselves beyond demographic differentiation from other social groups. We locate agency in the specific capacity to generate – through collective mobilization – collective definitions of interests, norms and values. Every mobilization has or creates its own culture. This creativity is, on the other hand, limited by the cultural resources that can be mobilized in collective action. Agency is thus intricately related to the cultural space that it creates and draws upon in order to constitute and reproduce itself as a collective capacity for action.

However, the way in which social movement research has treated the relationship between culture and mobilization, has until now remained rather unsystematic. The culture of mobilization has been analyzed by using middle range theories of mass psychology, relative deprivation or resource mobilization to account for collective mobilization.[30] Grand theory has taken whatever fashionable thesis there has been to expand

[29] This theory is opposed to the one that views the problem of social order as the basic problem of a theory of society. This does not imply that the problem of social order is irrelevant; it only states that it is a secondary problem arising out the capacity to act upon existing social orders. These orders are even defined in different ways: as equilibria of interests, normative orders or orders based upon shared values. The sociological tradition did not agree which one was the central aspect of social order. We simply see this as three different ways of creating social order, which implies that the theory has to explain why actors choose one of them. Therefore a theoretical primacy of the problem of agency is over the problem of order. This argument can draw upon theoretical arguments put forward, for example, by Giddens (1973, 1987) and Touraine (1981).

[30] For an overview see Chapter 3. With regard to mass psychology see Moscovici 1985, with regard to relative deprivation Gurr 1970; with regard to resource mobilization Zald and McCarthy 1979, 1987.

sweeping generalizations about the culture that underlies mobilization in social movements: postmaterialism, life-world colonization, individualization, and the emergence of a new risk culture are examples of such approaches.[31] These theories assume that the culture they measure in different ways is already given. Postmaterialism, for example, has been explicit on this assumption. Life-world theories assume some communitarian mode of existence prior to society. Individualization theories assume a modern culture of individualism as a general cultural orientation in modern societies. Risk culture approaches define the cultural world in a series of distinct but universal modes of cultural experience of risk. Rational-choice theories simply presuppose a shared culture of interests, norms and values, within which collective actors behave on the basis of calculating their available resources and the possible gains to be made given their 'preference structure".[32]

In opposition to such approaches, the construction of such cultures in the process of collective action has to be stressed which reduces these theories to mere hypotheses on alternative organizing principles of emerging cultures of mobilization.[33] The counterproductive effect of such theorizing is that the distinctive feature of the new social movements and its creative aspect, such as the rise of counterculture and alternative forms of life-forms and associations, does not figure in such accounts. The problem of agency has barely been considered.

The second element engages the context, i.e. the arena of social conflicts in which new social movements situate themselves. These are first of all cultural movements which transcend the field of industrial relations. The terms used to define the new field of social conflicts are: identity,

---

[31] In particular, reference is made to Inglehart 1977, 1990a; Habermas 1984, 1987; Beck 1992; Thompson et al. 1990.

[32] This idea has been taken up to reformulate the old theory of class relations in a new conceptual scheme. The work of the 'Analytical Marxists' is central here; see Roemer 1982, 1986 and Elster 1982, 1985b. The differential rationalist logic underlying the industrial class conflict has been shown very well in terms of the 'two logics' of collective action representing the two traditional classes; see Offe and Wiesenthal 1980. The paradoxical effect is that as soon as we argue in game-theoretic terms, the traditional image of class relations reappears; this theory makes sense of class relations characteristic of industrial relations which points to an implicit culture contained even in such 'culture-free' theories.

[33] A further problem has to do with the methodological individualism underlying survey research on collective beliefs and opinions. Methodological individualism gives people equal status: everybody has an opinion (with some marginal cases who never have an opinion) and it is enough to look at the distribution of such opinions. Everybody has resources (to have an opinion is just one of them) in order to indicate differences and even changes in culture. Postmaterialist values can be combined with old and new values in different ways, but they do not necessarily co-vary with ecological concerns; they have different impacts upon the capacity and potential of collective action, depending upon their action-relevance which can vary considerably. Thus we only have indicators that need extensive interpretation in order to be relevant for explaining cultures of mobilization.

expressivity, and the good life.[34] Defining the field of agency in this way implies types and rationalities of action beyond the utilitarian calculus constitutive of the model of industrial relations and industrial class conflict.

Defining a new field of social conflict does not necessarily imply that this field is no longer connected to possible class conflict and thus to a new type of class structure. This conclusion has dominated the theoretical idea of 'individualization' in modern societies. The alternative is to look at the new boundaries created in the process of individualization. Contrary to the image of a society of highly individualized people distinct from each other and engaged in marking such distinctions, we will defend the image of a society organized around the attempt to reestablish such a society that no longer uses exclusion from the means of production as the dichotomizing criterion. The social dichotomy that is invented and ultimately defended is one in which the exclusion from a society allowing for identity and expressive individualism is the dominant criterion. The culture of the new social movements contains an element of dichotomizing social reality, namely the idea of *exclusion from the social means of realizing identity*.

We can now specify our explanatory goal: does the mobilization of a new protest culture beyond the industrial protest culture have an effect upon the class structure? We can also specify a basic assumption of our theory, which is that the people in different social classes who are mobilized into social movements (as activists), or who identify at least with the goals of social movements (as bystanders), do so because they identify with cultural values and not because they experience a class-specific powerlessness (be it in economic, political or cultural terms). The mobilization mechanism appears not in response to class differentiation and class emulation but in response to the desire to take action on matters that are of concern to people. In doing so, such action creates a sense of collective identity between social groups. It defines who belongs to the action and its goals and who doesn't. In so far as such a setting of boundaries, such a creation of a collective identity can be related to social positions (to 'status', be they occupational, educational or political), this will change the class structure, both in its differentiation and in the forms of class emulation. Thus, the answer to our question will be: that classes do matter in the study of social movements, not only as causes of mobilization, but also as its effects. Social movements also create class relations. Class is not a social fact, but is – beyond being a theoretical construction – a social construction. This forces the abandonment of any idea of a natural existence of class. There is no lower, middle, and dominant class as such.

---

[34] The return of the problem of identity in the modern public discourse and its role in shaping social relationship are already proof of the power that such elements have upon society. It is also a signal that the traditional class relations no longer play an important role in the struggles characterizing modern societies. The shift in sociological theory towards the symbolic realm, towards a dramaturgical notion of social action is also significant. See for an example Gusfield's introduction to the work of Kenneth Burke (Burke 1990).

This constructivist approach to class, however, has limits which are set by the 'social opportunity structure' of advanced modern societies. Social opportunity structure is understood to be the social-structural processes (occupational differentiation, educational differentiation, income differentiation, life-style differentiation etc.) that open up the social space for class differentiation and class relations. The capacity of the new middle class to redefine the field of class conflict is dependent upon the objective situation of this middle class in terms of occupation and educational attainment. Countervailing processes on the level of institutions also have to be taken into account. The theory of the institutionalization of class conflict argues that institutions, above all institutionalized political regulation, define the boundaries between classes and shape class relationship. This theory has been especially successful regarding the institutionalization of industrial class conflict in modern Western societies. Whether it has an explanatory value regarding a postindustrial class conflict has to be seen. The conditions that limit the effectiveness of collective action have to be integrated as contextual conditions into the theoretical framework. Our theory nevertheless states that the mobilization of collective action is the basic mechanism that changes the boundaries between classes and shapes class relationships.[35] This theory will serve us in the following to reformulate the theory of middle class radicalism and to transform it into a new theory of the 'new social movements'.

### New social movements and the contemporary middle classes

The new middle classes of advanced modern societies have been labelled – and there is a political intention behind it – as manifesting a 'petit-bourgeois habitus' (Bourdieu 1984).[36] Our assumption is that they are more than that. They are the most visible part of an emerging new type of class antagonism centred on issues beyond exploitation and injustice. This leads to the following questions: Are the new social movements capable of making their cultural orientations the basis for a new class conflict? Or are they groups defined by ascriptive criteria which contribute to a cycle of protest in the history of modern middle class protest? We would like to follow the former explanatory strategy and argue that contemporary middle class radicalism is not a manifestation of cycles of protest, but a moment in the making of a new class relationship for the analysis of which the 'middle' class is the key.

Arguments in favour of a cyclical interpretation have been used in recent analyses of demographic changes in the population at stake in social

---

[35] Touraine (1985) sometimes argues in a way that comes close to such a theory, but he remains basically unclear about the status of class theory within his action theory.

[36] This is a recapitulation of a thesis formulated by Lederer in 1913! See Lederer 1979.

movement mobilization during the last two decades.[37] The argument is that the return to demographic normality, i.e. to 'normal' social stratification after the initial levelling effects of educational expansion since the seventies, will lead to a cultural normality in the sense of a return to a normal level of protest in society, a lessening of unconventional forms of political behaviour and a lessening of hedonist life-forms. Our argument against theories that deduce cultural cycles from demographic ones will be based on the distinction between 'triggering causes' and 'structural effects' of such demographic changes in the mobilization potential for protest behaviour. With regard to the triggering causes, we will take up the argument that the post-war generation is transitory with respect to its social structural characteristics: it experienced the reorganization of social differences in the social structure due to educational expansion, postponement of marriage decisions, and new life-course patterns. It is also taken for granted that we arrive at a situation where a reequilibration of social structure along the lines of traditional forms of inequality has taken place. Social structure has become 'normalized'. The generation following the protest generation will live again within a system characterized by modern stratification patterns; the difference between the lower, middle and upper classes will again become normal forms of modern social life (except for one factor, namely migration, that cannot be calculated regarding its effects upon social structure). We thus accept the argument that mobilization was tied to this 'exceptional' generation, but add the qualifying remark that this exceptionality has had a triggering effect for mobilization. As soon as this effect has been triggered, the consequences become independent of the causes.[38]

Against the methodologically sophisticated but theoretically mechanical interpretation which affirms that the movements will rise and fall with the social-structural reshuffling of these groups, a socio-cultural interpretation

[37] For such arguments see, among many others, Bürklin 1984, 1987, and recently Blossfeld 1990; Blossfeld et al. 1991. Bürklin has consequently turned to cyclical theories to explain the rise and fall of mobilization and protest assuming a latent stability of institutions over the vicissitudes of protest. Blossfeld radicalizes this approach by assuming a latent conservatism in social structure and social stratification, which takes protest as manifestations of a reequilibration of social structures, as a transitory phenomenon in the self-organization of social structures.

[38] This again points to the self-defeating types of class analysis that have been used in the discussion on class and social movements. They adhere to a deterministic idea of class which negates emergent socio-cultural properties coming out of the relations between classes by redefining the interests, norms and values which are at stake. It is obvious that a reductionist sociology, explaining social phenomena by their social-structural and even demographic characteristics, has had no problems in pointing out the lack of complexity of traditional class theory. See the revealing article by Sørensen (1991) in this context. These emergent effects, we will claim below, can be accounted for within a class-theoretical framework that defines classes as collective actors creating arenas for social struggles and contributing to class differentiation along lines that are different from those dominating in industrial society so far.

would argue that this generation succeeded in freeing traditional middle class cultures from their historical cultural bonds, cultural cage, and traditional ideological dependence upon the state. The exceptional generation of the sixties and seventies has been the promoter of a change in the culture of middle class groups, creating the 'new social movement culture' which has entered economic, political and cultural, and even religious life. This cultural effect can be traced back to a demographically atypical generation. But this atypicality does not explain why this generation produced the cultural effects it had. This has to do with the specific culture created in the mobilization of these structurally defined groups.

We see two main implications of this effect. First, the new social movements have reshaped the institutional system of modern societies.[39] They have – at least partially – introduced additional dimensions of political cleavages. Second, they are drawing new social boundaries in modern societies, thereby redefining the old class relations. The role of the new social movements for the process of democratization, and the intended as well as unintended consequences, have been the object of extensive discussion.[40] But the question as to what extent the culture of the new social movements has succeeded in redrawing not only political but also social boundaries in modern societies, has not been seriously addressed. The question itself and its theoretical fundament have already been laid a long time ago in the seminal work of Touraine.

Touraine's hypothesis is that the new social movements no longer identify with natural forces but with social forces (Touraine 1981). Traditionally, the working class has been tied to natural forces, the forces of production. The idea of the working class therefore carried within itself a fundamental ambivalence: it was at the same time a natural as well as a social phenomenon. The concept of class inherited from this tradition is a concept suited to a society that is itself still bound to naturalized forms. Defining modernity as denaturalization of social reality, industrial society appears as a 'semi-modern' society. Dissolving the naturalized view of social reality means realizing modernity. The theoretical critique of Historical Materialism as a naturalistic theory of society is an indicator of this 'modernization'. The new social movements are its concrete social indicator, and their common denominator is that they distance themselves from the naturalism underlying the world of the labour movement and

---

[39] I refrain from ascribing them a historical role. The effect is a change in the traditional political structures and institutional procedures of decision-making that as a result of the class compromise with the working class have dominated modern societies so far. This institutional system is put into question, and we have to analyze the ways this reorganization is going to be effected.

[40] The discussion on the new social movements is mainly centred – implicitly and even explicitly – on this question, from Habermas (1984, 1987) and Touraine (1985) to the more empirically oriented movement research (Rucht 1991).

the working class.[41] The denaturalization of the semi-modern industrial society forces us to define the arena and object of social conflicts and the classes of actors involved in a way that is not naturalistic but genuinely social. This means that the field of class conflict is not a given, but is itself produced in social practices, and that the collective actors involved are not predefined collectives (which is implied in the idea of a class 'in itself'), but are constituting themselves as a class through their collective action.

Regarding the first aspect, the social definition of the field of class conflict, the new social movements have contributed to its genuinely *social* definition. They have transformed the field of class conflict into 'arenas' that are created by these movements through their action. The concept of an 'arena' indicates the shift of emphasis away from a historically (and even world-historically) given field of class conflict to fluid arenas of social conflicts.[42] Regarding the second aspect, the notion of class, these new social movements no longer refer to class as defining their collective identity. Collective identity is sought outside prefabricated patterns of identity that have been carried within the semi-modern notion of class. Therefore we can no longer use the traditional model of class and class conflict with regard to the new social movements. Does it then still make sense to talk about a middle class basis of the new social movements?

We claim that it does. The concept of the middle class is an ideal case to study the modernization of collective action taking place in the context of the evolution of the labour movement and the rise of the new social movements. It allows us to develop a systematic critique of the concept of class and of its naturalization in the Marxist and socialist tradition. As soon as we conceive of class in a non-naturalistic way, we have to define class independently of naturalistic criteria. This will lead us in the following neither to the reduction of the class concept to a compound demographic variable, nor to its elimination. Instead, we will try to develop a concept of class that corresponds to a society that has crossed its semi-modern phase, and we will try to show that the concept of social movement is paramount to this endeavour.

---

[41] This, after all, remains the basic criterion of the 'newness' of the new social movements: that they conceive themselves as practices for which there exists no historical (= necessary = natural) reason to exist; rather, nature is seen as something to be created (or defended through practice). In this sense, the ecological movement is the most radical anti-naturalist movement that can be conceived of, for it takes nature not as a determinant of social action, but as a goal of action, which completely reverses the naturalism characteristic of the dominant social movements of the nineteenth and first half of the twentieth centuries. I developed this argument more fully in Eder 1988a.

[42] The increasing importance of 'public discourse' as a mechanism for creating such arenas is reflected in the turn that research in mass communication and public discourse analysis has taken in recent years. See as a prominent example the work of Gamson (1988, 1992) and Gamson and Modigliani (1987, 1989).

*A class-theoretical account of the new social movements*

The definition of a new conflictual field, centred on the social means of realizing identity, allows us to bring together two different phenomena: the 'new social movements' [43] and the 'new middle class'. [44] The conclusion that has been drawn from this coincidence is that the two are interrelated. But how do we explain this relationship? According to traditional class analysis we would simply check whether the 'members' (activists, supporters, protest voters etc.) of the new social movements are recruited from the new middle class (and/or other fractions of the middle class), defining middle class in terms of social-structural characteristics. [45] This explains why specific demographic processes (especially educational expansion and a changing occupational structure) provide opportunities for mobilization. But we can do equally well without the concept of class to explain such phenomena. We know that a social group, having had the experience of cultural upward mobility in terms of education and being active in the social service sector, is prone to more mobilization in this conflictual field. The discussion on middle class radicalism to which we refer demonstrates that there is a social opportunity structure for the 'making of a class'. These middle class groups are those engaged in qualified production and service occupations, i.e. those based on educational training which distinguishes them from the working class culture, and those who produce and reproduce the cultural resources in modern societies. Thus we have a first element in describing the making of a class (an element that has often been confused with class as such, leading to impressionistic conceptions of class).

A second element is the cultural space within which these groups of people make sense of themselves. Our historical analysis has shown that the history of the middle classes and their social-structural position between the working class and the capitalist class within the old class relationship have left in the middle classes the problem of *identity* as a

[43] This hypothesis has been defended by Cohen (1985), Offe (1985c) and most explicitly by Melucci (1985, 1988, 1989). See also the discussion in Olofsson (1988), who sees the new social movements as cultural movements; but he relativizes the role of these movements claiming that they are not – like the old movements – necessarily linked to societal changes. This latter argument allows for a 'weak' class-theoretical explanation.

[44] One of the interesting hypotheses is by Featherstone (1989), who argues that the new middle class has an effect on the rise of postmodernism. I put forward a similar argument regarding the new middle class intellectuals in Eder (1989). A general theory of middle class positions and middle class cultures is contained in Bourdieu 1984. The foregoing chapter is following this lead. See also Gans 1988 for an attempt to extend the idea of 'individualism' as a basic cultural orientation to the middle class as a whole.

[45] For such attempts see Bürklin 1984; Kriesi 1987; Hulsberg 1988. Kriesi (1989) argues in an empirical study of Dutch new social movements that the middle class is itself split, the most enthusiastic supporters being the younger generation of 'social and cultural specialists' which includes professionals and semiprofessionals in teaching, social and medical services, arts and journalism. For a sophisticated analysis on the basis of such a theory regarding the German case see Vester 1983, 1989.

central concern. Middle classes live with a traditional notion of a good life and of consensual social relations playing a prominent role. Thus we complement the idea of a social opportunity structure with the idea of a specific 'cultural opportunity structure'. Among the semantic resources available in this cultural opportunity structure, two concepts are of central importance: the concept of *good life* and the related ideas of community and life-world; and the concept of *consensual social relations* which has to be seen together with the concept of communication.

The first concept, good life, has been the quest of the middle classes for over a century. It is above all a religious notion: the good life is led by good people. Religious groups are based upon such goodness – and these religious notions have survived neither in the lower nor in the upper classes, making it a middle class phenomenon by elimination. The search by young people for alternatives to the greed and materialism and violence of the older generation is an expression of the inner dynamic of middle class culture that never escaped its search for the good life. Outrage against middle class values expressed itself in sexual freedom, opposition to the Vietnam war, etc. Today, middle classes are obsessed with personal aggrandizement, autonomy and competition. This is the cultural basis upon which new social movements were being built, and from which they drew their motivational and ideational sources.[46] The culture of good life is more than a philosophical idea: it is the expression of a class-specific life-form. We can apply such an idea to contemporary social protest and unrest relating mainly to environmental issues: environmental risks and damage are exactly those things that most threaten a good life because they threaten the physical and increasingly the psychic world.

The second concept, consensual social relations, fosters the idea of an authentic life-form where people interact as equals and free persons. Communication is a central feature of the middle class life-form. From didactic material (how to educate children) to personal affairs (how to solve conflicts with your partners) this culture of communication has started to serve as an integrating code of middle class culture.[47] The lower classes were traditionally and objectively bound to negate the primacy of communication (they just were not able to communicate the way the other classes could). The communication of the dominating classes on the other hand had to be exclusive (they therefore engaged in ritualized and specialized codes of communication). Risk communication seems to be the newest version of a rise of middle class culture in protest and collective

---

[46] There are two very different books relating to the same topic: Baritz 1989 and Bourdieu 1984.

[47] This holds true above all for the new middle class; but it is also an important aspect of the other middle class groups which use communicative competence to mark their difference from the lower classes. It has found a mirror in the classic social-scientific discussion on restricted and elaborated codes as underlying lower class and middle class life-forms.

mobilization.[48] It seems that all this has given to consensual social relations the role the early bourgeois ascribed to it 200 years ago.

But the theory, we propose, goes one step further by adding a third element beyond the social and the cultural opportunity structure. It claims that the new social movements contain more than specific social-structural and historical-cultural characteristics. Rather, it interprets these movements within the class structure of an emerging type of society. To the extent that class theory has been applied to these movements, it turns out to be an application that is dominated by the class model of the old industrial society. The 'orthodox' theory is to associate the new middle class to the traditional class relationship by extending the dominated class beyond the traditional working class. Then the new social movements are simply variations of the class conflict based 'ultimately' on the working class. The 'heterodox' theory is to define middle classes as falling outside of or in between social classes. Then these movements appear in a negative way; they are concerned with issues that are kept out of traditional class conflicts; they are concerned with non-class issues; instead of struggling for a share in societal resources, they 'defend' a life-world.[49] Against such orthodox and heterodox class theories of the new social movements we will propose the theory that the new middle class is an element of a new type of class relationship.

The above-mentioned theory argues that there is a new emerging class relationship which has its own and different logic. This argument does not deny the existence of non-class relationships outside these middle classes. Certainly, gender and ethnicity are alternative and competing forms of social relationships and social conflicts, but these are collectivities socially constructed on the basis of 'natural symbols'. Classes, on the contrary, exist as social facts, i.e. as collectivities socially constructed on the basis of socially defined symbols. This is the basic difference between class and any other criterion identifying collectivities. The middle classes are related to each other no longer by objective conditions of existence but by their collective practices to define a mode of social existence. The basic antagonism underlying this mode of existence is, as we argued above, the conflict over the means of an 'identitarian' existence. Furthermore, this conflict over the means of realizing an 'identitarian' existence does not resolve the question of what the identity is. The middle-class-specific form of experiencing and perceiving the world is – as has already been stated – characterized by using two key and favourite concepts: *good life* and

---

[48] Risk communication is intricately entwined in the culture of the middle classes. Historically seen, middle class life has been risky, because of the impact of the capitalist economy. Its alignment with the state has turned its sensitivity to problems of the life-world as such, above all in today's environmental risks.

[49] For 'heterodox' attempts to integrate the class perspective into a broader macro-sociological and socio-historical framework see Habermas (1987), Offe (1985b, 1985c), Luke (1989) and Brand (1990), who try to combine the 'European' type of explanation of new social movements with class analysis.

*consensual social relations*. Thus what gives the middle classes the status of a potential class is not their history, which ties them to an old class conflict, but their direct insertion into a new antagonistic social relationship which is defined by the control over the means of creating an identity, an identitarian life-form. This conflict has a class character because there is no other solution to this antagonism than by structural changes in the distribution of power. Because identity is a good that is indivisible, the conflict over identity cannot be litigated; the conflict is structurally inscribed into the problem and the groups involved in it.

Our theory thus consists of three elements. The first element is the social opportunity structure that has developed out of the class conflicts of the period preceding contemporary forms of mobilization and conflict. Within this social opportunity structure, the middle classes are defined merely by their specific location in traditional class relationships. This middle position continues to provide for a specific type of experiencing and perceiving the world that makes these groups prone to engage in issues beyond the traditional class issues. The second element is the cultural themes characteristic of the history of middle class radicalism that are intricately related to the social-structural location of the middle classes. The third – and decisive – element of our theory is to base a new class relationship on the criterion of the control of the means of an 'identitarian' social existence in the sense of guaranteeing identity and expressive social relations. These means of social existence are no longer described as means of production, but as means of cultural expression. Power differences refer to the way in which the chance of realizing identity is defined and its assets are unevenly distributed. These three elements have contributed to a form of mobilization that has succeeded in redefining social reality in dichotomic terms. This makes the middle class groups that have so far been defined as a problematic case in traditional class theory the unproblematic centre of a new class relationship. We have argued that the 'middle classes' are potential classes, and we must identify the specific conditions under which class will dominate the contemporary struggles over an identitarian existence.

### Social class does matter

Our original question can then be answered with a clear 'yes': social class does matter. Class is a social construction which puts together social categories in order to form a more encompassing whole. This presupposes a collective praxis. We have analyzed the praxis of the middle classes as such a collective and creative praxis and identified in it the social construction of the field of class conflict as well as the social construction of a collective identity as a social class beyond natural and naturalized determinants of social existence. Class therefore turned out to become the variable in need of explanation. The main result of our theory is thus a radical change in the research question. This question is: What are the

factors that contribute to the capacity of collective agency in order to
define their concerns in terms of structural conflicts or antagonisms? Here
we identified social-structural variables (the rise of middle class groups
within the traditional class structure) and cultural variables (a history of
middle class concerns as expressed in the diverse forms of middle class
radicalism). We ultimately added a third variable in order to distinguish
social conflicts and antagonisms that can become the field of class
relationships, and those that do not. The theoretical proposition is to
define as an element of a new emerging class relationship any conflict that
has to do with the exclusion from the means of an 'identitarian' social
existence. The new social movements concerned with the realization of an
'identitarian' existence are therefore those that foster the construction of
new class relationships. In this sense class does matter in the new social
movements.

The question of whether the new social movements cut across class lines
or whether they manifest new emerging class cleavages in advanced
industrial societies has led to the competing hypotheses of 'middle class
radicalism' versus 'individualized protest behaviour'. An analysis of the
history of petit-bourgeois radicalism allowed for the identification of some
developmental continuities with actual forms of protest. Additional variables are located in changes in social structure (in the emergence and
internal differentiation of the non-proletarian social groups). The argument for a class perspective has further been backed up by a methodological critique of the 'anti-class' literature on social movements, showing that
the anti-class assumption is the product of individualistic methodological
presuppositions in actual social movement research. The new social
movements are certainly not a class movement in the traditional
nineteenth-century sense. They can, however, be seen as a manifestation
of a new type of class relationship within which the 'making of the middle
class' in advanced modern societies takes place.

# CONCLUSION

# BEYOND TRADITIONAL CLASS THEORY

## 10

## FROM THE CRISIS OF CLASS POLITICS TO THE CRITIQUE OF CLASS POLITICS
### Reflecting the Role of 'Crisis Discourses' in Modern Society

**Situating the discourse on the crisis of class politics**

The concept of class is an eminent part of the history of the crisis discourse that modern society has produced about itself. Capital has been considered the foremost mechanism of the generation of developmental crises of modern society. Class has been seen as the remedy for this crisis through its capacity for collective action on society. The intimate connection of modernity with class in Marx's discourse on modern society led him to a sweeping theory on the course of modern society regarding its crisis-ridden form and its crisis resolution. Unlike traditional explanations, this theory no longer looked for something outside society to explain what happens within it. Instead, it 'internalized' the reasons for the production and reproduction of society into society. *Crisis* ensues when social changes lead to a situation where the capacity of a society to control the course and direction of its own development is blocked. Thus class can be perceived – together with capital – as a constitutive part of a genuinely *modern* discourse of society on itself. It has been mainly a discourse on the crises that pervade it.[1]

The idea of a crisis of class politics continues this discourse. The remedy for crisis is now itself in crisis. Society is blocking its capacity to act on itself. The discourse on crisis becomes one on the *self-blockage* of society, on the incapacity to act on its crises. It puts together the threads of *crisis*, *class* and *politics* in a new way. The connection between *class and crisis* is

---

[1] It belongs to the basic experience of early modern society to be born within and through a societal crisis. See for this link Koselleck 1973 and the discussion in note 18 below.

applied to class itself: class no longer is something outside the crisis of modern society, but part of and subject to its crisis; the connection of *crisis and politics* that has dominated much of class theory no longer holds. The discourse on a crisis of class politics claims there is a crisis because class and politics are decoupled, which erodes the capacity of classes to act on society and for society to overcome its endemic crises. The 'crisis of class politics' thus refers to the idea that the capacity of class-specific collective action is systematically restricted. It puts crisis into perspective as the result of the failure of classes to act as the carriers of the self-production of modern society.

The radicalization of the discourse on the crisis of class politics not only puts into question the political relevance of class, but also the social-structural relevance of class as a central feature of modern society. Then the crisis of class politics is interpreted as an interlude in the process leading to the *end of class politics*. This means not only accepting the argument that classes are no longer (if they have ever been) political actors, but also the argument that classes have disappeared as an organizing principle of social structure. Thus the crisis of class politics is ultimately an argument for proving that we enter a classless society.

As a substitute for class theory, social movement theory (especially the theory of the new social movements) stepped in, relating the phenomenon of new social movements to the crisis of 'fordism' or to the 'materialism' of capitalist societies and viewing them as carriers to 'postfordism' or 'postmaterialism'.[2] Such a linking of crisis and politics can be conceptualized as an alternative to class theory. Social movements are now seen as the actors destined to resolve the crises inherent in modern society.[3] Social movement theory therefore is to be explained as part of an attempt to fill the gap left by class politics. It is a way out of the crisis of class politics. However, as soon as social movements no longer dominate the political and ideological arena, even this substitute no longer works. The discourse on crisis could simply add another crisis: the crisis of the new social movements.[4]

This controversy over the character of the link between crisis, class, and

[2] The optimistic version, prevalent in the seventies and eighties, is that crisis can be solved by collective political action. I refer to Habermas and Touraine for such explanations. Apart from these normatively oriented approaches, the question often remains open as to whether social movements are conscious actors or functional mechanisms of such changes. This is the case in the argument of postfordism (Hirsch 1988) and of postmaterialism (Inglehart 1990b). The argument of postmodernism is even more radical. It argues for the end of social movements! It is obvious that in this case a functional explanation prevails.

[3] This is the basic thrust of the theory of social movements proposed by Touraine. See a very clear statement in Touraine 1992, where he defends this perspective even in times of a decline of social movements.

[4] Melucci (1984) has added a question mark to the formula of an 'end to social movements'. In the meantime, this end has become the focus of an extensive discussion that could be read as a new crisis discourse, this time on social movements. See as balanced statements, but with obvious implications, Oberschall 1978 and Zald 1988.

politics points to a pertinent element in the discussion: the role of discourse on the crisis of class politics as a part of the never-ending discourse on crisis in modern society. But how to end the inflationary use of such crisis discourses? The problem that all these discourses address is the problem of collective political action in modern societies. What varies is the type of crisis discourse that accompanies historical forms of collective political action in modern societies. Instead of continuing this theorizing the crisis discourses become the object of social-science discourse. This will separate the close relationship between crisis discourse and social-science discourse and lead to an analysis of their social function in the production and reproduction of collective political action; this leads to the question of how crisis discourses construct (and deconstruct) forms of collective political action.[5]

Thus the link between class and politics is not simply a 'realistic' one emerging quasi-naturalistically from conjunctures of historical processes and real events. It is also a *constructed* one – which means that discourses play a decisive role in historical conjunctures of processes and events. Our claim is that in modern societies crisis discourses are a decisive element in giving meaning to the link between class and politics. An adequate theory of the crisis of class politics therefore forces us to think about the social role of crisis discourses for the reproduction of class politics, which ultimately will take the form of a reflexive theory.

In the following sections the theoretical analysis of the relationship of crisis discourse and class politics proceeds in three steps. First, the classical Marxian analysis and the related theoretical discourse on crisis will be discussed. Second, the counterattack of modernization theory and its end-of-crisis discourse will be analyzed. Third, the reflexive turn which allows social theory to make sense of the paradoxes and contradictory evidence it has created is discussed. Finally, some elements of a reflexive theory beyond the crisis-of-class-politics discourse are put forward.

### Reconstructing the link of class and crisis in modern society

*From accumulation crisis to legitimation crisis*

The classic conception of crisis is to be found in Marx's theory of the crisis-ridden process of capitalist accumulation. This systemic conception of a crisis contains, paradoxically, its negation: since the system reproduces itself irrespective of the 'iron law of capitalist development' there must be something that intervenes into this crisis-ridden process: namely self-correcting processes. This idea has been generalized in modern sociological systems theory, which places the emphasis on *system integration* through

---

[5] This is the theoretical perspective that underlies recent research on the media coverage of social movements, assuming that this coverage is a decisive factor in the social reproduction of social movements. As an early example of this approach see Gitlin 1980.

differentiation. This attempts to explain why crises never end. Crisis is seen as a byproduct of the processes which lead to more and more complex social systems.[6] The dominant theories of social change derive primarily from this objectivist concept of crisis.[7]

The central problem, which neither Marx nor anyone after him has been able to solve, is how to relate the objectivity of systemic processes to the adaptive capacities of social systems. This problem has been solved by Marx – in an unsatisfactory way – through the voluntaristic act of a class to interrupt crisis-ridden processes. As this did not happen, the question of why this intervention did not take place had to be answered. This question points to a property of the system which Marx did not consider as relevant: the legitimacy of the system. For Marx the illegitimacy was self-evident. He therefore excluded systematically the possibility of the relative (and even rising) legitimacy of the system. Giving up this assumption has led to an alternative crisis discourse: the discourse on a *legitimation crisis* (Habermas 1976) that tried to identify limits of legitimacy beyond which crisis-ridden processes lead to the destruction of the system.[8]

This has led to a *social-psychological* conception of crisis. A legitimation crisis is based on the assumption of psychological limits of accepting crisis-ridden processes. It is therefore bound to the social-psychological habitus of social actors.[9] In order to know how severe such a systemic crisis is, we must know to what extent it is transformed into a crisis of the social-psychological acceptance (which equals 'legitimacy') of systemic processes. Thus one can transform a systemic concept of crisis into a social-psychological one. This at least is the idea of a 'legitimation crisis'. A crisis in this sense arises when the psychological resources necessary for legitimating social institutions of power and inequality have been exhausted.

However, the underlying assumption of the argument is not wholly

---

[6] The systems-theoretical approach has changed the classic paradigm of crisis. Contrary to Marxian tradition, such crises are seen as temporary. The evolutionary approach supports such optimistic reformulations; the only question is what kind of evolution is to take place? From the point of view of a radical systems theory, however, such a question is nonsense. For such an argument see Luhmann 1984. For a Marxist interpretation of Luhmann's autopoietic optimism see Berger 1988. An exemplary analysis in terms of a systemic concept, but without its optimistic implications, is found in the idea of a fiscal crisis (O'Connor 1973).

[7] The most important example is traditional modernization theory. It makes a critique of crisis theories, which see structural strains as unavoidable and unresolvable. Zapf (1983, 1986) is the most explicit on this point. This stance, however, leads only to a hybrid of Marx and Schumpeter. It does not address the problem that cultural identity is what is at stake in the resolution of social crises; it merely reduces the concept of crisis to one of adaptive problems that are to be solved by the strategic action of professional elites.

[8] Crisis theories themselves can be considered to be part of the symbolic resources and symbolic limits defining the acceptability of a system. Seen in this way, their specific effect in a cultural crisis is either to contribute to the 'normalization' or to the 'intensification' of structural strains in society. This argument will be taken up systematically later.

[9] Whether these theories rely on behaviourist or on cognitivist assumptions does not affect their systematic place within this argumentation.

convincing, in the sense that at a given level of the development of society only a limited amount of such resources are available for social legitimation. Expectations are not a scarce resource. On the contrary, the possibilities for creating and changing expectations are endless. The solution is in an expansion of the symbolic resources that are necessary for the cultural reproduction of social systems, which is achieved through learning processes of people (Eder 1987a). This implies that crises can go on for ever. Therefore, the theory of social-psychological limits to systemic crises must include a self-limiting mechanism in the production of legitimating symbols. This could be a crisis in the capacity of social actors to learn in a given socio-historical context. The theory of legitimation crisis turns out to be based on the theory of a *pathogenic path* to learning processes. The problem raised then is where to find the criteria for 'pathologies' of learning processes.[10]

The social-psychological concept of crisis implies a theoretical vision of society rejecting the philosophy-of-history vision, which has accompanied the thematization of crisis in the first phase of the modernization of modern societies. However, it still shares with this philosophy-of-history vision the assumption of 'objective' (in the sense of normative) limits built into the legitimation of the institutional framework which regulates systemic crises. These limits cannot be sought within the idea of systemic crises, because such an idea already presupposes such limits. We must therefore go beyond this social-psychological notion of crisis.

The basic problem has already been stated in Habermas's attempt to ground the social-psychological limits in a theory of the cultural evolution of criteria of validity (Habermas 1979, 1984): such criteria are part of the culture within which we ourselves live. Another way of looking at the same problem is to define it as a problem of 'self-reference' (Luhmann 1990a). A limitation of the Habermasian project is that 'modernity' as such is an insufficient basis for describing the culture that defines the limits of acceptability in modern society. It is too general a criterion. It takes a particular outcome of producing modern culture as its general substance. Since what is considered 'modern' varies more than this approach assumes, the process of producing such outcomes gains in importance. Thus the social-psychological approach needs to shift in scrutiny from the outcomes to the processes that generate them. Methodologically speaking, we have to consider modernity as a social construction and take into account the processes underlying this construction. Theoretically speaking, the results of social constructions are to be located within social relations of power and competition which are again embedded in social structures. This argument destroys the certainties that underlie the legitimationist dis-

---

[10] This has been solved by Habermas by referring to social-psychological theories of cognitive competence, above all to Kohlberg's theory of moral development; see Habermas 1979 and Kohlberg 1981. Incidentally, this conceptualization is a psychologizing version of the old theory of class consciousness and its attempt to find criteria for the wrong class consciousness.

course. The post-historicist discourse within which the crisis of modernity has become manifest[11] has to struggle with the problem of 'self-reference'.[12]

## Back to Marx and beyond

A step back to Marx is necessary in order to clarify whether the notion of crisis has to be subject to radical theoretical critique, or whether it still has something to say about the dynamics that are built into the development of modern societies. This will be done by analyzing more closely the way in which Marx tried to link crisis and class politics. Marx was certainly wrong regarding the link between class politics and crisis – but we already know this.[13] This, however, does not imply that the theoretical tools he worked with are obsolete. First, we must reconstruct the theoretical tools, and then decide whether they are fundamentally misplaced, or whether they are simply trapped within a political discourse that blocked his scientific way of analyzing modern societies.

The central concept of Marx's theoretical construction of social reality pertinent to the notion of crisis and class politics is 'contradiction', which is used to grasp two types of phenomena: on the one hand the contradiction between the relations of production; and on the other the forces of production and the contradiction between classes. The way in which these two contradictions are related is a controversial point in the interpretation of Marx's thinking,[14] for it poses the question of how social groups are related to 'fundamental' and/or 'objective' contradictions within society. Class conflict is defined as the social conflict that refers to the developmental possibilities of society, and to its alternative paths of development. This type of conflict can be defined as being about the alternative directions of social development that are opened by the contradictions at the level of the system of society. The contradictory character of the system is translated into contradictions between classes.

The theory of class conflict, however, is not fully developed in Marx's theoretical argument. It is rather reduced to a voluntaristic theory of collective action based on historical narratives and political wishful

[11] Habermas's analysis of the discourse of modernity still contains a teleological element (Habermas 1985a) by situating itself within the history of discourses of modernity, which can be seen as a first step towards what is called 'reflexivity'. But ultimately this reflexive discourse is again considered as the 'necessary' outcome of this history which places the analysis again outside the history to which it belongs.

[12] The project of enlightenment did not see this self-reference. In Luhmann's earlier writings this has been corrected by what he called 'sociological enlightenment' (a series of five volumes with essays on every aspect of society). This is probably not enough, because it insinuates that sociology can enlighten. The next step would be a 'sociology of enlightenment', a self-application of enlightenment thinking taking sociology as its medium. This project has already begun; see Bourdieu 1990.

[13] This was the basic argument in the writings of Habermas in the seventies; see Habermas 1979.

[14] See for this context the discussion in Chapter 2.

thinking. We only find the postulate that classes *an sich* have to be transformed into classes *für sich*. Marx gives a teleological answer to this problem by looking for the end of this process.[15] The process, within which a class constitutes itself as class *für sich*, is predetermined by its *telos*, the 'true' class consciousness; and the true class consciousness is defined as the adequate semantic representation of the contradictory character of reality which ultimately has to resonate in the individual mind in order to guide collective action.

This reconstruction leads straight to the weakness in this theoretical strategy: the notion of contradiction at the level of the constitution of class. By misconceiving the social constitution of class, the idea of class conflict is given up in favour of historicism. The theoretical task is to develop an adequate *theory of class conflict* which avoids the pitfalls of historicism as well as the pitfalls of objectivism (the latter being the major theoretical strategy in post-Marxist thinking).

The problem of conceptualizing and explaining class conflict guides the revisions which are necessary for their further theoretical treatment. The key to such a revision is an understanding of the *political* nature of contradictions. Such an understanding of the dynamics of contradictions for political action can neither be reduced to objective contradictions (on the level of societal systems) nor to subjective contradictions (on the level of the individual actors). We need a theoretical 'middle ground', a theory pointing out the role of antagonistic definitions of the social world, that creates and reproduces a reality outside individual motivations and beyond their social-structural determinants. This is the world of social conflict. It is, 'in the last instance',[16] shaped by class politics, since the issues around which social conflicts are organized refer to processes that separate and coordinate social actors quasi-objectively into classes of actors. This has been true for the issue of work conditions and of adequate pay from the nineteenth century until now. What we observe today is a shift in issue relevance that points to changes in the underlying logic of separation and coordination. The proposition that can be tested is that issues that generate present-day conflicts, such as environmental issues, have the same conflictual and coordinating potential as the classic issues centred on work. This is what is meant by the proposition that they are *potential class conflicts*.[17]

This reformulation of the Marxist notion of contradictions situated at the

---

[15] Marxist theory has grappled with this problem for a century. An interesting new answer has been given by 'Analytical Marxism', which sees itself as a complement and correction of Marx's general theory. See Elster's attempt to 'make sense of Marx' (Elster 1985b).

[16] This formula is a short-cut for a basic premise, which assumes an analytical difference between a surface structure of social conflicts (conflicts centred on any type of concrete issue) and a deep level structure that assumes that social conflicts are embedded in a logic of separation and coordination explaining the resulting conflicts on the surface level. This assumption is basic in so far as it is the condition of a scientific objectification beyond a mere descriptive account of social processes.

[17] See chapter 7 above on nature as a field of class conflict.

level of class conflict is a starting point for introducing a theoretical perspective that connects the discourse on class politics and the discourse on crisis. Reducing the Marxian notion of contradiction to its objectified existence in terms of social positions and social status would lead us to the discourse of systemic crisis. Reducing it to its subjectified existence in the mind of actors would lead us to the legitimationist discourse of pathologies of collective consciousness. Refocusing it on social conflicts and politicizing the notion of contradiction instead serves as a proposition for another theory of crisis. Its first element is that *the crisis endemic to modern society is the result of blocked class politics*. It is neither in the objective location nor in the mind of classes, but in the social relationships between classes that we must look for a theory of crisis in modern societies.[18] A second element is that *crisis discourses give meaning to the constitution and reproduction of social class relationships*. Since class relationships are based on interpreted contradictions, crisis discourses are a means to give meaning to contradictions. Crisis discourses serve as the medium of social contradictions.

Thus the term 'crisis' gains a connotation beyond its mere objectivity in so far as crisis denotes a situation in which actors try to regain a sovereignty that has been blocked by systemic and psychic reasons. Crisis therefore has a double meaning: it is a process of social self-blockading *and* a critique of this process. It is a process the understanding of which implies its critique. Critique, however, is bound to conflictual social relationships.[19] This changed perspective implies the abandonment of philosophies of history as a theory explaining the alternative to a crisis-ridden development. Philosophies of history, as they have guided the emergence and development of modern society from its enlightenment period through Marx to its socialist experiments, no longer serve as the critique built into the discourse on the crisis of modern society and its modernity. They have been replaced by new ways of thematizing the crisis endemic to modern society. The proposition made is to replace them by a theory of crisis discourse within which the theory of the crisis of class politics is situated.

There is, however, also a further point, which is that there is also a real

---

[18] The origins of the crisis of modern society have been well analyzed by Koselleck in his famous book on *Kritik und Krise* which originally appeared in 1959 (Koselleck 1973). The crisis of state-centred society – engendered by the critique constitutive for modern society – was accompanied by a philosophy of history that contained the solution to this crisis: the enlightened society. Marx can be seen as a transitory figure transforming this early modern crisis discourse to one in which the solution to the crisis was class politics.

[19] The close relationship of the terms 'crisis' and 'critique' can be traced back to the Greek word *krinein* which means to separate, select, or split on the one hand, and to contend, contest, or struggle on the other. This close connection of both terms is reconstructed in Koselleck's above-mentioned analysis of early modern social and political thinking (Koselleck 1973), which demonstrates that the beginning of modernity is grounded in the conscience of critique as the basis of the crisis leading to modern society. Crisis discourses are the ones that have kept the idea of their close interrelationship; to talk about crisis only makes sense when we criticize through it a given state of affairs.

crisis in class politics. Not only is the legitimationist discourse being exhausted, but its object is also vanishing. The object of class politics no longer concerns either the systemic logic of modern societies or its regulation.[20] The proposition is that constitutive of class politics is the situation in which alternate ways of perceiving and reacting to adaptive problems collide. The object can be any problem creating such situations (ranging from issues concerning capital–labour relations and the welfare state to environmental issues). It means that irreconcilable cultural orientations arise in society. This concept sees crisis as produced by social contradictions based on alternate cultural models for directing social development.[21]

Two factors contribute to the crisis-of-class-politics discourse: firstly, the internal problems of the legitimationist discourse concerning its insufficient reflexivity, and, secondly, external problems that have to do with a shift in the object of class politics. The crisis of class politics therefore is not only one of changing locus (a shift away from the steering problems of society towards cultural definitions of where to steer it), but one of a basic change in the discourse that observes and gives meaning to crisis.

### Reconnecting crisis and critique

The discussion on the crisis of class politics marks a new stage in a long history of crisis discourses in modern society. It also indicates that neither systemic processes nor pathogenic learning processes are sufficient to explain the crisis-ridden course of the development of modernity. Capitalism still works, and pathogenic learning processes continue without necessarily producing a bad outcome.[22] The notion of crisis no longer seems to have an empirical referent. However, this conclusion is valid only given the premise that modern societies reproduce themselves irrespective of politics. Politics is the dimension that is excluded from the conceptions of crisis we have discussed so far. Systems are bound to their parameters, and learning processes to their normative developmental logic. Both

---

[20] This proposition takes for granted that the crisis that is due directly to the process of capitalist accumulation is already solved by regulatory processes, i.e. the welfare state and systems of collective bargaining. This has historically changed the locus of crisis. The theories of crisis have turned to these regulatory agencies as objects of a crisis theory; see, for example, Offe 1972, 1985b. Today a new object of crisis theories is emerging: the environmental problems of modern societies. There are attempts to relate these problems back to basic contradictions of capitalism, such as a second contradiction of capitalism (O'Connor 1990). But the critique that such theories engender does not resonate, which is an indicator of their obsoleteness as a medium of critique.

[21] This formula owes its origins to Touraine (1978, 1981).

[22] This has to do with the phenomenon that micro-level phenomena do not necessarily determine macro-outcomes. Good intentions might produce bad collective results and bad intentions good collective results. This argument alone is sufficient to go on to the next question of what the mechanism is that mediates the individual intentions and the collective results.

aspects certainly are important elements of a theory of crisis, but they are not sufficient elements. They do not constitute a model that could grasp real crises in modern societies, namely crises that result from the incapacity of societies to change such parameters and to redress learning pathologies. The assumption of a crisis of class politics claims that the crisis of modernity is neither of a systemic nor of a legitimationist kind. It is a crisis of the capacity of a society of acting upon itself. This capacity is created and reproduced through social conflicts between social groups. Without such 'contradictions' modern society runs into crises for two reasons: (1) because such societies are not able to react to their systemic problems; and (2) because they are not able to correct pathogenic learning processes. The crisis of class politics occurs when there is not enough politics.

The crisis-of-class-politics argument implies that there has been class politics acting upon society. This is traditional class politics, a form which is 'withering away'. The creation of the welfare state and anti-fascist politics have become historical phenomena. They only serve for creating a euphemistic historical image. Whether the disappearance of traditional class politics signifies the end of class politics is a matter for debate. The notion of an end of class politics is therefore the alternative to the notion of a crisis of class politics as proposed here.

The argument of an end of class politics assumes that modern societies have become stable societies, at both the systemic and the socio-psychological levels. It is based on the theoretical model of self-regulating social systems, and a radical decoupling of systemic processes and legitimating conditions such as motivations of acceptance. This in fact is the assumption guiding recent sociological systems theory.[23] Against this end-of-class-politics discourse I defend a crisis-of-class-politics discourse that takes the political context within which social systems and their action environments are reproduced seriously (accepting that these elements are at the same time systematic restrictions of politics). This crisis discourse criticizes traditional class politics not in order to bring an end to it but in order to make it work on the level of complexity that advanced modern societies require. The crisis discourse criticizes the lack of a culture of contradictions that is seen as constitutive of modernity and which makes the modern society distinctive from non-modern societies.

Thus the crisis discourse cannot be separated from the critical observation this discourse implies. The end-of-class-politics discourse is just another variant of a critical discourse, with a decisive difference: the end-of-class-politics discourse argues as if it were outside the world it analyzes. It hypostatizes its critique. The crisis-of-class-politics discourse often hypostatizes the opposite stand. A reflexive turn to both ways of talking about class politics is to see their hidden complementarity. They need each other to foster the critique that is necessary for continuing the critique.

---

[23] Its main protagonist is Luhmann, who bases his theory of social systems exactly on these two premises. See as his main statement on these points Luhmann 1984.

Without their contradictory evidence due to different positions in the observatory of the world there would be no mechanism of continuing the discourse on class politics.

The systematic argument is that scientific knowledge is only a special case of the type of cultural knowledge that characterizes modern societies. Modern societies, instead of reducing contradictory evidence, are confronted by its increase. Modernization not only seems to produce more contradictory evidence; it even seems to become dependent on this dynamic of contradictory evidence. This is the new paradox of modernization: society reproduces itself by producing contradictory knowledge about itself. This paradox leads to a reflexive turn in social theory. It is also going to reach modernization theory.[24] This reflexive turn changes the perspective guiding the crisis discourse and its counterpart. Therefore a 'reflexive' turn in modernization theory is warranted showing how modernization is a process that is mediated by conflictual interpretations of its direction.

After its objectivist phase which took place mainly in the nineteenth century the discourse on modernization has been dominated by a normative discourse. Modern society takes equality as the factor which distinguishes it from traditional society. Hence modernization has been conceptualized as a process leading toward equality in the different spheres of social life: economic, political, and cultural. This approach to modernization belongs to the theorizing of those one can call the 'legitimationists'. This legitimationist discourse can be extended to the cognitive or the aesthetic spheres. In all of these cases it remains a legitimationist discourse, which blocks sociological analysis because such discourses grant themselves a special status towards their object.[25] This excludes the possibilities of making the discourses themselves the object of analysis. Within this framework they cannot be studied as part of the culture that is constitutive of modernity.

This is not sufficient to support the claim that the theory of modernization as such is still alive (Wallerstein 1979). On the contrary, what *is* dead is a theory of modernization that does not reflect on its own function in the modernization process. A reflexive theory of modernization is needed.[26] It

[24] The work of Beck, Giddens and Lash is pertinent here. See Beck 1992; Giddens 1990, 1991; Lash 1990.

[25] Among such attempts, the Hegelian solutions are the most interesting ones: they ascribe some kind of historical necessity to the normative description, which implies taking into account the time dimension of normative descriptions of society. In the final analysis, they are based on the optimistic assumption that a normative description has normative effects in the description. But this is a rather heroic assumption that does not help us understand the unintended consequences of normative theories of modern societies, which are much needed at a time when such normative ideals are crumbling.

[26] This has nothing to do with postmodernity, with deconstructivism or with feminism, each of which simply provides nothing but different descriptions of modernity. They vary with respect to the degree of reflexivity built into them. This degree of reflexivity is quite low. See also the discussion by Tiryakian (1991).

is interesting to note that the classic theory of modernization has been put into question by critiques that refer to its cultural assumptions. The critique of its ethnocentrism has been a first blow. A result of this rebuttal is the theory of antimodernity. Modern society – this theory of anti-modernity or antitheory of modernity argues – is nothing other than, and ultimately the most disgusting case of, the destruction of human sociality. This general attack is bound to a moral message – one that ends theorizing about modernity and modernization. This attack substitutes social analysis with moral concern. Morality is therefore also a subject of discussion, but in a way that makes morality the beginning, not the end of sociological thinking.

Modern society may not be less cruel, destructive, or suppressive than traditional societies have been (and are). What makes the difference is that it contains the social and cultural conditions to *rationalize* these features of society in a different way. The structure and logic of this different thinking has been the starting point for this discussion. I no longer describe modernity in terms of a legitimationist discourse but rather in terms of communicating normative codes that allow the producers of such discourses to identify something as modern. What is needed is a constructivist approach in the theory of modernization.[27] This theoretical and methodological perspective of a 'constructivist reflexivity' is a means for uncovering and reconstructing the close link between crisis and critique and with it the critical potential of the new-politics-of-class discourse.

[27] This is the central message of modern autopoietic systems theory – and here as well we can see that the legitimationist discourse (describing systems theory as technological or technocratic) has produced paradoxical effects: systems theory turns out to be much more cultural than any of the legitimationist discourses on modernity so far!

# References

Abercrombie, N. and Urry, J. (1988). *Capital, Labour and the Middle Classes*. London: Allen & Unwin.

Abrams, P. and McCulloch, A. (With Sheila Abrams and Pat Gore.) (1976). *Communes, Sociology and Society*. Cambridge: Cambridge University Press.

Ahlemeyer, H. (1989). Was ist eine soziale Bewegung? Zur Distinktion und Einheit eines sozialen Phänomens. *Zeitschrift für Soziologie*, 18, 175–91.

Alber, J. (1985). Modernisierung, neue Spannungslinien und die politischen Chancen der Grünen. *Politische Vierteljahreschrift*, 3, 211–26.

Alexander, J.C. (ed.) (1985). *Neo-functionalism*. Beverly Hills, CA: Sage.

Alexander, J.C. (1992). Durkheim's problem and differentiation theory today. In H. Haferkamp and N.J. Smelser (eds), *Social Change and Modernity* (pp. 179–204). Berkeley/ Los Angeles, CA: University of California Press.

Alexander, J.C., Giesen, B., Münch, R. and Smelser, N.J. (eds) (1987). *The Micro–Macro Link*. Berkeley, CA: University of California Press.

Allan-Michaud, D. (1990). *L'avenir de la société alternative*. Paris: Harmattan.

Allcock, J.B. (1971). 'Populism': A brief biography. *Sociology*, 5, 371–87.

Alvesson, M. and Berg, P.O. (1990). *Corporate Culture and Organizational Symbolism. Development, Theoretical Perspectives, Practice and Current Debate*. Berlin/New York: de Gruyter.

Anderson, B. (1983). *Imagined Communities. Reflections on the Origins and Spread of Nationalism*. London: Verso.

Anderson, J.A. and Meyer, T.P. (1988). *Mediated Communication. A Social Action Perspective*. Newbury Park, CA: Sage.

Axelrod, R. (1984). *The Evolution of Cooperation*. New York: Basic Books.

Baker, K.L., Dalton, R.J. and Hildebrandt, K. (1981). *Germany Transformed. Political Culture and the New Politics*. Cambridge, MA: Harvard University Press.

Baritz, L. (1989). *The Good Life. The Meaning of Success for the American Middle Class*. New York: Knopf.

Bechhofer, F. and Elliott, B. (eds) (1981). *The Petite Bourgeoisie. Comparative Studies of the Uneasy Stratum*. New York: St. Martin's Press.

Bechhofer, F. and Elliott, B. (1985). The petite bourgeoisie in late capitalism. *Annual Review of Sociology*, 11, 181–207.

Bechhofer, F., Elliott, B. and McCrone, D. (1978). Structure, consciousness and action: A sociological profile of the British middle class. *British Journal of Sociology*, 29, 410–36.

Beck, U. (1983). Jenseits von Stand und Klasse? In R. Kreckel (ed.), *Soziale Ungleichheiten (= Soziale Welt, Sonderband 2)* (pp. 25–74). Göttingen: Schwartz.

Beck, U. (1992). *Risk Society: Towards a New Modernity*. London: Sage.

Beck, U. and Bonß, W. (eds) (1989). *Weder Sozialtechnologie noch Aufklärung? Analysen zur Verwendung sozialwissenschaftlichen Wissens*. Frankfurt: Suhrkamp.

Beck, U. and Brater, M. (1978). *Berufliche Arbeitsteilung und soziale Ungleichheit. Eine gesellschaftlich-historische Theorie der Berufe*. Frankfurt: Campus.

Beck, U. and Lash, S. (in press). *Reflexive Modernisierung*. Frankfurt: Suhrkamp.

Becker, H.S. (1986). Culture: A Sociological View. In H.S. Becker (ed.), *Doing Things Together* (pp. 11–24). Evanston, IL: Northwestern University Press.

Beckford, J.A. and Levasseur, M. (1986). New religious movements in Western Europe. In

J.A. Beckford (ed., on behalf of Research Committee 22 of the International Sociological Association), *New Religious Movements and Rapid Social Change* (pp. 29–54). Paris/London: UNESCO/Sage.

Bellah, R.N., Madsen, R., Sullivan, W.M., Swidler, A. and Tipton, S.M. (1985). *Habits of the Heart.* Berkeley, CA: University of California Press.

Bellmann, L., Gerlach, K. and Hübler, O. (1984). *Lohnstruktur in der Bundesrepublik Deutschland. Zur Theorie und Empirie der Arbeitseinkommen.* Frankfurt: Campus.

Bendix, R. (1978). *Kings or People. Power and the Mandate to Rule.* Berkeley, CA: University of California Press.

Benseler, F., Heinze, R.G. and Klönne, A. (eds) (1982). *Die Zukunft der Arbeit.* Hamburg: VSA.

Berger, J. (ed.) (1986). *Die Moderne – Kontinuitäten und Zäsuren.* Göttingen: Schwartz.

Berger, J. (1988). Modernitätsbegriffe und Modernitätskritik in der Soziologie. *Soziale Welt,* 39, 224–36.

Berger, P.A. (1986). *Entstrukturierte Klassengesellschaft. Klassenbildung und Strukturen sozialer Ungleichheit im historischen Wandel.* Opladen: Westdeutscher Verlag.

Berger, P.A. (1987). Klassen und Klassifikationen. Zur 'neuen Unübersichtlichkeit' in der soziologischen Ungleichheitsdiskussion. *Kölner Zeitschrift für Soziologie und Sozialpsychologie,* 39, 59–85.

Berger, P.A. (1988). Die Herstellung sozialer Klassifikationen: Methodische Probleme der Ungleichheitsforschung. *Leviathan,* 16, 501–20.

Berger, P.A. (1990). Ungleichheitsphasen. Stabilität und Instabilität als Aspekte ungleicher Lebenslagen. In P.A. Berger and S. Hradil (eds), *Lebenslagen, Lebensläufe, Lebensstile (Soziale Welt, Sonderband 7)* (pp. 319–50). Göttingen: Otto Schwartz.

Berger, P.A. and Hradil, S. (1990). Die Modernisierung sozialer Ungleichheit – und die Konturen ihrer Erforschung. In P.A. Berger and S. Hradil (eds), *Lebenslagen, Lebensläufe, Lebensstile (Soziale Welt Sonderband 7)* (pp. 3–24). Göttingen: Otto Schwartz.

Bergmann, W. (1987). Was bewegt die soziale Bewegung? Überlegungen zur Selbstkonstitution der 'neuen' sozialen Bewegungen. In D. Baecker, J. Markowitz, R. Stichweh, H. Tyrell and H. Willke (eds), *Theorie als Passion. Niklas Luhmann zum 60. Geburtstag* (pp. 362–93). Frankfurt: Suhrkamp.

Berman, M. (1984). *The Reenchantment of the World.* New York: Free Press.

Béteille, A. (1965). *Caste, Class, and Power. Changing Patterns of Stratification in a Tanjore Village.* Berkeley, CA: University of California Press.

Birnbaum, P. (1988). *States and Collective Action: The European Experience.* Cambridge: Cambridge University Press.

Bischoff, J. et al. (1982). *Jenseits der Klassen? Gesellschaft und Staat im Spätkapitalismus.* Hamburg: VSA.

Blossfeld, H.P. (1985). *Bildungsexpansion und Berufschancen. Empirische Analysen zur Lage der Berufsanfänger in der Bundesrepublik.* Frankfurt: Campus.

Blossfeld, H.P. (1990). Changes in educational careers in the Federal Republic of Germany. *Sociology of Education.* 63, 165–77.

Blossfeld, H.P. and Huinink, J. (1991). Human capital investments or norms of role transition? How women's schooling and career affect the process of family formation. *American Journal of Sociology,* 97, 143–68.

Blossfeld, H.P. and Shavit, Y. (1992). Persisting barriers: changes in educational opportunities in thirteen countries. In Y. Shavit and H.P. Blossfeld (eds), *Persistent Inequality.* Boulder, CO: Westview Press.

Blossfeld, H.P., Gianelli, G. and Mayer, K.U. (1991). *Expansion of the Tertiary Sector and Social Inequality. Is there a New Service Proletariat Emerging in the Federal Republic of Germany?* (EUI Working Paper SPS No. 91/8). Florence: European University Institute.

Blossfeld, H.P., Hamerle, A. and Mayer, K.U. (1989). *Event History Analysis.* Hillsdale, NJ: Erlbaum.

Bögenhold, D. (1985). *Die Selbständigen. Zur Soziologie dezentraler Produktion.* Frankfurt: Campus.

Böhme, H. and Böhme, G. (1983). *Das Andere der Vernunft. Zur Entwicklung von Rationalitätsstrukturen am Beispiel Kants*. Frankfurt: Suhrkamp.

Boltanski, L. (1982). *Les cadres. La formation d'un groupe social*. Paris: Minuit.

Bolte, K.M. and Hradil, S. (1984). *Soziale Ungleichheit in der Bundesrepublik Deutschland* (4th ed.). Opladen: Leske and Budrich.

Bonß, W. and Hartmann, H. (1985). Zum Wirklichkeitscharakter soziologischer Diskurse. In Wolfgang Bonß and Heinz Hartmann (eds), *Entzauberte Wissenschaft. Soziale Welt. Sonderband 3* (pp. 1–46). Göttingen: Schwartz.

Bourdieu, P. (1966). Condition de classe et position de classe. *Archives européennes de sociologie*, 7, 201–23.

Bourdieu, P. (1970). *La reproduction*. Paris: Minuit.

Bourdieu, P. (1974). Avenir de classe et causalite du probable. *Revue française de sociologie*, 15, 3–42.

Bourdieu, P. (1980). *Le sens pratique*. Paris: Minuit.

Bourdieu, P. (1982). *La distinction. Critique sociale du jugement* (2nd edn). Paris: Minuit.

Bourdieu, P. (1984). *The Distinction. A Social Critique of the Judgment of Taste*. Cambridge, MA: Harvard University Press.

Bourdieu, P. (1985). The social space and the genesis of groups. *Theory and Society*, 14, 723–44.

Bourdieu, P. (1986). Forms of capital. In J.G. Richardson (ed.), *Handbook of Theory and Research for the Sociology of Education* (pp. 241–58). Westport, CT: Greenwood.

Bourdieu, P. (1987). What makes a social class? On the theoretical and practical existence of groups. *Berkeley Journal of Sociology*, 32, 1–17.

Bourdieu, P. (1990). *In Other Words. Essays Towards a Reflexive Sociology*. Cambridge: Polity Press.

Bourdieu, P., Boltanski, L., Castel, R., Chamboredon, J.C., Lagneau, G. and Schnapper, D. (1981). *Eine illegitime Kunst. Die sozialen Gebrauchsweisen der Photographie*. Frankfurt: Europäische Verlagsanstalt.

Boyte, H. (1980). *The Backyard Revolution: Understanding the New Citizen Movement*. Philadelphia, PA: Temple University Press.

Boyte, H.C., Booth, H. and Max, S. (1986). *Citizen Action and the New American Populism*. Philadelphia, PA: Temple University Press.

Boyte, H.C. and Riessman, F. (eds). (1986). *The New Populism. The Politics of Empowerment*. Philadelphia, PA: Temple University Press.

Bramwell, A. (1989). *Ecology and History: The Greening of the West Since 1880*. New Haven, NJ: Yale University Press.

Brand, K.W. (1990). Cyclical aspects of new social movements: waves of cultural criticism and mobilization cycles of new middle-class radicalism. In R.J. Dalton and M. Kuechler (eds), *Challenging the Political Order. New Social and Political Movements in Western Democracies* (pp. 23–42). Oxford: Polity Press.

Brunschwig, H. (1975). *Gesellschaft und Romantik in Preußen im 18. Jahrhundert. Die Krise des preußischen Staates am Ende des 18. Jahrhunderts und die Entstehung*. Frankfurt: Ullstein.

Bürklin, W.P. (1984). Ansatzpunkte einer sozialstrukturellen Verankerung der neuen sozialen Bewegungen. In J. Falter et al. (eds), *Politische Willensbildung und Interessenvermittlung* (pp. 566–79). Opladen: Westdeutscher Verlag.

Bürklin, W.P. (1987). Governing left parties frustrating the radical non-established left: The rise and inevitable decline of the Greens. *European Sociological Review*, 3, 109–26.

Burke, K. (1990). *On Symbols and Society*. (Edited and with an Introduction by Joseph R. Gusfield.) Chicago, IL: University of Chicago Press.

Burris, V. (1980). Class formation and transformation in advanced capitalist societies: A comparative analysis. *Social Praxis*, 7, 147–79.

Burris, V. (1986). The discovery of the new middle class. *Theory and Society*, 15, 317–49.

Calhoun, C.J. (1981). *Community, Class and Collective Action*. Chicago, IL: University of Chicago Press.

Calhoun, C.J. (1982). *The Question of Class Struggle. Social Foundations of Popular Radicalism during the Industrial Revolution*. Chicago, IL: University of Chicago Press.

Calhoun, C.J. (1988). The radicalism of tradition and the question of class struggle. In M. Taylor (ed.), *Rationality and Revolution* (pp. 129–75). Cambridge: Cambridge University Press.

Calhoun, C.J. (1991). The problem of identity in collective action. In J. Huber (ed.), *Macro–Micro Linkages in Sociology* (pp. 51–75). Newbury Park, CA: Sage.

Canovan, M. (1981). *Populism*. London.

Carter, R. (1985). *Capitalism, Class Conflict and the New Middle Class*. London: Routledge & Kegan Paul.

Case, J. and Taylor, R.C.R. (eds) (1979). *Coops, Communes and Collectives. Experiments in Social Change in the 1960s and 1970s*. New York: Pantheon Books.

Centers, R. (1949). *The Psychology of Classes. A Study of Class Consciousness*. New York: Russell & Russell.

Clegg, S.R. (ed.) (1989). *Organization Theory and Class Analysis. New Approaches and New Issues*. Berlin/New York: de Gruyter.

Cohen, G.A. (1978). *Karl Marx's Theory of History. A Defence*. Oxford: Clarendon Press.

Cohen, J.L. (1985). Strategy or identity: new theoretical paradigms and contemporary social movements. *Social Research*, 52–4, 663–716.

Collins, R. (1992). The romanticism of agency/structure versus the analysis of micro/macro. *Current Sociology*, 40, 77–97.

Colomy, P. (1985). Uneven structural differentiation: toward a comparative approach. In J. Alexander (ed.), *Neofunctionalism* (pp. 130–56). Beverly Hills, CA: Sage Publications.

Conze, W. (1973). Der Beginn der deutschen Arbeiterbewegung. In G.A. Ritter (ed.), *Die deutschen Parteien vor 1918* (pp. 331–41). Cologne: Kiepenheuer & Witsch.

Conze, W. and Groh, D. (1966). *Die Arbeiterbewegung in der nationalen Bewegung. Die deutsche Sozialdemokratie vor, während und nach der Reichsgründung*. Stuttgart: Klett.

Conze, W. and Kocka, J. (eds). (1985). *Bildungsbürgertum im 19. Jahrhundert. Teil 1: Bildungssystem und Professionalisierung in internationalen Vergleichen*. Stuttgart: Klett-Cotta.

Cotgrove, S. and Duff, A. (1980). Environmentalism, middle-class radicalism and politics. *Sociological Review*, 28, 333–51.

Cotgrove, S. and Duff, A. (1981). Environmentalism, values, and social change. *British Journal of Sociology*, 32, 92–110.

Dahrendorf, R. (1959). *Class and Class Conflict in Industrial Society* (6th edn). Stanford: Stanford University Press.

Dalton, R.J. and Küchler, M. (eds) (1990). *Challenging the Political Order: New Social and Political Movements in Western Democracies*. Cambridge: Polity Press.

DeMott, B. (1990). *The Imperial Middle: Why Americans Can't Think Straight About Class*. New York: Morrow.

Denzin, N.K. (1991). *Images of Postmodern Society. Social Theory and Contemporary Cinema*. London: Sage.

Destler, C.M. (1966). *American Radicalism 1865–1901*. New York.

Diani, M. (1992). Analysing social movement networks. In M. Diani and R. Eyerman (eds), *Studying Collective Action* (pp. 107–35). London: Sage.

Diani, M. and Eyerman, R. (1992). The study of collective action: Introductory remarks. In M. Diani and R. Eyerman (eds), *Studying Collective Action* (pp. 1–21). London: Sage.

DiMaggio, P.J. and Anheier, H.K. (1990). The sociology of nonprofit organizations and sectors. *Annual Review of Sociology*, 16, 137–59.

DiMaggio, P.J. and Mohr, J. (1985). Cultural capital, educational attainment and marital selection. *American Journal of Sociology*, 90, 1231–61.

Douglas, M. (1966). *Purity and Danger. An Analysis of Concepts of Pollution and Taboo*. London: Routledge & Kegan Paul.

Douglas, M. (1975). *Implicit Meanings. Essays in Anthropology*. London: Routledge & Kegan Paul.

Dreitzel, H.P. (1981). The socialization of nature: Western attitudes towards body and emotions. In P. Heelas and A. Lock (eds), *Indigenous Psychologies. The Anthropology of the Self* (pp. 205–23). London: Academic Press.

Dreyfuss, C. (1933). *Beruf und Ideologie der Angestellten*. München and Leipzig: Duncker & Humblot.

Dubiel. H. (ed.) (1986). *Populismus und Aufklärung*. Frankfurt: Suhrkamp.

Dumont, L. (1967). *Homo Hierarchicus*. Paris: Gallimard.

Dumont, L. (1970). Religion, Politics and Society in the Individualistic Universe. *Proceedings of the Royal Anthropological Institutions of Great Britain and Ireland 1970*, 31–41.

Dumont, L. (1977). *Homo Aequalis, I. Genèse et épanouissement de l'idéologie économique*. Paris: Gallimard.

Dumont, L. (1991). *Homo Aequalis, II. L'idéologie allemande – France–Allemagne et retour*. Paris: Editions Gallimard.

Durkheim, E. (1969). *Leçons de sociologie. Physique des moeurs et du droit* (2nd edn). Paris: Presses Universitaires de France.

Eder, K. (1976). *Die Entstehung staatlich organisierter Gesellschaften. Ein Beitrag zu einer Theorie sozialer Evolution*. Frankfurt: Suhrkamp.

Eder, K. (1985). *Geschichte als Lernprozeß? Zur Pathogenese politischer Modernität in Deutschland*. Frankfurt: Suhrkamp.

Eder, K. (1986a). Der permanente Gesellschaftsvertrag. Zur Kritik der ökonomischen Theorie des Sozialen. In L. Kern and H.P. Müller (eds), *Gerechtigkeit, Diskurs oder Markt? Die neuen Ansätze in der Vertragstheorie* (pp. 67–81). Opladen: Westdeutscher Verlag.

Eder, K. (1986b). Soziale Bewegung und kulturelle Evolution. Überlegungen zur Rolle der neuen sozialen Bewegungen in der kulturellen Evolution der Moderne. In J. Berger (ed.), *Die Moderne – Kontinuitäten und Zäsuren. Sonderband 4 der Sozialen Welt* (pp. 335–57). Göttingen: Schwartz.

Eder, K. (1987a). Learning and the evolution of social systems. An epigenetic perspective. In M. Schmid and F.M. Wuketits (eds), *Evolutionary Theory in Social Science* (pp. 101–25). Dordrecht/Boston: Reidel.

Eder, K. (1987b). The origin of class societies: a systems analysis. In V. Meja, D. Misgeld and N. Stehr (eds), *Modern German Sociology* (pp. 278–90). New York: Columbia University Press.

Eder, K. (1988a). *Die Vergesellschaftung der Natur. Studien zur sozialen Evolution der praktischen Vernunft*. Frankfurt: Suhrkamp.

Eder, K. (1988b). Wertwandel: Ein Beitrag zur Diagnose der Moderne? In H.O. Luthe and H. Meulemann (eds), *Wertwandel – Faktum oder Fiktion? Bestandsaufnahmen und Diagnosen aus kultursoziologischer Sicht* (pp. 257–94). Frankfurt: Campus.

Eder, K. (1988c). Critique of Habermas's contribution to the sociology of law. *Law and Society Review*, 22, 931–44.

Eder, K. (1989). Klassentheorie als Gesellschaftstheorie. Bourdieus dreifache kulturtheoretische Brechung der Klassentheorie. In K. Eder (ed.), *Klassenlage, Lebensstil und kollektive Praxis* (pp. 15–43). Frankfurt: Suhrkamp.

Eder, K. (1990). The cultural code of modernity and the problem of nature: a critique of the naturalistic notion of progress. In J. Alexander and P. Sztompka (eds), *Rethinking Progress: Movements, Forces and Ideas at the End of the Twentieth Century* (pp. 67–87). London/New York: Unwin Hyman.

Eder, K. (1992a). *Framing and communicating environmental protest. A discourse analysis of environmentalism* (EUI, Project No 42, Research paper No 6). Florence: Unpublished manuscript, European University Institute.

Eder, K. (1992b). Il paradosso de la cultura. Oltre una teoria consensualista della cultura. *Fenomenologia e Società* 15/2, 17–39, errata corrige (bibliography) 15/3.

Ehrenreich, B. (1989). *The Fear of Falling: The Inner Life of the Middle Class*. New York: Pantheon.

Eisenstadt, S.N. (1973). *Traditional Patrimonialism and Modern Neopatrimonialism.* Beverly Hills, CA: Sage.

Eisenstadt, S.N. (1981). Cultural traditions and political dynamics: The origins and modes of ideological politics. *British Journal of Sociology,* 32, 155 ?1

Eisenstadt, S.N. (1992). A reappraisal of theories of social change. In H. Haferkamp and N.J. Smelser (eds), *Social Change and Modernity* (pp. 412–29). Berkeley and Los Angeles, CA: University of California Press.

Elias, N. (1969). *Die höfische Gesellschaft. Untersuchungen zur Soziologie des Königtums und der höfischen Aristokratie.* Neuwied/Berlin: Luchterhand.

Elliott, B., Bechhofer, F., McCrone, D. and Black, S. (1982). Bourgeois social movements in Britain: Repertoires and responses. *The Sociological Review,* 30, 71–96.

Elster, J. (1978). *Logic and Society.* New York: John Wiley.

Elster, J. (1982). Marxism, functionalism, and game theory. The case for methodological individualism. *Theory and Society,* 11, 453–82.

Elster, J. (1985a). Drei Kritiken am Klassenbegriff. In N. Luhmann (ed.), *Soziale Differenzierung* (pp. 96–118). Opladen: Westdeutscher Verlag.

Elster, J. (1985b). *Making Sense of Marx.* Cambridge: Cambridge University Press.

Elster, J. (ed.). (1986). *Rational Choice.* Oxford: Blackwell.

Elster, J. (1989). *The Cement of Society. A Study of Social Order.* New York: Cambridge University Press.

Esping-Andersen, G. (1990). *The Three Worlds of Welfare Capitalism.* Cambridge/Princeton: Polity Press/Princeton University Press.

Esping-Andersen, G. (1992). Post-industrial class structures: An analytical framework. Florence: Unpublished manuscript, European University Institute.

Esping-Andersen, G. (ed.) (in press). *Changing Classes. Mobility Regimes in Post-Industrial Economies.* London: Sage.

Eyerman, R. and Jamison, A. (1991). *Social Movements: A Cognitive Approach.* Cambridge: Polity Press.

Falter, J.W. (1982). Radikalisierung des Mittelstandes oder Mobilisierung der Unpolitischen? Die Theorien von Seymour Martin Lipset und Reinhard Bendix über die Wählerschaft der NSDAP im Lichte neuerer Forschungsergebnisse. In P. Steinbach (ed.), *Probleme politischer Partizipation im Modernisierungsprozeß* (pp. 438–69). Stuttgart: Klett-Cotta.

Falter, J.W. (1984). Die Wähler der NSDAP 1928–1933: Sozialstruktur und parteipolitische Herkunft. In W. Michalka (ed.), *Die nationalsozialistische Machtergreifung* (pp. 47–59). Paderborn: Schöningh.

Feagin, J.R. and Çapek, S.M. (1991). Grassroots movements in a class perspective. *Research in Political Sociology* (5, 27–53). Greenwich, CT: JAI Press.

Featherstone, M. (1988). In the pursuit of the postmodern: An introduction. *Theory, Culture and Society,* 5, 195–216.

Featherstone, M. (1989). Towards a sociology of postmodern culture. In H. Haferkamp (ed.), *Social Structure and Culture* (pp. 147–74). Berlin: de Gruyter.

Featherstone, M. (1990). *Consumer Culture and Postmodernism.* London: Sage.

Featherstone, M. (1992a). Postmodernism and the aesthetization of everyday life. In S. Lash and J. Friedman (eds), *Modernity and Identity* (pp. 265–90). Oxford: Blackwell.

Featherstone, M. (ed.) (1992b). *Cultural Theory and Cultural Change.* London: Sage.

Francis, J., Turk, J. and Willman, P. (eds) (1983). *Power, Efficiency and Institutions: A Critical Approach to the 'Markets and Hierarchies' Paradigm.* London: Heinemann.

Frankenberg, G. (1984). Ziviler Ungehorsam und rechtsstaatliche Demokratie. *Juristenzeitung,* 39, 266–75.

Frecot, J. (1976). Die Lebensreformbewegung. In K. Vondung (ed.), *Das wilhelminische Bildungsbürgertum. Zur Sozialgeschichte seiner Ideen* (pp. 138–52) Göttingen: Vandenhoeck & Ruprecht.

Friedman, J. (1988). Cultural logics of the global system: A sketch. *Theory, Culture and Society,* 5, 447–60.

Friedman, S.R. (1985). Worker opposition movements. In L. Kriesberg (ed.), *Research in Social Movements, Conflicts and Change* (Vol. 8, pp. 133–70). Greenwich, CT: JAI Press.

Gale, R.P. (1986). Social movements and the state: The environmental movement, countermovement, and government agencies. *Sociological Perspectives*, 29, 202–40.

Galtung, J. (1986). *The green movement: A socio-historical explanation* (Vol. 1, pp. 75–90). International Sociology.

Gamson, W.A. (1988). Political discourse and collective action. In B. Klandermans, H. Kriesi and S. Tarrow (eds), *From Structure to Action: Comparing Social Movement Research across Cultures* (Vol. 1, International Social Movement Research, pp. 219–44). Greenwich, CT: JAI Press.

Gamson, W.A. (1992). *Talking Politics*. Cambridge, MA: Harvard University Press.

Gamson, W.A. and Modigliani, A. (1987). The changing culture of affirmative action. In R.D. Braungart and M.M. Braungart (eds), *Research in Political Sociology* (Vol. 3, pp. 137–77). Greenwich, CT: JAI Press.

Gamson, W.A. and Modigliani, A. (1989). Media discourse and public opinion on nuclear power: a constructionist approach. *American Journal of Sociology*, 95, 1–38.

Gans, H. J. (1988). *Middle American Individualism*. New York, NY: Free Press.

Geertz, C. (1966). Religion as a cultural system. In M. Banton (ed.), *Anthropological Approaches to the Study of Religion*. London: Tavistock.

Geertz, C. (1973). *The Interpretation of Cultures*. New York: Basic Books.

Gershuny, J.I. (1978). *After Industrial Society? The Emerging Self-Service Economy*. London: MacMillan.

Gershuny, J.I. (1983). *The New Service Economy. The Transformation of Employment in Industrial Societies*. London: Pinter.

Giddens, A. (1973). *The Class Structure of Advanced Societies*. London: Hutchinson.

Giddens, A. (1987). *Social Theory and Modern Sociology*. Cambridge: Polity Press.

Giddens, A. (1990). *The Consequences of Modernity*. Cambridge: Cambridge University Press.

Giddens, A. (1991). *Modernity and Self-Identity*. Stanford, CA: Stanford University Press.

Giesen, B. (1983). Moralische Unternehmer und öffentliche Diskussion. *Kölner Zeitschrift für Soziologie und Sozialpsychologie*, 2, 230–54.

Giesen, B. (1987). Natürliche Unglcichhcit, soziale Ungleichheit, ideale Ungleichheit. Zur Evolution von Deutungsmustern sozialcr Unglcichheit. In B. Giesen and H. Haferkamp (eds), *Soziologie der sozialen Ungleichheit* (pp. 314–45). Opladen: Westdeutscher Verlag.

Gitlin, T. (1980). *The Whole World is Watching: Mass Media in the Making and Unmaking of the New Left*. Berkeley, CA: University of California Press.

Glock, C.Y. and Bellah, R.N. (eds) (1976). *The New Religious Consciousness*. Berkeley/Los Angeles, CA: University of California Press.

Gluckman, M. (1963). *Order and Rebellion in Tribal Africa*. London: Cohen and West.

Godelier, M. (1973). Anthropologie und Ökonomie. In M. Godelier (ed.), *Ökonomische Anthropologie. Untersuchungen zum Begriff der sozialen Struktur primitiver Gesellschaften* (pp. 23–91). Reinbek: Rowohlt.

Godelier, M. (1978). Infrastructures, societies, and history. *Current Anthropology*, 19, 763–8.

Goldthorpe, J.H. (1978). Comment on: Bechhofer, F., et al., Structure, Consciousness and Action. A Sociological Profile of the British Middle Class. *British Journal of Sociology*, 29, 436–8.

Goodland, R. (ed.) (1991). *Environmentally Sustainable Development: Building on Brundtland*. Paris: UNESCO.

Goodwyn, L. (1976). *Democratic Promise: The Populist Movement in America*. New York: Oxford University Press.

Gouldner, A.W. (1979). *The Future of the Intellectuals and the Rise of the New Class*. New York: Seabury.

Grebing, H. (1986). *Arbeiterbewegung, sozialer Protest und kollektive Interessenvertretung bis 1914*. Munich: Deutscher Taschenbuch Verlag.

Greverus, I.M. (1979). *Auf der Suche nach Heimat*. Munich: Beck.

Gurr, T.R. (1970). *Why Men Rebel*. Princeton, NJ: Princeton University Press.

Gusfield, J.R. (1966). *Symbolic Crusade. Status Politics and the American Temperance Movement*. Urbana, IL: University of Illinois Press.

Gusfield, J.R. (1981a). Social movements and social change: Perspectives of linearity and fluidity. In L. Kriesberg (ed.), *Research in Social Movements, Conflict and Change* (Vol. 4, pp. 317–39). Greenwich, CT: JAI Press.

Gusfield, J.R. (1981b). *The Culture of Public Problems: Drinking-Driving and the Symbolic Order*. Chicago, IL: University of Chicago Press.

Habermas, J. (1968a). *Nachwort zu Nietzsche. Erkenntnistheoretische Schriften*. Frankfurt: Suhrkamp.

Habermas, J. (1968b). Technik und Wissenschaft als 'Ideologie'. *Technik und Wissenschaft als 'Ideologie'* (pp. 48–103). Frankfurt: Suhrkamp.

Habermas, J. (1976). *Legitimation Crisis*. London: Heinemann.

Habermas, J. (1979). *Communication and the Evolution of Society*. London: Heinemann.

Habermas, J. (1983). *Moralbewußtsein und kommunikatives Handeln*. Frankfurt: Suhrkamp.

Habermas, J. (1984). *The Theory of Communicative Action: Reason and the Rationalization of Society. Volume I*. Boston, MA: Beacon Press.

Habermas, J. (1985a). *Der philosophische Diskurs der Moderne. Zwölf Vorlesungen*. Frankfurt: Suhrkamp.

Habermas, J. (1985b). *Die neue Unübersichtlichkeit*. Frankfurt: Suhrkamp.

Habermas, J. (1987). *The Theory of Communicative Action. Lifeworld and System. A Critique of Functionalist Reason. Volume II*. Boston: Beacon Press.

Habermas, J. (1989a). *The Structural Transformation of the Public Sphere: An Inquiry into a Category of Bourgeois Society*. Cambridge, MA: MI Press.

Habermas, J. (1989b). Volkssouveränität als Verfahren. Ein normativer Begriff von Öffentlichkeit. *Merkur*, 43, 465–77.

Haferkamp, H. (1987). Angleichung ohne Gleichheit. In B. Giesen and H. Haferkamp (eds), *Soziologie der sozialen Ungleichheit* (pp. 146–88). Opladen: Westdeutscher Verlag.

Hamilton, R.F. (1982). *Who Voted for Hitler?* Princeton, NJ: Princeton University Press.

Hamilton, R.F. and Wright, J.D. (1986). *The State of the Masses*. New York: Aldine.

Hardy, D. (1979). *Alternative Communities in Nineteenth Century England*. London: Longman.

Harré, R. (1980). Social being and social change. In M. Brenner (ed.), *The Structure of Action* (pp. 287–312). Oxford: Blackwell.

Harwood, D. (1928). *Love of Animals, and How it Developed in Great Britain*. New York: Columbia University Library.

Hechter, M. (1989). *Principles of Group Solidarity*. Berkeley/Los Angeles, CA: University of California Press.

Hechter, M. (1990). The emergence of cooperative social institutions. In M. Hechter, K.D. Opp and R. Wippler (eds), *Social Institutions. Their Emergence, Maintenance and Effects* (pp. 13–34). New York: Aldine de Gruyter.

Hechter, M. (1991). *Should values be written out of the social scientists' lexicon?* Stanford, CA: Unpublished manuscript.

Hepp, C. (1987). *Avantgarde – Moderne Kunst, Kulturkritik und Reformbewegungen nach der Jahrhundertwende*. Munich: Deutscher Taschenbuch Verlag.

Hill, C.E. (ed.) (1975). *Symbols and Society. Essays on Belief Systems in Action*. Athens, GA: University of Georgia Press.

Hintze, O. (1970). *Staat und Verfassung. Gesammelte Abhandlungen zur allgemeinen Verfassungsgeschichte* (3rd edn). Göttingen: Vandenhoeck and Ruprecht.

Hirsch, J. (1988). The crisis of fordism, transformations of the 'Keynesian' security state, and new social movements. In L. Kriesberg (ed.), *Research in Social Movements, Conflicts and Change* (Vol. 10, pp. 43–55). Greenwich, CT: JAI Press.

Hirschman, A.O. (1977). *The Passions and the Interests. Political Arguments for Capitalism*. Princeton, NJ: Princeton University Press.

Hirschman, A.O. (1982). *Shifting Involvements: Private Interests and Public Action*. Princeton, NJ: Princeton University Press.

Holdermeier, M. (1979). Agrarian social protest, populism, and economic development: Some problems and some rèsults from recent studies. *Social History*, 4, 319–32.

Hollstein, W. (1981). *Die Gegengesellschaft. Alternative Lebensformen*. Bonn: Verlag Neue Gesellschaft.

Horkheimer, M. (1967). *Zur Kritik der instrumentellen Vernunft*. Frankfurt: Suhrkamp.

Horkheimer, M. and Adorno, T.W. (1947). *Dialektik der Aufklärung*. Amsterdam.

Hradil, S. (1987). *Sozialstrukturanalyse in einer fortgeschrittenen Gesellschaft. Von Klassen und Schichten zu Lagen und Milieus*. Opladen: Leske & Budrich.

Hulsberg, W. (1988). *The German Greens: A Social and Political Profile*. London: Verso.

Hurrelmann, K. (1985). Soziale Ungleichheit und Selektion im Erziehungssystem. Ergebnisse und Implikationen aus der sozialstrukturellen Sozialisationsforschung. In H. Strasser and J.H. Goldthorpe (eds), *Die Analyse sozialer Ungleichheit. Kontinuität, Erneuerung, Innovation* (pp. 48–69). Opladen: Westdeutscher Verlag.

Inglehart, R. (1977). *The Silent Revolution. Changing Values and Political Styles Among Western Publics*. Princeton, NJ: Princeton University Press.

Inglehart, R. (1981). Post-materialism in an environment of insecurity. *The American Political Science Review*, 75, 880–900.

Inglehart, R. (1990a). *Culture Shift in Advanced Industrial Societies*. Princeton, NJ: Princeton University Press.

Inglehart, R. (1990b). Values, ideology, and cognitive mobilization in new social movements. In R.J. Dalton and M. Kuechler (eds), *Challenging the Political Order. New Social and Political Movements in Western Democracies* (pp. 43–66). Oxford: Polity Press.

Jantke, C. and Hilger, D. (eds) (1965). *Die Eigentumslosen. Der deutsche Pauperismus und die Emanzipationskrise in Darstellungen und Deutungen der zeitgenössischen Literatur*. Freiburg/Munich: Alber.

Japp, K.P. (1984). Selbsterzeugung oder Fremdverschulden? Thesen zum Rationalismus in den Theorien sozialer Bewegungen. *Soziale Welt*, 35, 313–29.

Japp, K.P. (1986). Neue soziale Bewegungen und die Kontinuität der Moderne. In J. Berger (ed.), *Die Moderne – Kontinuitäten und Zäsuren. Soziale Welt Sonderband 4* (pp. 311–34). Göttingen: Schwartz.

Jenson, S. (1984) Aspekte der Medientheorie. *Zeitschrift für Soziologie*, 13, 154–64.

Jerome, J. (1974). *Families of Eden. Communes and the New Anarchism*. London: Thames and Hudson.

Joas, H. (1989). The democratization of collective action: on the creativity of collective action. In J. Alexander and P. Sztompka (eds), *Rethinking Progress. Movements, Forces and Ideas at the End of the Twentieth Century* (pp. 182–201). Boston, MA: Unwyn Hyman.

Johnson, B.B. (1987). The environmentalist movement and grid/group analysis: A modest critique. In B.B. Johnson and V.T. Covello (eds), *The Social and Cultural Construction of Risk. Essays on Risk Selection and Perception* (pp. 147–75). Dordrecht: Reidel.

Johnson, D.L. (ed.). (1982). *Class and Social Development: A New Theory of the Middle Class*. Beverly Hills, CA: Sage.

Joppke, C. (1986). The cultural dimension of class formation and class struggle: On the social theory of Pierre Bourdieu. *Berkeley Journal of Sociology*, 21, 53–78.

Kaase, M. and Klingemann, H.D. (1979). Sozialstruktur, Wertorientierung und Parteiensystem: Zum Problem der Interessenvermittlung in westlichen Demokratien. In J. Matthes (Ed.), *Sozialer Wandel in Westeuropa* (pp. 534–73). Frankfurt: Campus.

Kann, M.E. (1983). The new populism and the new Marxism. *Theory and Society*, 12, 365–73.

Kann, M.E. (1986). *Middle Class Radicalism in Santa Monica*. Philadelphia, PA: Temple University Press.

Kendall, W. (1975). *The Labour Movement in Europe*. London: Allen Lane.

Kern, H. and Schumann, M. (1984). *Das Ende der Arbeitsteilung? Rationalisierung in der industriellen Produktion: Bestandsaufnahme, Trendbestimmung*. Munich: Beck.

Kitschelt, H. (1984). *Der ökologische Diskurs. Eine Analyse von Gesellschaftskonzeptionen in der Energiedebatte.* Frankfurt: Campus.

Kitschelt, H. (1985). New social movements in West Germany and the United States. In M. Zeitlin (ed.), *Political Power and Social Theory* (Vol. 5, pp. 273–324). Greenwich, CT: JAI Press.

Kitschelt, H. (1990). New social movements and the decline of party organization. In R.J. Dalton and M. Kuechler (eds), *Challenging the Political Order. New Social and Political Movements in Western Democracies* (pp. 179–208). Oxford: Polity Press.

Kitschelt, H. (1991). Resource mobilization theory: A critique. In D. Rucht (ed.), *Research on Social Movements. The State of the Art in Western Europe and the USA* (pp. 323–47). Frankfurt/Boulder, CO: Campus/Westview Press.

Klages, H. (1984). *Wertorientierungen im Wandel.* Frankfurt: Campus.

Klandermans, B. (1984). Mobilization and participation: Social-psychological expansions of resource mobilization theory. *American Sociological Review*, 49, 583–600.

Klandermans, B. (1988). The formation and mobilization of consensus. In B. Klandermans, H. Kriesi and S. Tarrow (eds), *From Structure to Action: Comparing Social Movement Research across Cultures* (Vol. 1, International Social Movement Research, pp. 173–96). Greenwich, CT: JAI Press.

Klandermans, B. (1990). Linking the 'old' and 'new': Movement networks in the Netherlands. In R.J. Dalton and M. Kuechler (eds), *Challenging the Political Order. New Social and Political Movements in Western Democracies* (pp. 122–36). Oxford: Polity Press.

Klandermans, B. (1991). New social movements and resource mobilization: The European and American Approach revisited. In D. Rucht (ed.), *Research on Social Movements. The State of the Art in Western Europe and the USA* (pp. 17–44). Frankfurt/Boulder, CO: Campus/Westview Press.

Klandermans, B. (1992). The case for longitudinal research on movement participation. In M. Diani and R. Eyerman (eds), *Studying Collective Action* (pp. 55–75). London: Sage.

Klandermans, B. and Oegema, D. (1987). Potentials, networks, motivations and barriers: Steps toward participation in social movements. *American Sociological Review*, 51, 519–31.

Klandermans, B. and Tarrow, S. (1988). Mobilization into social movements: synthesizing European and American approaches In B. Klandermans, H. Kriesi and S. Tarrow (eds), *From Structure into Action* (Vol. 1, International Social Movement Research, pp. 1–38). Greenwich, CT: JAI Press.

Klandermans, B., Kriesi, H. and Tarrow, S. (eds). (1988). *From Structure to Action. Comparing Social Movement Research across Cultures* (Vol. 1, International Social Movement Research). Greenwich, CT: JAI Press.

Kluckhohn, F.R. and Strodtbeck, F.L. (1961). *Variations in Value Orientations.* Westport, CT: Greenwood Press.

Knorr-Cetina, K. (1981). The micro-sociological challenge of macro-sociology. In K. Knorr-Cetina and A.V. Cicourel (eds), *Advances in Social Theory and Methodology* (pp. 1–47). Boston and London: Routledge and Kegan Paul.

Knorr-Cetina, K. (1988). The micro-social order: Towards a reconception. In N.G. Fielding (ed.), *Actions and Structure: Research Methods and Social Theory* (pp. 21–53). London: Sage.

Kocka, J. (1983). *Lohnarbeit und Klassenbildung. Arbeiter und Arbeiterbewegung in Deutschland 1800–1875.* Berlin/Bonn: Dietz.

Kocka, J. and Prinz, M. (1983). Vom 'neuen Mittelstand' zum angestellten Arbeitnehmer. Kontinuität und Wandel der deutschen Angestellten seit der Weimarer Republik. In W. Conze and R.M. Lepsius (eds), *Sozialgeschichte der Bundesrepublik Deutschland* (pp. 210–55). Stuttgart: Klett.

Kohlberg, L. (1981). *The Philosophy of Moral Development. Moral Stages and the Idea of Justice.* San Francisco, CA: Harper and Row.

Konrad, G. and Szelenyi, I. (1979). *The Intellectuals on the Road to Class Power.* New York: Harcourt Brace Jovanovich.

Koselleck, R. (1973). *Kritik und Krise. Eine Studie zur Pathogenese der bürgerlichen Welt.* Frankfurt: Suhrkamp (Original 1959).

Krabbe, W.R. (1974). *Gesellschaftsveränderung durch Lebensreform. Strukturmerkmale einer sozialreformerischen Bewegung im Deutschland der Industrialisierungsepoche.* Göttingen: Vandenhoeck & Ruprecht.

Kracauer, S. (1985). *Die Angestellten. Aus dem neuesten Deutschland.* Frankfurt: Suhrkamp.

Kreckel, R. (ed.) (1983). *Soziale Ungleichheiten. Sonderband 2 der Sozialen Welt.* Göttingen: Schwartz.

Kriesi, H. (1987). Neue soziale Bewegungen: Auf der Suche nach ihrem gemeinsamen Nenner. *Politische Vierteljahresschrift,* 28, 315–34.

Kriesi, H. (1988). The interdependence of structure and action: Some reflections on the state of the art. In B. Klandermans, H. Kriesi and S. Tarrow (eds), *From Structure to Action: Comparing Social Movement Research across Cultures* (Vol. 1, International Social Movement Research, pp. 249–368). Greenwich, CT: JAI Press.

Kriesi, H. (1989). New social movements and the new class in the Netherlands. *American Journal of Sociology,* 94, 1078–117.

Kriesi, H. (1992). Support and mobilization potential for new social movements: Concepts, operationalizations and illustrations from the Netherlands. In M. Diani and R. Eyerman (eds), *Studying Collective Action* (pp. 22–54). London: Sage.

Kuechler, M. and Dalton, R.J. (1990). New social movements and the political order: Inducing change for long-term stability? In R.J. Dalton and M. Kuechler (eds), *Challenging the Political Order. New Social and Political Movements in Western Democracies* (pp. 277–300). Oxford: Polity Press.

Kumar, K. (1983). Class and political action in nineteenth-century England. Theoretical and comparative perspectives. *Archives Européennes de Sociologie,* 24, 3–43.

Laclau, E. (1977). Towards a theory of populism. In E. Laclau (ed.), *Politics and Ideology in Marxist Theory* (pp. 143–98). New Left Books.

Landsberger, H.A. (ed.) (1973). *Rural Protest. Peasant Movements and Social Change.* New York: Barnes & Noble.

Lane, R.E. (1991). *The Market Experience.* Cambridge: Cambridge University Press.

Lapeyronnie, D. (1988). Mouvements sociaux et action politique. Existe-t-il une théorie de la mobilisation des ressources? *Revue française de sociologie,* 29, 593–619.

Lash, S. (1990). *Sociology of Postmodernism.* London: Routledge.

Lash, S. and Urry, J. (1984). The new Marxism of collective action. *Sociology,* 18, 33–50.

Lash, S. and Urry, J. (1987). *The End of Organized Capitalism.* Cambridge: Polity Press.

Leach, E. (ed.) (1968). *Dialectic of Practical Religion.* Cambridge: Cambridge University Press.

Leach, E. (1976). *Culture and Communication. The Logic by which Symbols are Connected.* Cambridge: Cambridge University Press.

LeBon, G. (1963). *La psychologie des foules.* Paris: Presses Universitaires de France (Original 1903).

Lechner, F.J. (1985). Modernity and its discontents. In J. Alexander (ed.), *Neofunctionalism* (pp. 157–76). Beverly Hills, CA: Sage.

Lederer, E. (1912). *Die Privatangestellten in der modernen Wirtschaftsentwicklung.* Tübingen: Mohr.

Lederer, E. (1979). Die Gesellschaft der Unselbständigen. Zum sozialpsychologischen Habitus der Gegenwart (1913/19). In J. Kocka (ed.), *Kapitalismus, Klassenstruktur und Probleme der Demokratie in Deutschland 1910–1940. Ausgewählte Aufsätze von Emil Lederer* (pp. 14–32). Göttingen: Vandenhoeck & Ruprecht.

Leineweber, B. (1981). *Pflugschrift. Über Politik und Alltag in Landkommunen und anderen Alternativen.* Frankfurt: Verlag Neue Kritik.

Levitt, B. and March, J.G. (1988). Organizational learning. *Annual Review of Sociology,* 14, 319–40.

Lewy, G. (1974). *Religion and Revolution.* New York: Oxford University Press.

Linse, U. (1983a). *Barfüßige Propheten. Erlöser der zwanziger Jahre.* Munich: Siedler.

Linse, U. (ed.). (1983b). *Zurück, o Mensch, zur Mutter Erde. Landkommunen in Deutschland 1890–1933*. Munich: Deutscher Taschenbuch Verlag.

Lipset, S.M. (1959). Democracy and working class authoritarianism. *American Sociological Review*, 24, 482–501.

Lipset, S.M. (1988). *Revolution and Counterrevolution* (rev. edn). New Brunswick, NJ: Transaction Books.

Lockwood, D. (1981). The weakest link in the chain? Some comments on the Marxist theory of action. *Research in the Sociology of Work*, 1, 435–81. Greenwich, CT: JAI Press.

Lockwood, D. (1987). Staatsbürgerliche Ungleichheit. In B. Giesen and H. Haferkamp (eds), *Soziologie der Sozialen Ungleichheit* (pp. 31–48). Opladen: Westdeutscher Verlag.

Luhmann, N. (1982). *The Differentiation of Society*. New York: Columbia University Press.

Luhmann, N. (1984). *Soziale Systeme. Grundriß einer allgemeinen Theorie*. Frankfurt: Suhrkamp.

Luhmann, N. (1985). Zum Begriff der sozialen Klasse. In N. Luhmann (ed.), *Soziale Differenzierung* (pp. 119–62). Opladen: Westdeutscher Verlag.

Luhmann, N. (1989). *Ecological Communication*. Chicago, IL: University of Chicago Press.

Luhmann, N. (1990a). *Essays on Self-Reference*. New York: Columbia University Press.

Luhmann, N. (1990b). *Soziologische Aufklarung 5. Konstruktivistische Perspektiven*. Opladen: Westdeutscher Verlag.

Lukács, G. (1971). *History and Class Consciousness*. Cambridge, MA: MI Press.

Luke, T. W. (1988). The dreams of deep ecology. *Telos*, 76, 65–92.

Luke, T. W. (1989). *Screens of Power. Ideology, Domination, and Resistance in Informational Society*. Urbana, IL: University of Illinois Press.

Lukes, S. (1991). *Moral Conflicts and Politics*. Oxford: Clarendon Press.

Luthe, H.O. and Meulemann, H. (eds) (1988). *Wertwandel – Faktum oder Fiktion? Bestandsaufnahmen und Diagnosen aus kultursoziologischer Sicht*. Frankfurt: Campus.

Macpherson, C.B. (1967). *Die politische Theorie des Besitzindividualismus. Von Hobbes bis Locke*. Frankfurt: Suhrkamp.

McAdam, D. (1988). Micromobilization contexts and recruitment to activism. In B. Klandermans, H. Kriesi and S. Tarrow (eds), *From Structure to Action: Comparing Social Movement Research Across Cultures* (Vol. 1, International Social Movement Research, pp. 125–54). Greenwich, CT: JAI Press.

McAdams, J. (1987). Testing the theory of the new class. *Sociological Quarterly*, 28, 23–49.

McCarthy, J.D. (1987). Pro-life and pro-choice mobilization: Infrastructure deficits and new technologies. In M.N. Zald and J.D. McCarthy (eds), *Social Movements in an Organizational Society* (pp. 49–66). New Brunswick/Oxford: Transaction Books.

McCarthy, J.D. and Wolfson, M. (1990). Consensus movements, conflict movements, and the cooptation of civic and state infrastructures. In A. Morris and C. Mueller (eds), *Frontiers of Social Movement Theory*. New Haven, CT: Yale University Press.

McCarthy, J.D. and Zald, M.N. (1973). *The Trend of Social Movements in America: Professionalization and Resource Mobilization*. Morristown, NJ: General Learning Corporation.

McKenna, G. (1974). Populism: the American ideology. In G. McKenna (ed.), *American Populism* (pp. 11–21). New York: Capricorn Books.

McNall, S.G. (1988). *The Road to Rebellion: Class Formation and Kansas Populism, 1865–1900*. Chicago, IL: University of Chicago Press.

Mangham, I. and Overington, M. (1987). *Organization as Theatre. A Social Psychology of Dramatic Appearances*. New York: Wiley & Sons.

Mannheim, K. (1936). *Ideology and Utopia. An Introduction to the Sociology of Knowledge*. New York: Harcourt.

Manuel, F.E. and Manuel, F.P. (1979). *Utopian Thought in the Western World*. Cambridge, MA: Harvard University Press.

March, J.G. and Olsen, J.P. (1989). *Rediscovering Institutions: The Organizational Basis of Politics*. New York: Free Press.

Marshall, T.H. (1950). *Citizenship and Social Class*. Cambridge, MA: Harvard University Press.

Martens, W. (1968). *Die Botschaft der Tugend. Die Aufklärung im Spiegel der deutschen Moralischen Wochenschriften.* Stuttgart: Metzler.

Marwell, G., Oliver, P.E. and Prahl, R. (1989). Social networks and collective action. A theory of the critical mass III. *American Journal of Sociology*, 94, 502–35.

Matthes, J. (1984). Über die Arbeit mit lebensgeschichtlichen Erzählungen in einer nicht-westlichen Kultur. In H. Kohli and G. Robert (eds), *Biographie uns soziale Wirklichkeit* (pp. 284–96). Stuttgart: Metzler.

Matthes, J. (1985). Anmerkungen zum Wirklichkeitsverhältnis der Soziologie. In W. Bonß and H. Hartmann (eds), *Entzauberte Wissenschaft. Zur Relativität und Geltung soziologischer Forschung* (pp. 49–64). Göttingen: Schwartz.

Matthiesen, U. (1989). 'Bourdieu' und 'Konopka'. Imaginäres Rendezvous zwischen Habitus-Konstruktion und Deutungsmuster-Rekonstruktion. In K. Eder (ed.), *Klassenlage, Lebensstil und kulturelle Praxis* (pp. 221–99). Frankfurt: Suhrkamp.

Mayer, K.U. and Blossfeld, H.P. (1990). Die gesellschaftliche Konstruktion sozialer Ungleichheit im Lebensverlauf. In P.A. Berger and S. Hradil (eds), *Lebenslagen, Lebensläufe, Lebensstile (Soziale Welt, Sonderband 7)* (pp. 297–318). Göttingen: Otto Schwartz.

Meillassoux, C. (1973). Y a-t-il des castes aux Indes? *Cahiers Internationaux de Sociologie*, 54, 5–24.

Mcillassoux, C. (1976). *'Die wilden Früchte der Frau'. Über häusliche Produktion und kapitalistische Wirtschaft.* Frankfurt: Syndikat.

Melucci, A. (1980). The new social movements: A theoretical approach. *Social Science Information*, 19, 199–226.

Melucci, A. (1984). An end to social movements? Introductory paper to the sessions on 'New Movements and Change in Organizational Forms'. *Social Science Information*, 23, 819–35.

Melucci, A. (1985). The symbolic challenge of contemporary movements. *Social Research*, 52, 789–816.

Melucci, A. (1988). Getting involved: Identity and mobilization in social movements. In B. Klandermans, H. Kriesi and S. Tarrow (eds), *From Structure to Action: Comparing Social Movement Research across Cultures* (Vol. 1, International Social Movement Research, pp. 329–48). Greenwich, CT: JAI Press.

Melucci, A. (1989). *Nomads of the Present. Social Movements and Individual Needs in Contemporary Society.* (Edited by John Keane and Paul Mier.) London: Hutchinson Radius.

Melucci, A. and Diani, M. (1992). *Nazioni senza stato. I movimenti etnico-nazionali in Occidente* (2nd edn). Milan: Feltrinelli.

Mesch, H. (ed.) (1990). *Ecoresistance / Ökowiderstand (Gulliver, Bd. 27).* Berlin/Hamburg: Argument Verlag.

Meyer, J.W. and Rowan, B. (1977). Institutionalized organizations: Formal structure as myth and ceremony. *American Journal of Sociology*, 83, 340–63.

Meyer, J.W. and Scott, W.R. (1983). *Organizational Environments: Ritual and Rationality.* Beverly Hills, CA: Sage.

Milbrath, L.W. (1989). *Envisioning a Sustainable Society: Learning Our Way Out.* Buffalo, NY: State University of New York Press.

Miller, M. (1986). *Kollektive Lernprozesse. Studien zur Grundlegung einer soziologischen Lerntheorie.* Frankfurt: Suhrkamp.

Miller, M. (1987). Culture and collective argumentation. *Argumentation*, 1, 127–54.

Miller, M. (1989). Verzerrte Legitimationsdiskurse. In K. Eder (ed.), *Klassenlage, Lebensstil und kulturelle Praxis* (pp. 191–220). Frankfurt: Suhrkamp.

Miller, M. (1992). Discourse and morality – two case studies of social conflicts in a segmentary and a functionally differentiated society. *Archives Européennes de Sociologie.*

Mills, C.W. (1956). *The Power Elite.* London: Oxford University Press.

Misra, B. and Preston, J. (eds) (1978). *Community, Self, and Identity.* The Hague: Mouton.

Moore, B. (1966). *Social Origins of Dictatorship and Democracy. Lord and Peasant in the Making of the Modern World.* Boston, MA: Beacon Press.

Moore, B. (1978). *Injustice: The Social Bases of Obedience and Revolt*. White Plains, NY: Sharpe.

Mooser, J. (1983a). Abschied von der 'Proletarität' Sozialstruktur und Lage der Arbeiterschaft in der Bundesrepublik Deutschland in historischer Perspektive. In W. Conze and M.R. Lepsius (eds), *Sozialgeschichte der Bundesrepublik Deutschland. Beiträge zum Kontinuitätsproblem* (pp. 143–86). Stuttgart: Klett.

Mooser, J. (1983b). Auflösung der proletarischen Milieus. *Soziale Welt*, 34, 270–306.

Mooser, J. (1984). *Arbeiterleben in Deutschland 1900–1970*. Frankfurt: Suhrkamp.

Moscovici, S. (1968). *L'histoire humaine de la nature*. Paris: Flammarion.

Moscovici, S. (1972). *La société contre nature*. Paris: Union Générale d'Editions.

Moscovici, S. (1976). Die Wiederverzauberung der Welt. In A. Touraine, H.P. Dreitzel, S. Moscovici, R. Sennet et al. (eds), *Jenseits der Krise. Wider das politische Defizit der Ökologie* (pp. 94–131). Frankfurt: Syndikat.

Moscovici, S. (1979). *Sozialer Wandel durch Minoritäten*. Munich: Urban and Schwarzenberg.

Moscovici, S. (1985). *L'âge des foules. Un traité historique de psychologie des masses*. Brussels: Editions Complexe.

Moscovici, S. (1990). Questions for the twenty-first century. *Theory, Culture and Society*, 7, 119.

Mousnier, R. (1974). *Les institutions de la France sous la monarchie absolue. Vol. 1, Société et Etat*. Paris: Presses Universitaires de France.

Mousnier, R. (1980). *Les institutions de la France sous la monarchie absolue. Vol. 2, Les classes sociales*. Paris: Presses Universitaires de France.

Müller-Rommel, F. (ed.) (1989). *New Politics in Western Europe: The Rise and Success of Green Parties and Alternative Lists*. Boulder, CO: Westview Press.

Musgrave, F. (1974). *Ecstasy and Holiness. Counterculture and the Open Society*. London: Methuen.

Mutz, G. (1987). Arbeitslosigkeit in der Dienstleistungsgesellschaft. *Soziale Welt*, 3, 255–81.

Na'aman, S. (1978). *Zur Entstehung der deutschen Arbeiterbewegung. Lernprozesse und Vergesellschaftung 1830–1868*. Hanover: SOAK.

Nash, R.F. (1989). *The Rights of Nature: A History of Environmental Ethics*. Madison, WI: University of Wisconsin Press.

Neidhardt, F. and Rucht, D. (1991). The analysis of social movements: The state of the art and some perspectives for further research. In D. Rucht (ed.), *Research on Social Movements: The State of the Art in Western Europe and the USA* (pp. 421–64). Frankfurt/ Boulder, CO: Campus and Westview Press.

Niehues-Pröbsting, H. (1988). *Der Kynismus des Diogenes und der Begriff des Zynismus*. Frankfurt: Suhrkamp.

Nipperdey, T. (1972). Verein als soziale Struktur in Deutschland im späten 18. und frühen 19. Jahrhundert. In H. Boockmann et al. (ed.), *Geschichtswissenschaft und Vereinswesen im 19. Jahrhundert* (pp. 1–44). Göttingen: Vandenhoeck & Ruprecht.

Oberschall, A. (1973). *Social Conflicts and Social Movements*. Englewood Cliffs, NJ: Prentice-Hall.

Oberschall, A. (1978). The decline of the 1960s social movements. In L. Kriesberg (ed.), *Research in Social Movements, Conflicts and Change* (Vol. 1, pp. 257–89). Greenwich, CT: JAI Press.

O'Connor, J. (1973). *The Fiscal Crisis of the State*. London: St. Martin's Press.

O'Connor, J. (1990). The second contradiction of capitalism: Causes and consequences. Santa Cruz, CA: Unpublished manuscript, University of California.

Offe, C. (1972). *Strukturprobleme des kapitalistischen Staates*. Frankfurt: Suhrkamp.

Offe, C. (1985a). Bemerkungen zur spieltheoretischen Neufassung des Klassenbegriffs bei Wright und Elster. *Prokla*, 15, 83–8.

Offe, C. (1985b). *Disorganized Capitalism. Contemporary Transformations of Work and Politics*. Cambridge: Polity Press.

Offe, C. (1985c). New social movements: Challenging the boundaries of institutional politics. *Social Research*, 52, 817–68.

Offe, C. and Wiesenthal, H. (1980). Two logics of collective action: Theoretical notes on social class and organizational form. In M. Zeitlin (ed.), *Political Power and Social Theory* (Vol. 1, pp. 67–115). Greenwich, CT: JAI Press.

Oliver, P.E. (1980). Rewards and punishments as selective incentives for collective action: Theoretical investigations. *American Journal of Sociology*, 585, 1356–75.

Oliver, P.E. and Marwell, G. (1988). The paradox of group size in collective action: A theory of the critical mass II. *American Sociological Review*, 53, 1–8.

Oliver, P.E., Marwell, G. and Teixeira, R. (1985). Interdependence, group heterogeneity, and the production of collective goods. A theory of the critical mass I. *American Journal of Sociology*, 91, 522–56.

Olofsson, G. (1988). After the working-class movement? An essay on what's 'new' and what's 'social' in the new social movements. *Acta Sociologica*, 31, 15–34.

Opp, K.D. (1989). *The Rationality of Political Protest. A Comparative Analysis of Rational Choice Theory*. Boulder, CO: Westview Press.

O'Riordan, T. (1990). The politics of sustainability. In R. K. Turner (ed.), *Sustainable Environmental Management. Principles and Practice* (pp. 29–50). London/Boulder, CO: Belhaven Press/Westview Press.

Pakulski, J. (1990). Mass Movements and Social Class. Paper prepared for the World Congress of Sociology in Madrid, Spain, 9–13 July 1990.

Pappi, F.U. (1981). The petite bourgeoisie and the new middle class. Differentiation and homogenisation of the middle strata in Germany. In F. Bechhofer and B. Elliott (eds), *The Petite Bourgeoisie. Comparative Studies of the Uneasy Stratum* (pp. 105–20). New York: St. Martin's Press.

Parkin, F. (1968). *Middle Class Radicalism*. Manchester: Manchester University Press.

Pearce, F. (1991). *Green Warriors. The People and the Politics Behind the Environmental Revolution*. London: The Bodley Head.

Peters, J. (ed.) (1980). *Die Geschichte alternativer Projekte von 1800 bis 1975*. Berlin: Verlag Klaus Guhl.

Piven, F.F. and Cloward, R.A. (1972). *Regulating the Poor. The Function of Public Welfare*. London: Tavistock.

Pizzorno, A. (1986). Some other kinds of otherness: A critique of 'rational choice' theories. In A. Foxley, M.S. McPherson and G. O'Donnell (eds), *Development, Democracy and the Art of Trespassing: Essays in Honor of Albert O. Hirschman* (pp. 355–73). Notre Dame, IN: University of Notre Dame Press.

Plotkin, H.C. (ed.) (1982). *Learning, Development, and Culture*. Chichester/New York: Wiley & Sons.

Poggi, G. (1978). *The Development of the Modern State: A Sociological Introduction*. Stanford, CA: Stanford University Press.

Poguntke, T. (1987). The organization of a participatory party – the German Greens. *European Journal of Political Research*, 15, 609–33.

Polanyi, K. (1957). *The Great Transformation. The Political and Economic Origins of Our Time*. Boston, MA: Beacon Press (Original 1943).

Prinz, M. (1981). Das Ende der Standespolitik. Voraussetzungen und Konsequenzen mittelständischer Interessenpolitik in der Weimarer Republik am Beispiel des Deutschnationalen Handlungsgehilfenverbandes. In J. Kocka (ed.), *Angestellte im europäischen Vergleich. Die Herausbildung angestellter Mittelschichten seit dem späten 19. Jahrhundert* (pp. 313–53). Göttingen: Vandenhoeck & Ruprecht.

Puhle, H.J. (1975). *Politische Agrarbewegungen in kapitalistischen Industriegesellschaften*. Göttingen: Vandenhoeck & Ruprecht.

Raschke, J. (1985). *Soziale Bewegungen. Ein historisch-systematischer Grundriß*. Frankfurt: Campus.

Rawls, J. (1971). *A Theory of Justice*. Cambridge, MA: Harvard University Press.

Reddy, W.M. (1985). *The Rise of Market Culture*. Cambridge: Cambridge University Press.

Renn, O. (1985). Die Alternativbewegung: Eine historisch-soziologische Analyse des Protests gegen die Industriegesellschaft. *Zeitschrift für Politik*, 32, 153–94.

Roemer, J.E. (1982). *A General Theory of Exploitation and Class*. Cambridge, MA: Harvard University Press.

Roemer, J.E. (ed.) (1986). *Analytical Marxism*. Cambridge and Paris: Cambridge University Press and Editions de la Maison des sciences de l'homme.

Rogowski, R. (1985). Causes and varieties of nationalism: A rationalist account. In E.A. Tiryakina and R. Rogowski (eds), *New Nationalisms of the Developed West* (pp. 87–146). Boston, MA: Allen & Unwin.

Roth, G. (1975). Socio-historical model and developmental theory. Charismatic community, charisma of reason and the counterculture. *American Sociological Review*, 40, 148–57.

Roth, R. (1989). Fordismus und neue soziale Bewegungen. In U.C. Wasmuht (ed.), *Alternativen zur alten Politik? Neue soziale Bewegungen in der Diskussion* (pp. 13–37). Darmstadt: Wissenschaftliche Buchgesellschaft.

Rucht, D. (1984). Recht auf Widerstand? Aktualität, Legitimität und Grenzen 'zivilen Ungehorsams'. In B. Guggenberger and C. Offe (eds), *An den Grenzen der Merhheits-demokratie* (pp. 254–81). Opladen: Westdeutscher Verlag.

Rucht, D. (1987). Von der Bewegung zur Institution? In R. Roth and D. Rucht (eds), *Neue soziale Bewegungen in der Bundesrepublik Deutschland* (pp. 238–62). Frankfurt: Campus.

Rucht, D. (ed.) (1991). *Research on Social Movements. The State of the Art in Western Europe and the USA*. Frankfurt: Campus.

Rüdig, W. (1990). *Anti-Nuclear Movements: A World Survey of Opposition to Nuclear Energy*. London: Longman.

Rüdig, W. (1991). *The Green Wave: A Comparative Analysis of Ecological Parties*. London: Polity Press.

Sahlins, M. (1976). *Culture and Practical Reason*. Chicago, IL: University of Chicago Press.

Salt, H.S. (1886). *A Plea for Vegetarianism*. Manchester.

Salt, H.S. (1980). *Animals' Rights Considered in Relation to Social Progress*. Revised edition with preface by Peter Singer (Original 1892). Clarks Summit, PA: Society for Animal Rights.

Schäfer, W. (1985). *Die unvertraute Moderne. Historische Umrisse einer anderen Natur- und Sozialgeschichte*. Frankfurt: Fischer.

Schelsky, H. (1975). *Die Arbeit tun die Anderen*. Opladen: Westdeutscher Verlag.

Schimank, U. (1983). *Neoromantischer Protest im Spätkapitalismus: Der Widerstand gegen die Stadt- und Landschaftsverödung*. Bielefeld: AJZ-Verlag.

Schindler, N. (1984). Spuren in der Geschichte der 'anderen' Zivilisation. Probleme und Perspektiven einer historischen Volkskulturforschung. In R. van Dülmen and N. Schindler (eds), *Volkskultur. Zur Wiederentdeckung des vergessenen Alltags (16.–20. Jahrhundert)* (pp. 13–77). Frankfurt: Fischer.

Schluchter, W. (1979). The paradoxes of rationalization. In G. Roth and W. Schluchter (eds), *Max Weber's Vision of History* (pp. 11–64). Berkeley/Los Angeles, CA: University of California Press.

Schluchter, W. (1981). *The Rise of Western Rationalism: Max Weber's Developmental History*. Berkeley/Los Angeles, CA: University of California Press.

Schmid, M. (1982). Habermas' theory of social evolution. In J.B. Thompson and D. Held (eds), *Habermas: Critical Debates* (pp. 162–80). London: Macmillan.

Schmidt, A. (1971). *Der Begriff der Natur in der Lehre von Marx* (2nd edn). Frankfurt: EVA.

Schwartz, B. (1981). *Vertical Classification. A Study in Structuralism and in the Sociology of Knowledge*. Chicago, IL: University of Chicago Press.

Sessions, G. (1987). The deep ecology movement: A review. *Environmental Ethics*, 8, 105–25.

Sicinski, A. and Wemegah, M. (eds) (1983). *Alternative Ways of Life in Contemporary Europe*. Tokyo: United Nations University.

Singer, P. (1976). *Animal Liberation. A New Ethics for our Treatment of Animals*. London: Cambridge University Press.

Singer, P. (1979). *Practical Ethics*. London: Cambridge University Press.

Sjoeberg, G. (1960). Contradictory functional requirements and social systems. *Journal of Conflict Resolution*, 4, 198–208.

Skinner, Q. (1978). *The Foundations of Modern Political Thought. Vols I-II*. Cambridge: Cambridge University Press.

Sloterdijk, P. (1983). *Kritik der zynischen Vernunft*. Frankfurt: Suhrkamp.

Smelser, N.J. (1962). *Theory of Collective Behavior*. New York: Free Press.

Smelser, N.J. (1985). Evaluating the model of structural differentiation in relation to educational change in the nineteenth century. In J. Alexander (ed.), *Neofunctionalism* (pp. 113–30). Beverly Hills, CA: Sage.

Smith, A.D. (1972). Ethnocentrism, nationalism and social change. *International Journal of Comparative Sociology*, 13, 1–20.

Smith, A.D. (1981). *The Ethnic Revival*. Cambridge: Cambridge University Press.

Smith, A.D. (1986). *The Ethnic Origins of Nations*. Oxford: Basil Blackwell.

Snow, D.A. and Benford, R.D. (1988). Ideology, frame resonance, and participant mobilization. In B. Klandermans, H. Kriesi and S. Tarrow (eds), *From Structure to Action: Comparing Social Movement Research Across Cultures* (Vol. 1, International Social Movement Research, pp. 197–217). Greenwich, CT: JAI Press.

Snow, D.A. and Benford, R.D. (1991). Collective action frames. In A. Morris and C. Mueller (eds), *Frontiers in Social Movement Theory*. New Haven: Yale University Press.

Snow, D.A., Rochford, E.B., Worden, S.K. and Benford, R.D. (1986). Frame alignment processes, micromobilization and movements participation. *American Sociological Review*, 51, 464–81.

Sørensen, A.B. (1991). On the usefulness of class analysis in research on social mobility and socioeconomic inequality. *Acta Sociologica*, 34, 71–87.

Speier, H. (1977). *Die Angestellten vor dem Nationalsozialismus. Ein Beitrag zum Verständnis der deutschen Sozialstruktur 1918–1933*. Göttingen: Vandenhoeck & Ruprecht.

Sprondel, W.L. (1986). Kulturelle Modernisierung durch antimodernistischen Protest. Der lebensreformerische Vegetarismus. In F. Neidhardt, M.R. Lepsius and J. Weiß (eds), *Kultur und Gesellschaft. Sonderheft der KZfSS* (Vol. 27, pp. 314–30). Opladen: Westdeutscher Verlag.

Steinmetz, G. and Wright, E.O. (1989). The fall and rise of the petty bourgeoisie: Changing patterns of self-employment in the postwar United States. *American Journal of Sociology*, 94, 973–1019.

Streeck, W. and Schmitter, P.C. (1985). Community, market, state – and associations? The prospective contribution of interest governance to social order. In W. Streeck and P.C. Schmitter (eds), *Private Interest Government. Beyond Market and State* (pp. 1–29). London: Sage.

Strydom, P. (1987). Collective Learning: Habermas' concessions and their theoretical implications. *Philosophy and Social Criticism*, 13, 265–81.

Symmons-Symonolewicz, K. (1965). Nationalist movements: An attempt at a comparative typology. *Comparative Studies in Society and History*, 4, 253–64.

Tarrow, S. (1982). *Social Movements, Resource Mobilization and Reform during Cycles of Protest: A Bibliographic and Critical Essay* (Western Societies Program. Occasional Paper No. 15. Center for International Studies, Cornell University). Center for International Studies, Cornell University.

Tarrow, S. (1989). *Democracy and Disorder. Protest and Politics in Italy 1965–1975*. Oxford: Clarendon Press.

Teubner, G. (1989a). 'And God Laughed . . .': Indeterminacy, self-reference and paradox in law. In C. Joerges and D.M. Trubek (eds), *Critical-Legal Thought: An American–German Debate* (pp. 399–434). Baden-Baden: Nomos.

Teubner, G. (1989b). *Recht als autopoietisches System*. Frankfurt: Suhrkamp.

Therborn, G. (1991). Cultural belonging, structural location and human action. Explanation in and sociology and social science. *Acta Sociologica*, 34, 177–91.

Thomas, K. (1983). *Man and the Natural World. A History of the Modern Sensibility*. New York: Pantheon Books.

Thompson, E.P. (1968). *The Making of the English Working Class*. Harmondsworth: Penguin.

Thompson, E.P. (1971). The moral economy of the English crowd in the eighteenth century. *Past and Present*, 50, 76–136.

Thompson, E.P. (1974). Patrician society, plebeian culture. *Journal of Social History*, 7, 382–405.

Thompson, E.P. (1978). Eighteenth-century English society: Class struggle without class. *Social History*, 3, 133–64.

Thompson, M., Ellis, R. and Wildavsky, A. (1990). *Cultural Theory, or, Why All that is Permanent is Bias*. Boulder, CO: Westview Press.

Tilly, C. (1977). Hauptformen kollektiver Aktion in Westeuropa 1500–1975. *Geschichte und Gesellschaft*, 3, 153–63.

Tilly, C. (1978). *From Mobilization to Revolution*. Reading, MA: Addison-Wesley.

Tilly, C. (1985). Models and realities of popular collective action. *Social Research*, 52, 717–48.

Tilly, C. (1988). Social movements, old and new. In L. Kriesberg (ed), *Research in Social Movements, Conflicts and Change* (Vol. 10, pp. 1–18). Greenwich, CT: JAI Press.

Tilly, C., Tilly, L. and Tilly R. (1975). *The Rebellious Century*. Cambridge, MA: Harvard University Press.

Timm, H. (1978). *Die heilige Revolution. Schleiermacher – Novalis – Friedrich Schlegel*. Frankfurt: Syndikat.

Tiryakian, E.A. (1991). Modernisation: exhumetur in pace (rethinking macrosociology in the 1990s). *International Sociology*, 6, 165–80.

Tiryakian, E.A. (1992). Dialectics of modernity: reenchantment and dedifferentiation as counter-processes. In H. Haferkamp and N.J. Smelser (eds), *Social Change and Modernity* (pp. 78–94). Berkeley/Los Angeles, CA: University of California Press.

Tiryakian, E.A. and Rogowski, R. (eds). (1985). *New Nationalisms of the Developed West*. Boston: Allen and Unwin.

Touraine, A. (1969). *La société postindustrielle*. Paris: Denoël.

Touraine, A. (1977). *The Self-Production of Society*. Chicago, IL: University of Chicago Press.

Touraine, A. (1978). *La voix et le regard*. Paris: Seuil.

Touraine, A. (1981). *The Voice and the Eye*. New York: Cambridge University Press.

Touraine, A. (1985). An introduction to the study of social movements. *Social Research*, 52, 749–88.

Touraine, A. (1992). Two interpretations of contemporary social change. In H. Haferkamp and N.J. Smelser (eds), *Social Change and Modernity* (pp. 55–77). Berkeley/Los Angeles, CA: University of California Press.

Touraine, A., Hegedus, Z., Dubet, F. and Wieviorka, M. (1980). *La prophétie anti-nucléaire*. Paris: Seuil.

Trow, M. (1958). Small businessmen, political tolerance, and support for McCarthy. *American Journal of Sociology*, 64, 270–81.

Tugendhat, E. (1980). Zur Entwicklung von moralischen Begründungsstrukturen im modernen Recht. *Archiv für Rechts- und Sozialphilosophie. Beiheft Neue Folge*, 14, 1–20.

Tumin, M.M. (1967). *Social Stratification. The Forms and Functions of Inequality*. Englewood Cliffs, NJ: Prentice-Hall.

Turner, B.S. (ed.) (1990). *Theories of Modernity and Postmodernity*. London: Sage.

Turner, J.H. (1988). *A Theory of Social Interaction*. Stanford, CA: Stanford University Press.

Turner, R.H. (1969). The public perception of protest. *American Sociological Review*, 34, 815–31.

Turner, R.K. (1990). Sustainability, resource conservation and pollution control: An overview. In R.K. Turner (ed.), *Sustainable Environmental Management: Principles and Practices* (pp. 1–25). London/Boulder, CO: Belhaven Press / Westview Press.

Unger, R.M. (1975). *Knowledge and Politics*. New York: Free Press.

Unger, R.M. (1987). *False Necessity: Anti-necessitarian Social Theory in the Service of Radical Democracy. Part 1 of Politics: A Work in Constructive Social Theory.* Cambridge: Cambridge University Press.

Van der Veen, G. and Klandermans, B. (1989). 'Exit' behavior in social movement organizations. In B. Klandermans (ed.), *Organizing for Change: Social Movement Organizations in Europe and the United States* (Vol. 2, International Social Movement Research, pp. 33–59). Greenwich, CT: JAI Press.

Venturi, F. (1960). *The Roots of Revolution.* London.

Vester, M. (1970). *Die Entstehung des Proletariats als Lernprozeß? Die Entstehung antikapitalistischer Theorie und Praxis in England 1792–1848.* Frankfurt: Europäische Verlagsanstalt.

Vester, M. (1983). Die 'Neuen Plebejer': Thesen zur Klassen- und Schichtstruktur und zu den Entwicklungsperspektiven der neuen sozialen Bewegungen. In H.H. Hartwich (ed.), *Gesellschaftliche Probleme als Anstoß und Folge von Politik* (pp. 213–24). Opladen: Westdeutscher Verlag.

Vester, M. (1989). Neue soziale Bewegungen und soziale Schichten. In U.C. Wasmuht (ed.), *Alternativen zur alten Politik? Neue soziale Bewegungen in der Diskussion* (pp. 38–63). Darmstadt: Wissenschaftliche Buchgesellschaft.

Vondung, K. (ed.) (1976). *Das wilhelminische Bildungsbürgertum. Zur Sozialgeschichte seiner Ideen.* Göttingen: Vandenhoeck & Ruprecht.

Wallerstein, I. (1979). Modernization: Requiescat in pace. In I. Wallerstein (ed.), *The Capitalist World Economy.* Cambridge/Paris: Cambridge University Press/Editions de la Maison des sciences de l'homme.

Weber, M. (1956). *Wirtschaft und Gesellschaft.* Tübingen: Mohr.

Wegener, B. (1985). Gibt es Sozialprestige? *Zeitschrift für Soziologie*, 14, 209–35.

Weiß, J. (1986). Wiederverzauberung der Welt? Bemerkungen zur Wiederkehr der Romantik in der gegenwärtigen Kulturkritik. In F. Neidhardt, R.M. Lepsius and J. Weiß (eds), *Kultur und Gesellschaft. Sonderheft 27 der KZfSS* (pp. 286–301). Opladen: Westdeutscher Verlag.

Werblowsky, R.J. (1976). *Beyond Tradition and Modernity. Changing Religions in a Changing World.* London: Athlone Press.

Weymann, A. (ed.) (1987). *Bildung und Beschäftigung – Grundzüge und Perspektiven eines Strukturwandels. Sonderband 5 der Sozialen Welt.* Göttingen: Schwartz.

Williamson, O. (1975). *Markets and Hierarchies.* New York: The Free Press.

Wilson, B.R. (ed.) (1967). *Patterns of Sectarianism. Organisation and Ideology in Social and Religious Movements.* London: Heinemann.

Winkler, H.A. (1971). Der rückversicherte Mittelstand: Die Interessenverbände von Handwerk und Kleinhandel im deutschen Kaiserreich. In W. Rüegg and O. Neuloh (eds), *Zur soziologischen Theorie und Analyse des 19. Jahrhunderts* (pp. 163–79). Göttingen: Vandenhoeck & Ruprecht.

Winkler, H.A. (1978). Vom Sozialprotektionismus zum Nationalsozialismus. Die Bewegung des gewerblichen Mittelstandes in Deutschland im Vergleich. In H.G. Haupt (ed.), *'Bourgeois und Volk zugleich?' Zur Geschichte des Kleinbürgertums im 19. und 20. Jahrhundert* (pp. 143–61). Frankfurt: Campus.

Winkler, H.A. (1979). Extremismus der Mitte? Sozialgeschichtliche Aspekte der nationalsozialistischen Machtergreifung. In H.A. Winkler (ed.), *Liberalismus und Antiliberalismus. Studien zur politischen Sozialgeschichte des 19. und 20. Jahrhunderts* (pp. 205–17/349–35). Göttingen: Vandenhoeck & Ruprecht.

Winkler, H.A. (1983). Stabilisierung durch Schrumpfung: Der gewerbliche Mittelstand in der Bundesrepublik. In W. Conze and M.R. Lepsius (eds), *Sozialgeschichte der Bundesrepublik Deutschland. Beiträge zum Kontinuitätsproblem* (pp. 187–209). Stuttgart: Klett-Cotta.

Winkler, H.A. (1985). *Von der Revolution zur Stabilisierung. Arbeiter und Arbeiterbewegung in der Weimarer Republik 1918–1924* (2nd edn). Berlin/Bonn: Dietz.

Winkler, H.A. (1986). *Der Schein der Normalität. Arbeiter und Arbeiterbewegung in der Weimarer Republik 1924–1930.* Berlin/Bonn: Dietz.

Winkler, H.A. (1987). *Der Weg in die Katastrophe. Arbeiter und Arbeiterbewegung in der Weimarer Republik 1930–1933*. Berlin/Bonn: Dietz.

Wippler, R. (1985). Kulturelle Ressourcen, gesellschaftlicher Erfolg und Lebensqualität. In B. Giesen and H. Haferkamp (eds), *Soziologie der sozialen Ungleichheit* (pp. 221–54). Opladen: Westdeutscher Verlag.

Wippler, R. (1990). Cultural resources and participation in high culture. In M. Hechter, K.D. Opp and R. Wippler (eds), *Social Institutions. Their Emergence, Maintenance and Effects* (pp. 187–204). New York: Aldine de Gruyter.

Wright, E.O. (1985). *Classes*. London: New Left Books.

Wright, E.O. (1986). What is middle about the middle class? In J. Roemer (ed.), *Analytical Marxism* (pp. 114–40). Cambridge: Cambridge University Press.

Wright, E.O. (1990). A general framework for the analysis of class structure. In E.O. Wright (ed.), *The Debate on Classes* (pp. 3–43). London: Verso.

Wuthnow, R. (1976). *The Consciousness Reformation*. Berkeley, CA: University of California Press.

Wuthnow, R. (1986). Religious movements and countermovements in North America. In J.A. Beckford (ed., on behalf of Research Committee 22 of the International Sociological Association), *New Religious Movements and Rapid Social Change* (pp. 1–28). Paris/London: UNESCO/Sage.

Wuthnow, R. (1987). *Meaning and Moral Order: Explorations in Cultural Analysis*. Berkeley, CA: University of California Press.

Wuthnow, R. and Witten, M. (1988). New directions in the study of culture. *Annual Review of Sociology*, 14, 4967.

Yinger, J.M. (1977). Countercultures. *American Sociological Review*, 42, 833–53.

Yinger, J.M. (1982). *Countercultures. The Promise and the Peril of a World Turned Upside Down*. New York: Free Press.

Zald, M.N. (1988). The trajectory of social movements in America. In L. Kriesberg (ed.), *Research in Social Movements, Conflicts and Change* (Vol. 10, pp. 19–41). Greenwich, CT: JAI Press.

Zald, M.N. (1991). The continuing vitality of resource mobilization theory: Response to Herbert Kitschelt's critique. In D. Rucht (ed.), *Research on Social Movements. The State of the Art in Western Europe and the USA* (pp. 323–47). Frankfurt/Boulder, CO: Campus/Westview Press.

Zald, M.N. and McCarthy, J.D. (eds) (1979). *The Dynamics of Social Movements*. Cambridge: Winthrop.

Zald, M.N. and McCarthy, J.D. (eds) (1987). *Social Movements in an Organizational Society*. New Brunswick/Oxford: Transaction Books.

Zald, M.N. and Useem, B. (1987). Movement and countermovement interaction: Mobilization, tactics, and state involvement. In M.N. Zald and J.D. McCarthy (eds), *Social Movements in an Organizational Society* (pp. 247–72). New Brunswick/Oxford: Transaction Books.

Zapf, W. (1983). Entwicklungsdilemmas und Innovationspotentiale in modernen Gesellschaften. In J. Matthes (ed.), *Krise der Arbeitsgesellschaft? Verhandlungen des 21. Deutschen Soziologentages in Bamberg 1982* (pp. 293–308). Frankfurt: Campus.

Zapf, W. (1986). Zur Diskussion um Krise und Innovationschancen in westlichen Demokratien. In M. Kaase (ed.), *Politische Wissenschaft und politische Ordnung. Analysen zu Theorie und Empirie demokratischer Systeme* (pp. 52–60). Opladen: Westdeutscher Verlag.

Zelizer, V. (1988). Beyond the polemics on the market: Establishing a theoretical and empirical agenda. *Sociological Forum*, 3, 614–34.

# Index